Street by Street

KINGSTON UP
RICHMOND, WIMBLEDON
HOUNSLOW, NEW MALDEN, SURBITON,
TEDDINGTON, TWICKENHAM

Barnes, Brentford, Chessington, Feltham, Ham, Hampton Court, Isleworth, Kew, Putney, Raynes Park, Stoneleigh, Sunbury, Worcester Park

2nd edition March 2008

Original edition printed August 2002

 © Automobile Association Developments Limited 2008

This product includes map data licensed from Ordnance Survey® with the permission of the Controller of Her Majesty's Stationery Office. © Crown copyright 2008.
All rights reserved. Licence number 100021153.

The copyright in all PAF is owned by Royal Mail Group plc.

Published by AA Publishing (a trading name of Automobile Association Developments Limited, whose registered office is Fanum House, Basing View, Basingstoke, Hampshire RG21 4EA. Registered number 1878835).

Produced by the Mapping Services Department of The Automobile Association. (A03562)

A CIP Catalogue record for this book is available from the British Library.

Printed by Oriental Press in Dubai

Ref: ML212z

Key to map pages	ii-iii
Key to map symbols	iv-1
Enlarged map pages	2-3
Main map pages	4-45
Index – towns & villages	46
Index – streets	47-62
Index – featured places	62-65
Acknowledgements	65

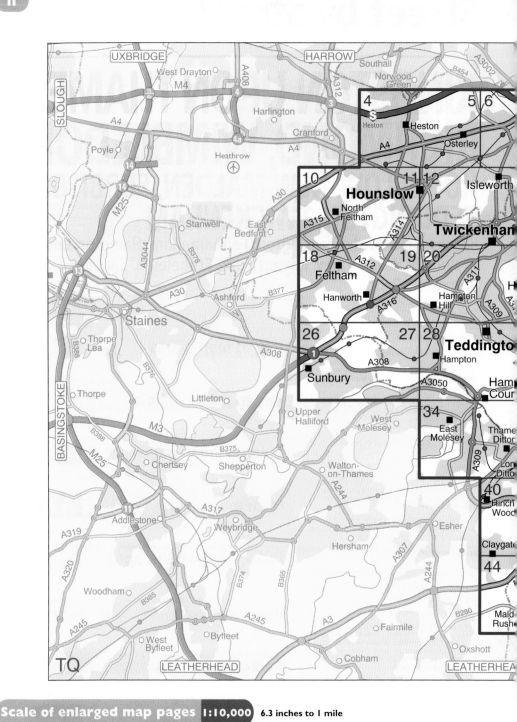

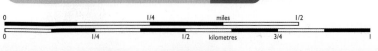

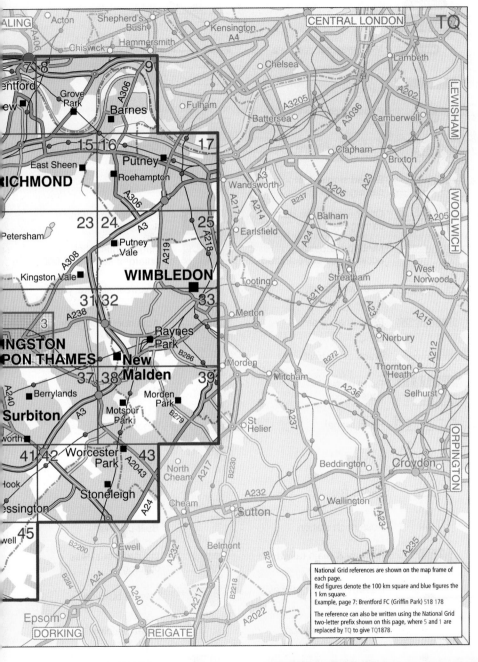

National Grid references are shown on the map frame of each page.
Red figures denote the 100 km square and blue figures the 1 km square.
Example, page 7: Brentford FC (Griffin Park) 518 178

The reference can also be written using the National Grid two-letter prefix shown on this page, where 5 and 1 are replaced by TQ to give TQ1878.

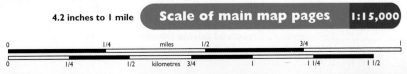

4.2 inches to 1 mile **Scale of main map pages** 1:15,000

Junction 9	Motorway & junction	*LC*	Level crossing
Services	Motorway service area	●—●—●—●	Tramway
	Primary road single/dual carriageway	- - - - - - -	Ferry route
Services	Primary road service area	··················	Airport runway
	A road single/dual carriageway	— · — · — · —	County, administrative boundary
	B road single/dual carriageway	▼▼▼▼▼▼▼▼▼	Mounds
	Other road single/dual carriageway	**I7**	Page continuation 1:15,000
	Minor/private road, access may be restricted	**3**	Page continuation to enlarged scale 1:10,000
← ←	One-way street		River/canal, lake, pier
	Pedestrian area		Aqueduct, lock, weir
- - - - - - -	Track or footpath	465 ▲ Winter Hill	Peak (with height in metres)
	Road under construction		Beach
	Road tunnel		Woodland
P	Parking		Park
P+	Park & Ride		Cemetery
	Bus/coach station		Built-up area
	Railway & main railway station		Industrial/business building
	Railway & minor railway station		Leisure building
⊖	Underground station		Retail building
⊖	Light railway & station		Other building
+++++++++	Preserved private railway		

City wall			Castle	
A&E	Hospital with 24-hour A&E department			Historic house or building
PO	Post Office		Wakehurst Place (NT)	National Trust property
	Public library			Museum or art gallery
i	Tourist Information Centre			Roman antiquity
i	Seasonal Tourist Information Centre			Ancient site, battlefield or monument
	Petrol station, 24 hour Major suppliers only			Industrial interest
†	Church/chapel			Garden
	Public toilets			Garden Centre Garden Centre Association Member
	Toilet with disabled facilities			Garden Centre Wyevale Garden Centre
PH	Public house AA recommended			Arboretum
	Restaurant AA inspected			Farm or animal centre
Madeira Hotel	Hotel AA inspected			Zoological or wildlife collection
	Theatre or performing arts centre			Bird collection
	Cinema			Nature reserve
	Golf course			Aquarium
	Camping AA inspected			Visitor or heritage centre
	Caravan site AA inspected			Country park
	Camping & caravan site AA inspected			Cave
	Theme park			Windmill
	Abbey, cathedral or priory			Distillery, brewery or vineyard

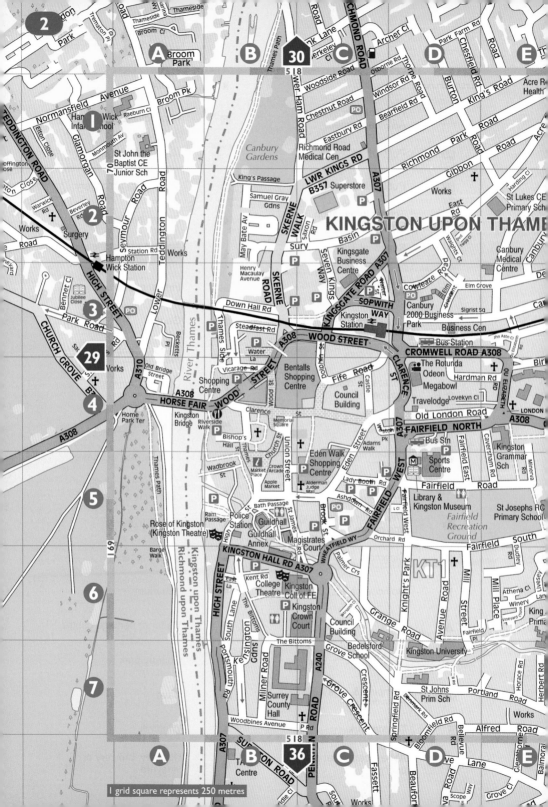

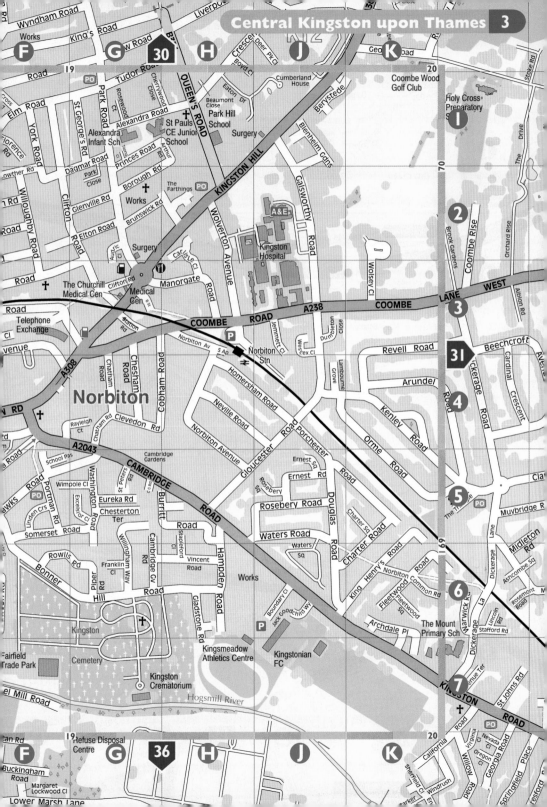

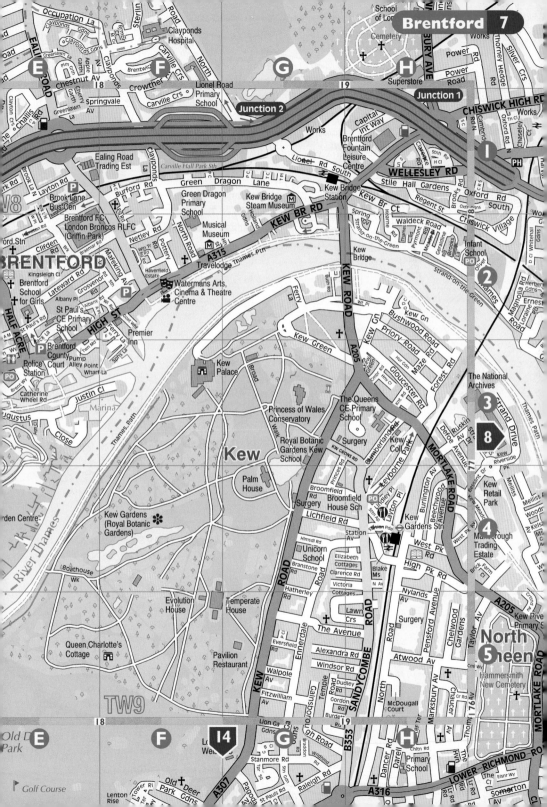

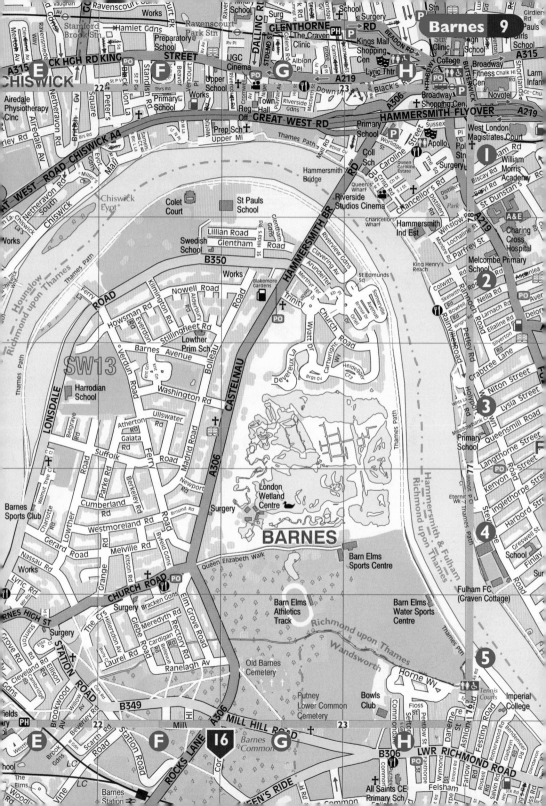

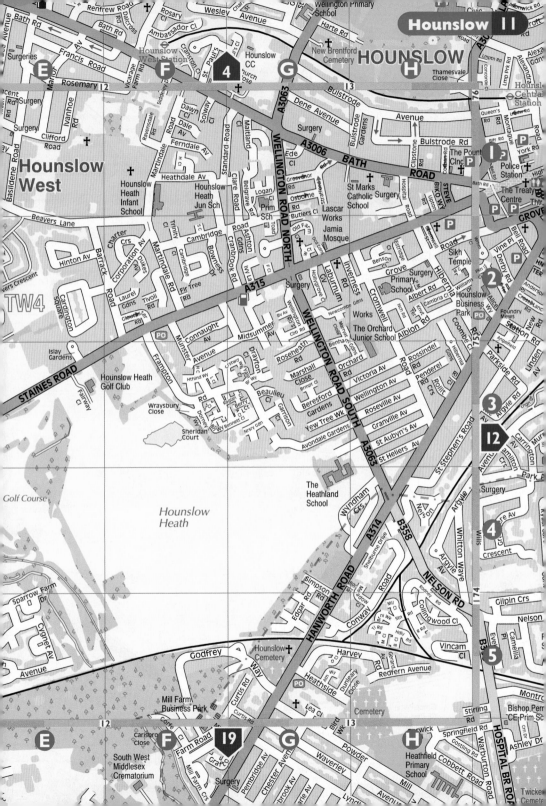

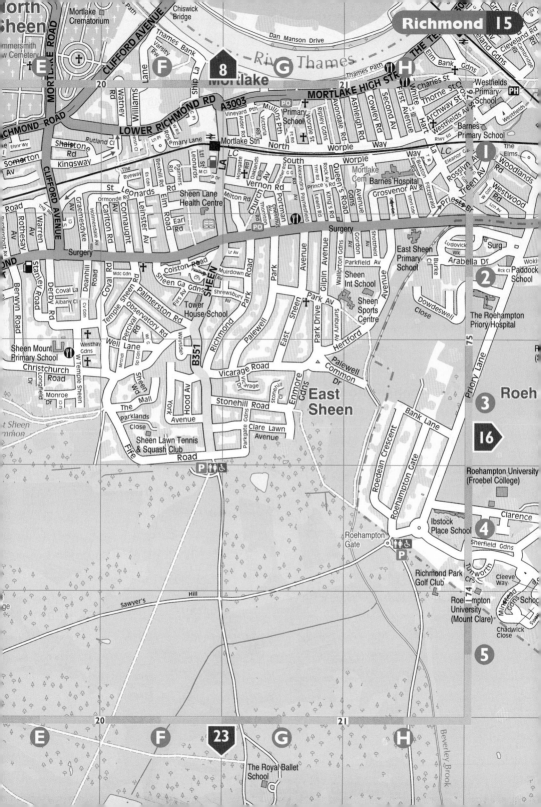

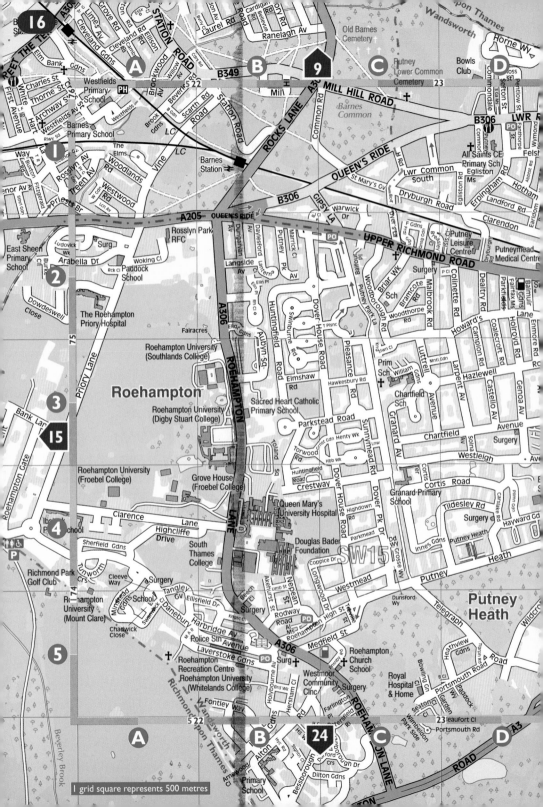

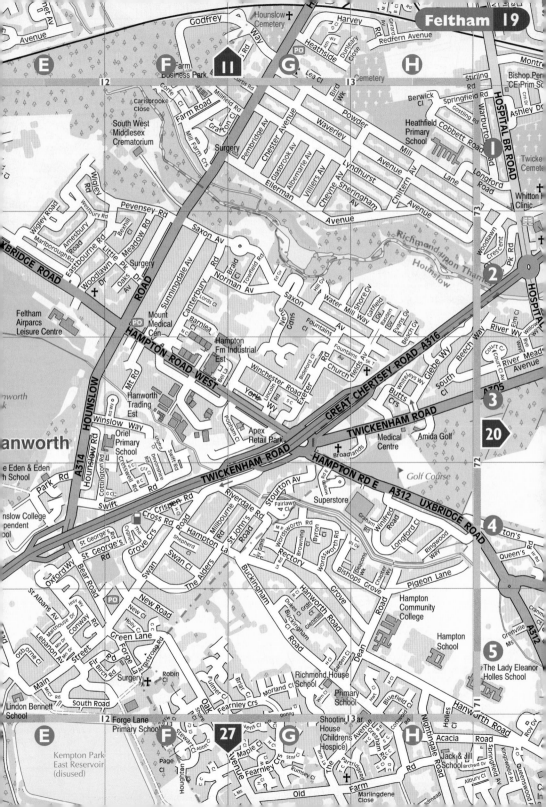

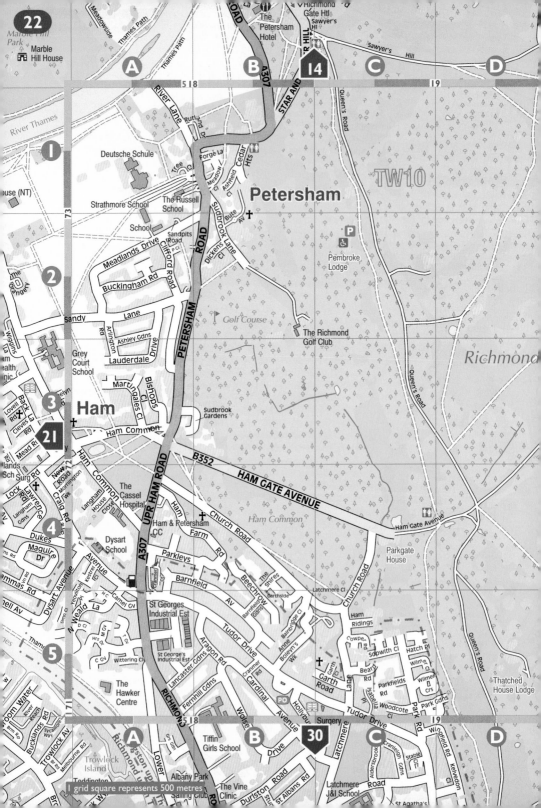

Close

E F **15** G H

20 21

I

Golf Course

73

The Royal Ballet School

2

Pen Ponds

National Nature Reserve

Park

P

Kingston University

ROEHAMPTON VAL

Friar

London Cornish RFC

3

P

Sawyer's Hill

24

72

PO

Isabella Plantation

Robinwood Place

KINGSTON VALE

Robin Hood Way

ROBIN

4

Woodview Cl

Derwent Avenue

Robin Hood

Vale Crs

Cedar Cl

Grasmere Avenue

Robin Hood Road

Ullswater Crs

HOOD

Kingston Hi Pl

Windermere Rd

A308

Sawyer's Hill

Richmond upon Thames
Kingston upon Thames

Kingston University

Robin Hood Primary School

Bowness Crescent

Rydal Gdns

WAY

5

Merton

Kingston upon Thames

71

KINGSTON

HILL

Coombe Pk

Coombe Wd

Coombe Rd

Coombe

Park

Park

Keswick Avenue

Ladderstile Ride

Coombe Ridings

Coombe

Park

Corscombe Cl

Kingston Vale

E F **31** G H

20 21

Canbury Sch

Warboys Road

Wby Ap

Golf Course

Astor Close

Fairlawn Cl

Warren Road

Warren House

Cotswold Cl

N HILL

KI

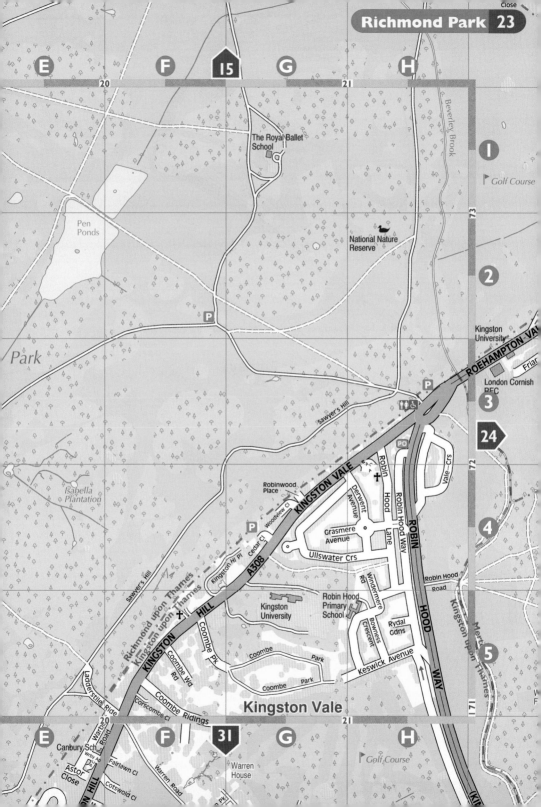

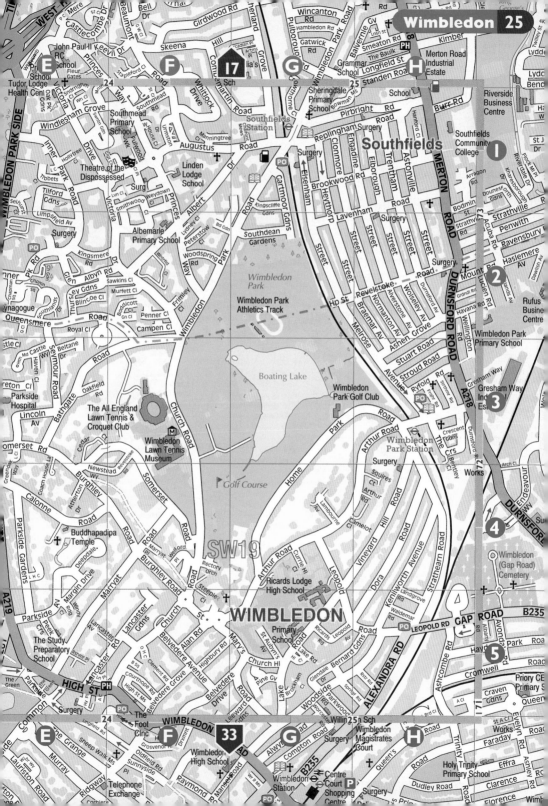

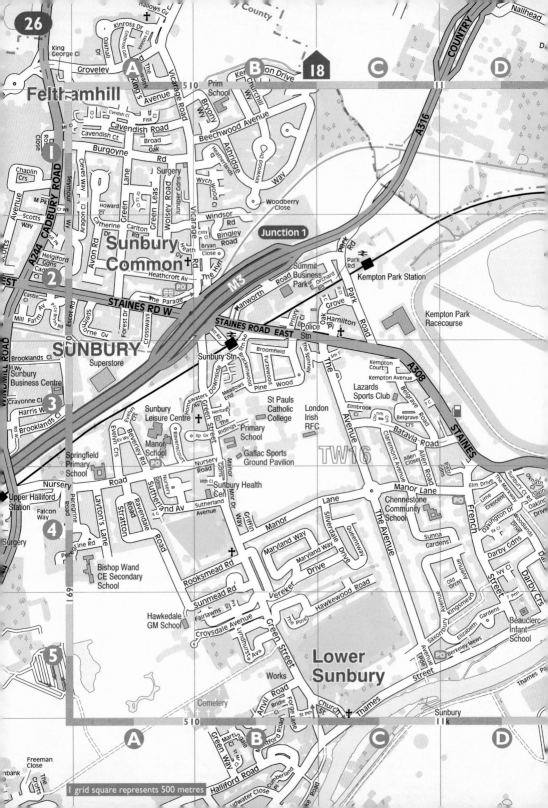

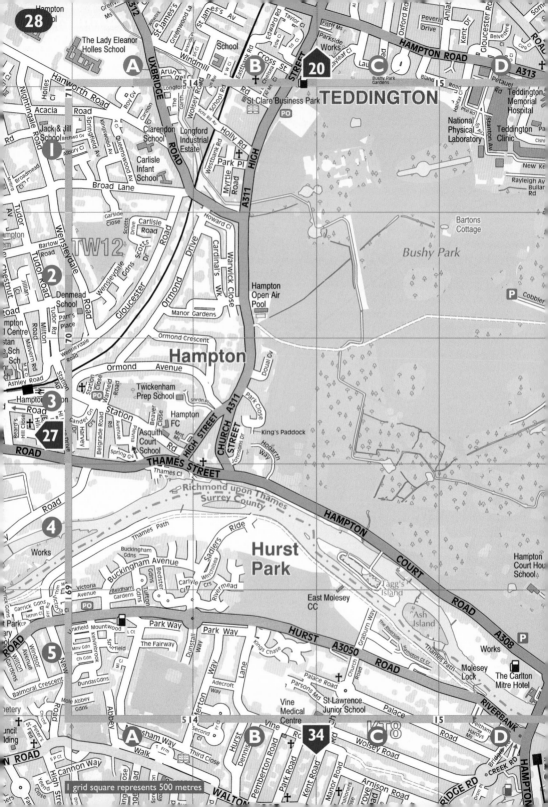

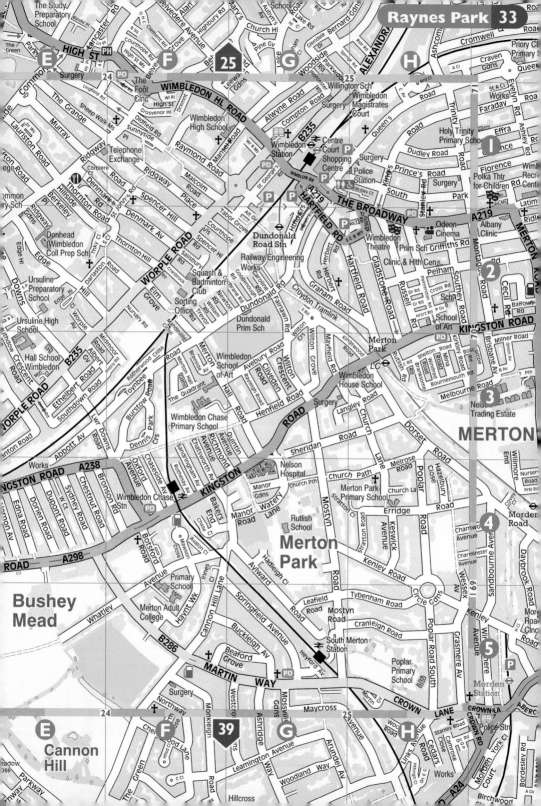

Hampton Court Palace

E

F

29

Stud House

G

H

16

17

I

Hampton Court Park

Golf Course

Hampton Court Palace Golf Club

Thames Path

Wolsey Av
Aragon Avenue
Queen's Road
Alexandra Rd
River Bank
Riverdale Rd

Summer
Speer Road

PH

Thames Ditton Island

Works

Richmond upon Thames

Richmond upon Thames

Kingston upon Thames

River Thames

Seething Wells

PORT SOUTH ROAD

68

Syna Cath

Grove

Cadogan R

Leonard's

Cleaveland Road

Westfield Road

The Mall

St Andrew's Sq

St Ann

2

BRIGHTON R

Surbiton Court

Thames Ditton Infant School

St Nicholas Rd
Old school

Church Walk

High St
Boyle Road

Farm Road

Fitzgerald

Ashley Rd

Council Building

PO

Burtenshaw Road

Queen's Drive

King's Drive

Ferry Road

Ferry

Ditton Reach

Choimley Road

Southbank

Howard

Houston Rd

PORTSMOUTH ROAD

Works

Simpson Way

Prospect Rd

Chadwick Pl

Williams

Akerman Road

Seething Wells

Balaclava

A243

36

Surb Busi Cent

STATION ROAD

Ditton

High Road

Basingfield Rd

Basing Way
Basing Close

Mercer Close

WATTS ROAD

Ditton Close

St Leonard's Road

Portsmouth Avenue

River Avenue

King's Drive

Vaughan Rd

Windmill Road

Saverly Dr
Saverly Dr

Jennings

St James

St John's

Victoria Avenue

Lovelace Gar

KT7

Thames Ditton Junior School

Surgery

Raphael Drive

Savile Cl
Hayward

B364
GIGGS HILL RD

Giggs Hill Rd

A307

Thames Ditton

Giggshill

Westville Rd

Southville Road

Rythe Court

Ewell Road

Rushett Rd

Angel Road

Kingston Liberal Synagogue

Effingham Road

Orchard Road

Windmill Close

Fleece Road

St Chads Cl

St Mary's Saxonbury Gardens

Pound Road

Sharon Close

Lovelace Road

Beechwood Rd

Lwr Sand Hills

Woodl

Sylvan Gdns

4

Longmead Rd

Surgery

Quinton Rd

Thorkhill Surgery

Thorkhill Gdns

Scott Farm Cl

St Andrews

Betts Way

King's Road

Rectory Lane

Long Ditton County Infant School

Ditton Hill Rd

SUR5TON

Ditton Grange Drive

Ditton Gra Cl

Lynwood Road

North Dene

Greenwood Road

Sugden Road

Mayfield Close

Orchard Road

Long Ditton

St Marys CE Junior School

Church Road

Cemetery

Rectory La

Church Meadow

Oaks Way

Hill

Devonshire

Wentwo

E

16

F

40

Bankside Drive

G

17

H

Brn Rd

Lynwd

Wessel Cl

Claygate Lane

Cumber

Hinchley Wood School & Sixth Form Centre

Hinchley Wood Primary Sch

Garden Centre

Woodstock Lane

Church Meadow

Love

Close

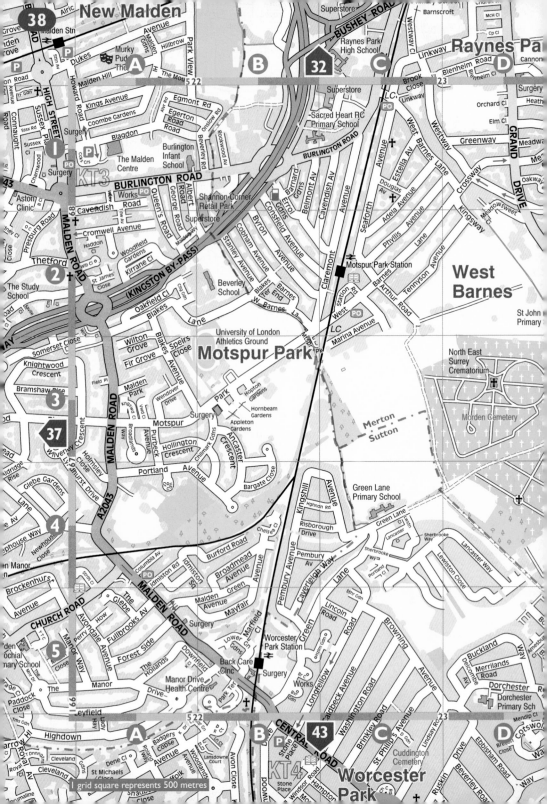

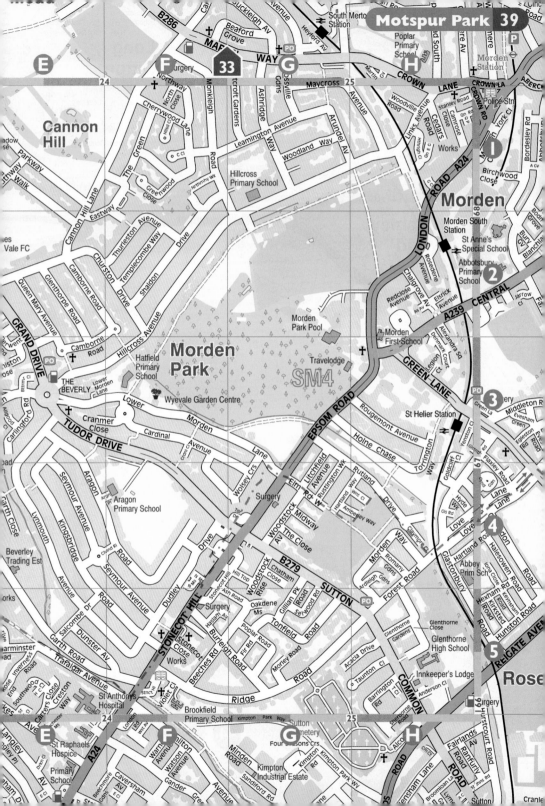

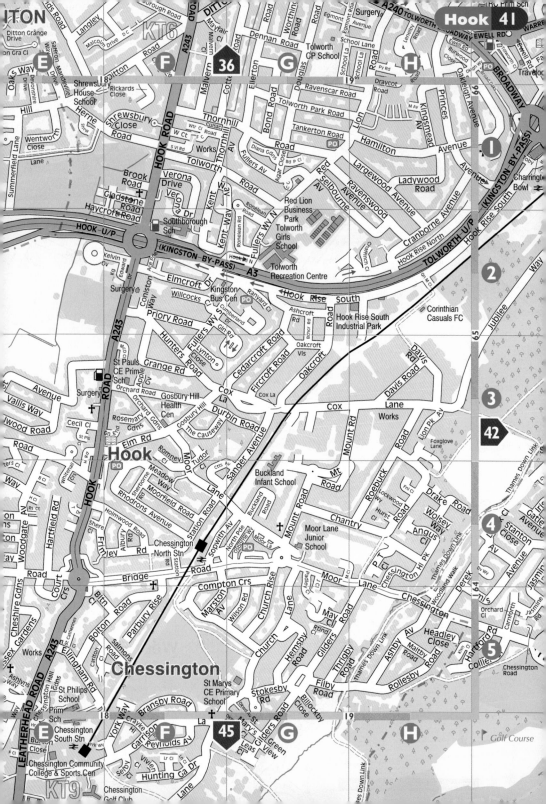

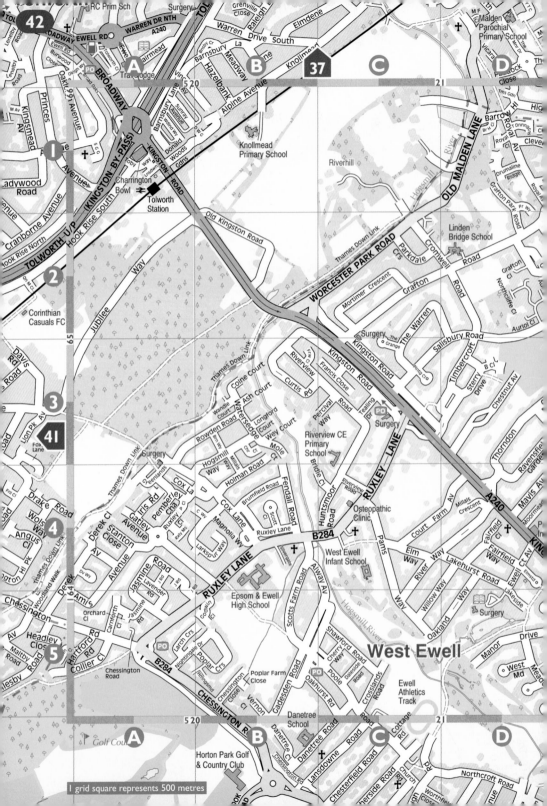

West Ewell

Tolworth Station

Knollmead Primary School

Riverview CE Primary School

Epsom & Ewell High School

West Ewell Infant School

Ewell Athletics Track

Horton Park Golf & Country Club

Danetree School

1 grid square represents 500 metres

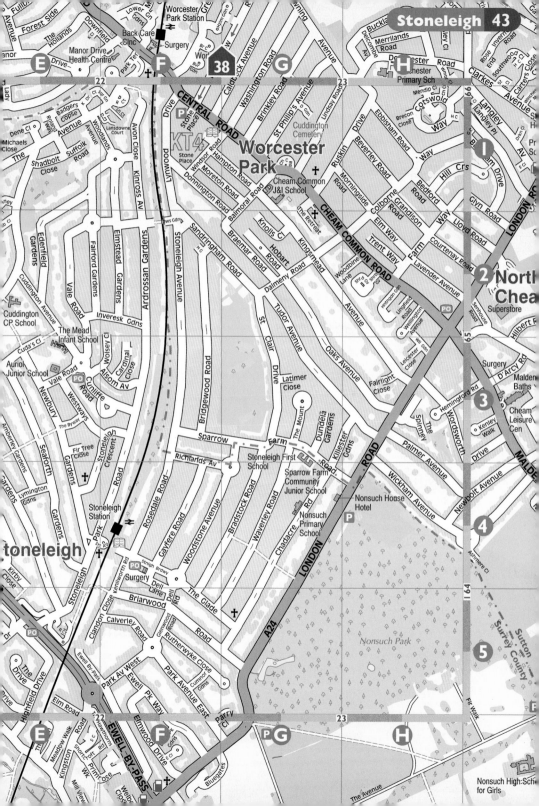

Barnes	9 G4	Hampton	28 A3	Morden	39 H1	Southfields	25
Barwell	44 D1	Hampton Hill	20 B4	Morden Park	39 F3	Spring Grove	5
Berrylands	36 C5	Hampton Wick	29 G3	Mortlake	8 B5	Stoneleigh	43
Brentford	7 E2	Hanworth	19 E3	Motspur Park	38 B3	Strawberry Hill	20
Brentford End	6 C2	Heston	4 C3	New Malden	32 A5	Sunbury	26
Bushey Mead	39 E5	Hinchley Wood	40 A2	Norbiton	3 G4	Sunbury Common	26
Cannon Hill	39 E1	Hook	41 F4	North Feltham	10 C3	Surbiton	35
Chessington	41 F5	Hounslow	4 D5	North Sheen	8 A5	Teddington	28
Claygate	40 A5	Hounslow West	11 E1	Old Malden	37 G4	Thames Ditton	35
Cole Park	13 F4	Hurst Park	28 B4	Osterley	5 F3	Tolworth	36
Coombe	31 H2	Isleworth	13 G1	Petersham	22 B1	Twickenham	20
Copse Hill	32 B2	Kew	7 G3	Putney	17 E3	Wandsworth	17
Cottenham Park	32 C3	Kingston upon Thames	2 C2	Putney Heath	16 D5	West Barnes	38
Crooked Billet	32 C1	Kingston Vale	23 G5	Putney Vale	24 B3	West Ewell	42
East Molesey	34 B2	Lampton	5 E4	Raynes Park	32 D5	West Hill	17
East Sheen	15 G3	Long Ditton	35 G5	Richmond	14 B3	Weston Green	34
Feltham	18 C2	Lower Sunbury	26 B5	Richmond Hill	14 B4	Whitton	12
Giggshill	35 F4	Malden Rushett	44 C5	Roehampton	16 A3	Wimbledon	25
Grove Park	8 C4	Merton	33 H3	St Margarets	13 H4	Woodlands	12
Ham	22 A3	Merton Park	33 G4	Seething Wells	35 G5	Worcester Park	43

USING THE STREET INDEX

Street names are listed alphabetically. Each street name is followed by its postal town or area locality, the Postcode District, the page number, and the reference to the square in which the name is found.

Standard index entries are shown as follows:

Abbey Ms *ISLW* TW7 .... **6** C4

Street names and selected addresses not shown on the map due to scale restrictions are shown in the index with an asterisk:

Abbotts Md *RCHPK/HAM* TW10 * **21** H4

GENERAL ABBREVIATIONS

ACC	ACCESS	E	EAST	LDG	LODGE	R	RIV
ALY	ALLEY	EMB	EMBANKMENT	LGT	LIGHT	RBT	ROUNDABO
AP	APPROACH	EMBY	EMBASSY	LK	LOCK	RD	RO
AR	ARCADE	ESP	ESPLANADE	LKS	LAKES	RDG	RID
ASS	ASSOCIATION	EST	ESTATE	LNDG	LANDING	REP	REPUB
AV	AVENUE	EX	EXCHANGE	LTL	LITTLE	RES	RESERVO
BCH	BEACH	EXPY	EXPRESSWAY	LWR	LOWER	RFC	RUGBY FOOTBALL CL
BLDS	BUILDINGS	EXT	EXTENSION	MAG	MAGISTRATES'	RI	R
BND	BEND	F/O	FLYOVER	MAN	MANSIONS	RP	RA
BNK	BANK	FC	FOOTBALL CLUB	MD	MEAD	RW	RO
BR	BRIDGE	FK	FORK	MDW	MEADOWS	S	SOU
BRK	BROOK	FLD	FIELD	MEM	MEMORIAL	SCH	SCHO
BTM	BOTTOM	FLDS	FIELDS	MI	MILL	SE	SOUTH EA
BUS	BUSINESS	FLS	FALLS	MKT	MARKET	SER	SERVICE AR
BVD	BOULEVARD	FM	FARM	MKTS	MARKETS	SH	SHO
BY	BYPASS	FT	FORT	ML	MALL	SHOP	SHOPPI
CATH	CATHEDRAL	FTS	FLATS	MNR	MANOR	SKWY	SKYW
CEM	CEMETERY	FWY	FREEWAY	MS	MEWS	SMT	SUMM
CEN	CENTRE	FY	FERRY	MSN	MISSION	SOC	SOCIE
CFT	CROFT	GA	GATE	MT	MOUNT	SP	SP
CH	CHURCH	GAL	GALLERY	MTN	MOUNTAIN	SPR	SPRI
CHA	CHASE	GDN	GARDEN	MTS	MOUNTAINS	SQ	SQUA
CHYD	CHURCHYARD	GDNS	GARDENS	MUS	MUSEUM	ST	STRE
CIR	CIRCLE	GLD	GLADE	MWY	MOTORWAY	STN	STATI
CIRC	CIRCUS	GLN	GLEN	N	NORTH	STR	STREA
CL	CLOSE	GN	GREEN	NE	NORTH EAST	STRD	STRAN
CLFS	CLIFFS	GND	GROUND	NW	NORTH WEST	SW	SOUTH WE
CMP	CAMP	GRA	GRANGE	O/P	OVERPASS	TDG	TRADI
CNR	CORNER	GRG	GARAGE	OFF	OFFICE	TER	TERRA
CO	COUNTY	GT	GREAT	ORCH	ORCHARD	THWY	THROUGHW
COLL	COLLEGE	GTWY	GATEWAY	OV	OVAL	TNL	TUNN
COM	COMMON	GV	GROVE	PAL	PALACE	TOLL	TOLLW
COMM	COMMISSION	HGR	HIGHER	PAS	PASSAGE	TPK	TURNPI
CON	CONVENT	HL	HILL	PAV	PAVILION	TR	TRA
COT	COTTAGE	HLS	HILLS	PDE	PARADE	TRL	TRA
COTS	COTTAGES	HO	HOUSE	PH	PUBLIC HOUSE	TWR	TOW
CP	CAPE	HOL	HOLLOW	PK	PARK	U/P	UNDERPA
CPS	COPSE	HOSP	HOSPITAL	PKWY	PARKWAY	UNI	UNIVERSI
CR	CREEK	HRB	HARBOUR	PL	PLACE	UPR	UPP
CREM	CREMATORIUM	HTH	HEATH	PLN	PLAIN	V	VA
CRS	CRESCENT	HTS	HEIGHTS	PLNS	PLAINS	VA	VALL
CSWY	CAUSEWAY	HVN	HAVEN	PLZ	PLAZA	VIAD	VIADU
CT	COURT	HWY	HIGHWAY	POL	POLICE STATION	VIL	VIL
CTRL	CENTRAL	IMP	IMPERIAL	PR	PRINCE	VIS	VIS
CTS	COURTS	IN	INLET	PREC	PRECINCT	VLG	VILLA
CTYD	COURTYARD	IND EST	INDUSTRIAL ESTATE	PREP	PREPARATORY	VLS	VILL
CUTT	CUTTINGS	INF	INFIRMARY	PRIM	PRIMARY	VW	VIE
CV	COVE	INFO	INFORMATION	PROM	PROMENADE	W	WE
CYN	CANYON	INT	INTERCHANGE	PRS	PRINCESS	WD	WO
DEPT	DEPARTMENT	IS	ISLAND	PRT	PORT	WHF	WHA
DL	DALE	JCT	JUNCTION	PT	POINT	WK	WA
DM	DAM	JTY	JETTY	PTH	PATH	WKS	WAL
DR	DRIVE	KG	KING	PZ	PIAZZA	WLS	WEL
DRO	DROVE	KNL	KNOLL	QD	QUADRANT	WY	W
DRY	DRIVEWAY	L	LAKE	QU	QUEEN	YD	YAR
DWGS	DWELLINGS	LA	LANE	QY	QUAY	YHA	YOUTH HOST

POSTCODE TOWNS AND AREA ABBREVIATIONS

ARN ...... Barnes
YLDS ...... Berrylands
FD ...... Brentford
EAM ...... Cheam
SGTN ...... Chessington
SWK ...... Chiswick
WMO/HCT ...... East & West Molesey/Hampton Court
...... Ealing
ED/NFELT ...... East Bedfont/North Feltham
SOM ...... Epsom
H/CLAY ...... Esher/Claygate
V ...... Ewell

FELT ...... Feltham
FUL/PGN ...... Fulham/Parsons Green
HEST ...... Heston
HMSMTH ...... Hammersmith
HNWL ...... Hanwell
HOR/WEW ...... Horton/West Ewell
HPTN ...... Hampton
HSLW ...... Hounslow
HSLWW ...... Hounslow west
HTHAIR ...... Heathrow Airport
ISLW ...... Isleworth
KUT/HW ...... Kingston upon Thames/Hampton Wick

KUTN/CMB ...... Kingston upon Thames north/Coombe
LHD/OX ...... Leatherhead/Oxshott
MORT/ESHN ...... Mortlake/East Sheen
MRDN ...... Morden
NWDGN ...... Norwood Green
NWMAL ...... New Malden
PUT/ROE ...... Putney/Roehampton
RCH/KEW ...... Richmond/Kew
RCHPK/HAM ...... Richmond Park/Ham
RYNPK ...... Raynes Park
SHPTN ...... Shepperton
SUN ...... Sunbury

SURB ...... Surbiton
SUT ...... Sutton
TEDD ...... Teddington
THDIT ...... Thames Ditton
TWK ...... Twickenham
WAND/EARL ...... Wandsworth/Earlsfield
WHTN ...... Whitton
WIM/MER ...... Wimbledon/Merton
WOT/HER ...... Walton-on-Thames/Hersham
WPK ...... Worcester Park

Index - streets

Abb - Ayl

A

bey Ms ISLW TW7 .....6 C4
bey Wk E/WMO/HCT KT8 .....28 A5
bbots Av HOR/WEW KT19 .....45 H4
bbotsmede Cl TWK TW1 .....21 E2
bbotstone Rd PUT/ROE SW15 .....16 D1
bbott Av RYNPK SW20 .....33 E4
bbott Cl HPTN TW12 .....27 F1
bbotts Md RCHPK/HAM TW10 * 21 H4
bercorn Ms RCHPK/HAM TW10 .....14 C3
binger Gdns ISLW TW7 .....12 D1
boyne Dr RYNPK SW20 .....32 B4
cacia Av BTFD TW8 .....6 C3
cacia Dr CHEAM SM3 .....39 G5
cacia Gv NWMAL KT3 .....38 A1
cacia Rd HPTN TW12 .....27 H1
ce Pde CHSGTN KT9 .....41 F2
corn Cl HPTN TW12 .....28 A1
cre Rd KUTN/CMB KT2 .....2 E1
dams Cl BRYLDS KT5 .....36 C3
dams Wk KUT/HW KT1 .....2 E4
dam Wk FUL/PGN SW6 * 9 H3
ddison Av HSLW TW3 .....5 F4
ddison Gdns BRYLDS KT5 .....36 C1
ddison Rd TEDD TW11 .....29 G1
decroft Wy E/WMO/HCT KT8 .....28 B5
dela Av NWMAL KT3 .....38 C2
delaide Rd
  PUT/ROE SW15 .....17 H5
  RCH/KEW TW9 .....14 C2
  SURB KT6 .....36 B2
  TEDD TW11 .....29 E1
delaide Ter BTFD TW8 * 7 E1
dmiralty Rd TEDD TW11 .....29 E1
gar Cl SURB KT6 .....41 G1
ilsa Av TWK TW1 .....13 F3
ilsa Rd TWK TW1 .....13 G3
iredale Av CHSWK W4 .....9 E1
iredale Av South CHSWK W4 * 9 E1
rtman Dr BTFD TW8 * 7 E1
kehurst St PUT/ROE SW15 .....16 B4
kerman Rd SURB KT6 .....35 G5
an Rd WIM/MER SW19 .....25 F5
bany Ms KUTN/CMB KT2 * 30 A1
bany Pl BTFD TW8 * 7 F2
bany Park Rd KUT/HW KT1 .....30 A1
bany Pl BTFD TW8 .....7 E2
bany Rd BTFD TW8 .....7 E2
  NWMAL KT3 .....37 G1
  RCHPK/HAM TW10 * 14 C3
bany Ter RCHPK/HAM TW10 * 14 C3
bemarle Av WHTN TW2 .....19 G1
bemarle Gdns NWMAL KT3 .....37 G1
bert Dr WIM/MER SW19 .....25 F2
bert Gv RYNPK SW20 .....33 E3
bert Rd HPTN TW12 .....20 B5
  HSLW TW3 .....11 H2
  KUT/HW KT1 .....2 E4
  NWMAL KT3 .....38 A1
  RCHPK/HAM TW10 * 14 C3
  TEDD TW11 .....29 E1
  TWK TW1 .....21 E1
bion Rd HSLW TW3 .....11 H2
  KUTN/CMB KT2 .....31 E3
  WHTN TW2 .....20 D3
bury Av ISLW TW7 .....6 A3
bury Cl HPTN TW12 .....27 F2
bury Rd CHSGTN KT9 .....41 F4
lcock Rd HEST TW5 .....4 A3
derbury Rd BARN SW13 .....9 F2
derman Judge Ml KUT/HW KT1 .....2 E5
derney Av HEST TW5 .....5 E3
der Rd MORT/ESHN SW14 .....15 C1
dersbrook Dr KUTN/CMB KT2 .....30 C1
dersgrove E/WMO/HCT KT8 .....34 B1
he Alders FELT TW13 .....19 F5
  HEST TW5 .....4 C2
derwick Dr HSLW TW3 .....12 C1
ldridge Ri NWMAL KT3 .....37 H4

Alexander Cl WHTN TW2 .....20 D2
Alexandra Dr BRYLDS KT5 .....36 D4
Alexandra Gdns HSLW TW3 .....5 E5
Alexandra Rd BTFD TW8 * 7 E2
  HSLW TW3 .....5 E5
  KUTN/CMB KT2 .....3 G1
  MORT/ESHN SW14 .....15 G1
  RCH/KEW TW9 .....7 H7
  THDIT KT7 .....35 E2
  TWK TW1 .....13 H4
  WIM/MER SW19 .....25 H5
Alexandra Sq MRDN SM4 .....39 H2
Alexandra Wy HOR/WEW KT19 .....45 H5
Alfred Rd FELT TW13 .....18 D1
  KUT/HW KT1 .....2 D7
Alfreton Cl WIM/MER SW19 .....25 E3
Alfriston BRYLDS KT5 .....36 C3
Alfriston Cl BRYLDS KT5 .....36 C3
Algar Rd ISLW TW7 .....13 F1
Alice Wy HSLW TW3 .....12 A2
Aikerden Rd CHSWK W4 .....8 D1
Allan Cl NWMAL KT3 .....37 G2
Allbrook Cl TEDD TW11 .....20 D5
Allcot Cl EBED/NFELT TW14 .....18 A1
Allen Cl SUN TW16 .....26 C3
Alleyn Pk NWDGN UB2 .....4 C1
Allgood Cl MRDN SM4 .....39 E3
Alliance Rd WIM/MER SW19 .....25 E5
Allington Cl WIM/MER SW19 .....25 E5
All Saints Pas WAND/EARL SW18 * 17 H3
Alma Rd ESH/CLAY KT10 .....34 D5
Aimer Rd RYNPK SW20 .....32 B2
Almond Cl FELT TW13 .....18 B1
Almond Gv BTFD TW8 .....6 C3
Aimorah Rd HEST TW5 .....4 A4
Almshouse La CHSGTN KT9 .....44 D1
Alpha Pl MRDN SM4 * 39 E4
Alpha Rd BRYLDS KT5 .....36 C3
  TEDD TW11 .....20 C5
Aipine Av BRYLDS KT5 .....42 B1
Alric Av NWMAL KT3 .....31 H5
Alsom Av WPK KT4 .....43 E3
Alston Cl SURB KT6 .....35 E5
Alt Gv WIM/MER SW19 .....33 G2
Alton Cl ISLW TW7 .....6 A5
Alton Gdns WHTN TW2 .....12 C4
Alton Rd PUT/ROE SW15 .....24 B1
  RCH/KEW TW9 .....14 B2
Alverstone Av WAND/EARL SW18 .....25 H2
Alverstone Rd NWMAL KT3 .....38 A1
Alway Av HOR/WEW KT19 .....42 B4
Alwyn Av CHSWK W4 .....8 C1
Alwyne Rd WIM/MER SW19 .....33 G1
Amalgamated Dr BTFD TW8 .....6 B2
Ambassador Cl HSLW TW3 .....4 D5
Amberley Gdns HOR/WEW KT19 .....43 E5
Amberley Wy HSLWW TW4 .....10 D5
  MRDN SM4 .....39 G4
Amberside Cl ISLW TW7 .....12 C4
Amberwood Ri NWMAL KT3 .....37 H3
Ambleside Dr EBED/NFELT TW14 .....18 A1
Amenity Wy MRDN SM4 .....38 D4
Amerland Rd PUT/ROE SW15 .....17 G4
Amesbury Cl WPK KT4 .....38 D5
Amesbury Rd FELT TW13 .....19 E2
Amhurst Gdns ISLW TW7 .....6 A4
Amis Av HOR/WEW KT19 .....41 H5
Amity Gv RYNPK SW20 .....32 D3
Amyand Cottages TWK TW1 .....13 G4
Amyand Park Gdns TWK TW1 .....13 G5
Amyand Park Rd TWK TW1 .....13 G5
Ancaster Crs NWMAL KT3 .....38 B3
Anchorage Cl WIM/MER SW19 .....25 H5
Anderson Cl CHEAM SM3 .....39 H5
Anderson's Pl HSLW TW3 .....12 A2
Andover Cl EBED/NFELT TW14 .....18 A1
Andover Rd WHTN TW2 .....20 C1
Angelfield HSLW TW3 .....12 A2
Angel Ms PUT/ROE SW15 .....24 A1
Angel Rd THDIT KT7 .....35 F5
Anglers Reach SURB KT6 * 36 A2
Anglesea Rd KUT/HW KT1 .....36 A1
Angus Cl CHSGTN KT9 .....41 H4

Anlaby Rd TEDD TW11 .....20 D5
Anne Boleyn's Wk KUTN/CMB KT2 .....22 B5
Anne Case Ms NWMAL KT3 * 31 G5
Anstice Cl CHSWK W4 .....8 D5
Anvil Rd SUN TW16 .....26 B5
Aplin Wy ISLW TW7 .....5 H4
Appleby Cl WHTN TW2 .....20 C2
Appleby Gdns EBED/NFELT TW14 * 18 A1
Applegarth ESH/CLAY KT10 .....40 A4
Apple Gv CHSGTN KT9 .....41 F3
Apple Market KUT/HW KT1 .....2 B5
Appleton Gdns NWMAL KT3 .....38 B3
Approach Rd RYNPK SW20 .....32 D4
April Cl FELT TW13 .....18 B1
Apsley Rd NWMAL KT3 .....31 F5
Aquarius TWK TW1 * 21 G1
Arabella Dr PUT/ROE SW15 .....15 H2
Aragon Av THDIT KT7 .....35 G2
Aragon Cl SUN TW16 .....26 A2
Aragon Pl MRDN SM4 .....39 E4
Aragon Rd KUTN/CMB KT2 .....22 B5
  MRDN SM4 .....39 E4
Arcade Pde CHSGTN KT9 * 41 F2
Arcadian Pl WAND/EARL SW18 .....17 F5
Archdale Pl NWMAL KT3 .....3 K6
Archer Cl KUTN/CMB KT2 .....30 B2
Archer Ct FELT TW13 .....18 B1
Archer Ms HPTN TW12 .....20 B2
Archway St BARN SW13 .....15 H1
Ardleigh Gdns CHEAM SM3 .....39 G4
Ardmay Gdns SURB KT6 * 36 B2
Ardrossan Gdns WPK KT4 .....43 E2
Ardshiel Cl PUT/ROE SW15 .....17 E1
Argent Ct SURB KT6 * 41 H4
Argyle Av HSLW TW3 .....12 A3
Argyle Rd HSLW TW3 .....12 A3
Ariel Wy HSLW TW4 .....10 C1
Arlington Cl TWK TW1 * 13 H5
Arlington Gdns CHSWK W4 .....8 B1
Arlington Rd RCHPK/HAM TW10 .....22 A2
  SURB KT6 .....36 A3
  TEDD TW11 .....21 E4
  TWK TW1 .....13 H5
Armadale Rd EBED/NFELT TW14 .....10 B3
Armoury Wy WAND/EARL SW18 .....17 H3
Armstrong Rd FELT TW13 .....19 F5
Armytage Rd HEST TW5 .....4 A3
Arnal Crs WAND/EARL SW18 .....17 F5
Arnewood Cl PUT/ROE SW15 .....24 B1
Arnison Rd E/WMO/HCT KT8 .....34 C1
Arnold Crs ISLW TW7 .....12 C4
Arnold Dr CHSGTN KT9 .....41 E5
Arosa Rd TWK TW1 .....14 A4
Arragon Rd TWK TW1 .....13 F5
  WAND/EARL SW18 .....25 H5
Artemis Pl WAND/EARL SW18 .....17 G5
Arterberry Rd RYNPK SW20 .....32 D2
Arthur Rd KUTN/CMB KT2 .....3 G1
  NWMAL KT3 .....38 C2
  WIM/MER SW19 .....25 G4
Arundel Av MRDN SM4 .....39 F5
Arundel Cl HPTN TW12 .....20 A5
Arundel Rd HSLWW TW4 .....10 B5
  KUT/HW KT1 .....3 K4
  KUT/HW KT1 .....2 E6
Arundel Ter BARN SW13 .....9 G2
Ashbourne Gv CHSWK W4 .....8 D1
Ashbourne Ter WIM/MER SW19 .....33 H2
Ashburnham Rd RCHPK/HAM TW10 .....21 G5
Ashby Av CHSGTN KT9 .....41 H5
Ash Cl NWMAL KT3 .....31 G4
Ashcombe Av SURB KT6 .....36 A4
Ashcombe Rd WIM/MER SW19 .....25 H5
Ashcombe Sq NWMAL KT3 .....37 G2
Ash Ct HOR/WEW KT19 .....42 B3
Ashcroft Rd CHSGTN KT9 .....41 H4
Ashdale Cl WHTN TW2 .....12 A5
Ashdown Pl THDIT KT7 .....35 F3
Ashdown Rd KUT/HW KT1 .....2 C5
Ashen Gv WIM/MER SW19 .....25 H4
Ashfield Av FELT TW13 .....18 C1
Ashfield Cl RCHPK/HAM TW10 .....21 H2
Ashford Rd FELT TW13 .....18 A3
Ash Gv HEST TW5 .....4 A4

Ashleigh Rd MORT/ESHN SW14 .....15 H1
Ashley Av MRDN SM4 .....39 H2
Ashley Dr ISLW TW7 .....5 H2
  WHTN TW2 .....20 A1
Ashley Gdns RCHPK/HAM TW10 .....22 A3
Ashley Rd HPTN TW12 .....27 H3
  RCH/KEW TW9 .....14 B1
  THDIT KT7 .....35 E3
Ashlone Rd PUT/ROE SW15 .....16 D1
Ashlyns Wy CHSGTN KT9 .....41 E5
Ashmead Rd EBED/NFELT TW14 .....18 B1
Ashridge Wy MRDN SM4 .....39 G1
  SUN TW16 .....26 B1
Ash Rd CHEAM SM3 .....39 F5
Ashton Gdns HSLWW TW4 .....11 G2
Ash Tree Cl SURB KT6 .....35 H5
The Ashway Centre KUTN/CMB KT2 * 2 D3
Askill Dr PUT/ROE SW15 .....17 E3
Aspen Wy FELT TW13 .....18 C3
Aston Rd RYNPK SW20 .....32 D4
Astonville St WAND/EARL SW18 .....25 H1
Astor Cl KUTN/CMB KT2 .....31 E1
Atbara Rd TEDD TW11 .....29 G1
Atcham Rd HSLW TW3 .....12 B2
Athelstan Rd KUT/HW KT1 .....36 C1
Athena Cl KUT/HW KT1 .....2 E6
Atherley Wy HSLWW TW4 .....11 G5
Atherton Dr WIM/MER SW19 .....25 E4
Atherton Rd BARN SW13 .....9 F3
Atney Rd PUT/ROE SW15 .....17 F2
Atwell Pl THDIT KT7 .....35 F5
Atwood Av RCH/KEW TW9 .....7 H5
Aubyn Sq PUT/ROE SW15 .....16 B2
Auckland Rd KUT/HW KT1 .....36 C1
Auden Pl CHEAM SM3 * 43 H5
Audley Rd RCHPK/HAM TW10 .....14 C3
Audric Cl KUTN/CMB KT2 .....3 G2
Augusta Cl E/WMO/HCT KT8 .....27 G5
Augusta Rd WHTN TW2 .....20 B2
Augustus Cl BTFD TW8 .....7 E3
Augustus Rd WIM/MER SW19 .....25 F1
Auriol Cl WPK KT4 .....42 D2
Auriol Park Rd WPK KT4 .....42 D2
Austin Cl TWK TW1 .....13 H3
Austyn Gdns BRYLDS KT5 * 37 E5
Avalon Cl RYNPK SW20 .....33 F4
Avebury Pk SURB KT6 * 36 A3
Avebury Rd WIM/MER SW19 .....33 G3
Avening Rd WAND/EARL SW18 .....17 H5
Avening Ter WAND/EARL SW18 .....17 H4
Avenue Elmers SURB KT6 .....36 B2
Avenue Gdns MORT/ESHN SW14 .....15 H1
  TEDD TW11 .....29 E2
Avenue Pde SUN TW16 .....26 C5
Avenue Rd BTFD TW8 .....6 D1
  FELT TW13 .....18 A3
  HPTN TW12 .....28 A3
  ISLW TW7 .....5 H4
  KUT/HW KT1 .....2 D6
  NWMAL KT3 .....31 H5
  RYNPK SW20 .....32 C4
  TEDD TW11 .....29 F2
Avenue South BRYLDS KT5 .....36 C4
Avenue Ter NWMAL KT3 .....31 F5
The Avenue BRYLDS KT5 .....36 C3
  HPTN TW12 .....27 G1
  HSLW TW3 .....12 A3
  LHD/OX KT22 .....44 A5
  RCH/KEW TW9 .....7 G5
  SUN TW16 .....26 C3
  TWK TW1 .....13 G4
  WPK KT4 .....43 E1
Avern Gdns E/WMO/HCT KT8 .....34 A1
Avern Rd E/WMO/HCT KT8 .....34 A2
Avon Cl WPK KT4 .....43 F1
Avondale Av ESH/CLAY KT10 .....40 B2
  WPK KT4 .....38 A5
Avondale Gdns HSLWW TW4 .....11 G3
Avondale Rd MORT/ESHN SW14 .....15 G1
Avon Rd SUN TW16 .....26 A2
Avonwick Rd HSLW TW3 .....5 E5
Aylett Rd ISLW TW7 .....5 H5
Aylward Rd RYNPK SW20 .....33 G4

B

Babbacombe Cl CHSGTN KT9 41 E4
Baber Bridge Pde EBED/NFELT TW14 * 10 D4
Baber Dr EBED/NFELT TW14 10 D4
Back La BTFD TW8 7 E3
RCHPK/HAM TW10 21 H3
Back Rd TEDD TW11 28 D2
Baden Powell Cl SURB KT6 41 G1
Badger Cl FELT TW13 18 C3
HSLWW TW4 10 D1
Badgers Copse WPK KT4 43 E1
Badgers Ct WPK KT4 * 43 E1
Badgers Wk NWMAL KT3 31 H4
Bailey Crs CHSGTN KT9 45 E1
Bailey Ms CHSWK W4 8 A2
Bainbridge Cl RCHPK/HAM TW10 22 B5
Bakers End RYNPK SW20 33 F4
Bakewell Wy NWMAL KT3 31 H4
Balaclava Rd SURB KT6 35 H4
Baldwin Gdns HSLW TW3 5 F4
Balfern Gv CHSWK W4 8 D1
Balfour Pl PUT/ROE SW15 16 C2
Balfour Rd HSLW TW3 12 A1
Balgowan Cl NWMAL KT3 37 H1
Ballard Cl KUTN/CMB KT2 31 G2
Balmoral Cl PUT/ROE SW15 * 17 E4
Balmoral Crs E/WMO/HCT KT8 27 H5
Balmoral Rd KUT/HW KT1 36 C1
WPK KT4 43 G2
Balmuir Gdns PUT/ROE SW15 16 D2
Balvernie Gv WAND/EARL SW18 17 G5
Bangalore St PUT/ROE SW15 16 D1
Bank La KUTN/CMB KT2 30 B2
PUT/ROE SW15 15 H3
Bankside Cl ISLW TW7 13 E2
Bankside Dr THDIT KT7 40 C1
Bannow Cl HOR/WEW KT19 42 D3
Bardolph Rd RCH/KEW TW9 14 C2
Bargate Cl NWMAL KT3 38 B4
Barge Wk KUT/HW KT1 2 A6
Barham Rd RYNPK SW20 32 B2
Barker Cl NWMAL KT3 37 E1
RCH/KEW TW9 8 A5
Barley Mow Pas CHSWK W4 8 C1
Barlow Rd HPTN TW12 27 H2
Barnard Cl SUN TW16 26 C2
Barnard Gdns NWMAL KT3 38 B1
Barneby Cl WHTN TW2 20 D1
Barnes Av BARN SW13 9 F3
Barnes Br CHSWK W4 8 D5
Barnes End NWMAL KT3 38 B2
Barnes High St BARN SW13 9 E5
Barnfield NWMAL KT3 37 H3
Barnfield Av KUTN/CMB KT2 22 A4
Barnfield Gdns KUTN/CMB KT2 22 B5
Barnlea Cl FELT TW13 19 F2
Barnsbury Cl NWMAL KT3 37 F1
Barnsbury Crs BRYLDS KT5 37 F5
Barnsbury La BRYLDS KT5 37 F5
Barnscroft RYNPK SW20 32 C5
Baronsfield Rd TWK TW1 * 13 G4
Baronsmead Rd BARN SW13 9 F4
The Barons TWK TW1 13 G4
Barrack Rd HSLWW TW4 11 E2
Barrington Rd CHEAM SM3 39 H5
Barrowgate Rd CHSWK W4 8 B1
Barrow Hl WPK KT4 42 D1
Barrow Hill Cl WPK KT4 42 D1
Barton Gn NWMAL KT3 31 G4
Barwell Ct CHSGTN KT9 * 44 D1
Barwell La CHSGTN KT9 44 D1
Basden Gv FELT TW13 19 H2
Basildene Rd HSLWW TW4 11 E1
Basing Cl THDIT KT7 35 E4
Basingfield Rd THDIT KT7 35 E4
Basing Wy THDIT KT7 35 E4
Bassett Gdns ISLW TW7 5 F3
Batavia Rd SUN TW16 26 C3
Batemans Cnr CHSWK W4 * 8 C1
Bathgate Rd WIM/MER SW19 25 E3
Bath Pas KUT/HW KT1 2 B5
Bath Rd HSLW TW3 11 G1
HSLW TW3 12 A1
HSLWW TW4 4 A5
The Baulk WAND/EARL SW18 17 H5
Bayleaf Cl HPTN TW12 20 C5
Baylis Ms TWK TW1 13 F5
Bazalgette Cl NWMAL KT3 37 F2
Bazalgette Gdns NWMAL KT3 37 G2
Beach Gv FELT TW13 19 H3
Beaconsfield Cl CHSWK W4 8 B1
Beaconsfield Rd NWMAL KT3 31 G4
SURB KT6 36 C4
TWK TW1 13 G4
Beaford Gv RYNPK SW20 33 F5
Beagle Cl FELT TW13 18 C4
Beard Rd KUTN/CMB KT2 22 C5
Beard's Hl HPTN TW12 27 H3
Beard's Hill Cl HPTN TW12 27 H3
Bearfield Rd KUTN/CMB KT2 2 C1
Bear Rd FELT TW13 19 E4
Beatrice Rd RCHPK/HAM TW10 14 C3
Beattie Cl EBED/NFELT TW14 10 A5
Beauchamp Rd E/WMO/HCT KT8 34 A2
TWK TW1 13 F5
Beauchamp Ter BARN SW13 16 C1
Beauclerk Cl FELT TW13 18 C1
Beaufort Cl PUT/ROE SW15 24 D1
Beaufort Ct RCHPK/HAM TW10 21 H4
Beaufort Gdns HEST TW5 4 B4
Beaufort Rd KUT/HW KT1 36 B1
RCHPK/HAM TW10 21 H4
TWK TW1 13 H5
Beaulieu Cl HSLWW TW4 11 G3
TWK TW1 14 A4
Beaumont Av RCH/KEW TW9 14 C1
Beaumont Cl KUTN/CMB KT2 3 H1
KUTN/CMB KT2 30 D2
Beaumont Pl ISLW TW7 13 E3
Beaumont Rd WIM/MER SW19 17 F5
Beaver Cl HPTN TW12 28 A3
MRDN SM4 38 D4
Beavers Crs HSLWW TW4 11 E2
Beavers La HSLWW TW4 10 D1
Beavor La HMSMTH W6 9 F1
Becketts Cl EBED/NFELT TW14 10 C4
Becketts Pl KUT/HW KT1 2 A3
Bective Rd PUT/ROE SW15 17 F2
Bedfont La EBED/NFELT TW14 18 B1
Bedfont Rd FELT TW13 18 A3
Bedford Cl CHSWK W4 8 D2
Bedford Rd WHTN TW2 20 C3
WPK KT4 43 H1
Bedford Vls KUT/HW KT1 * 3 F5
Bedgebury Gdns WIM/MER SW19 25 F2
Bedster Gdns E/WMO/HCT KT8 28 A4
Beech Av BTFD TW8 6 C3
Beech Cl PUT/ROE SW15 16 B5
SUN TW16 27 E4
WIM/MER SW19 32 D1
Beechcroft Av NWMAL KT3 31 F3
Beechcroft Cl HEST TW5 4 B3
Beechcroft Rd CHSGTN KT9 41 G3
MORT/ESHN SW14 * 15 F1
Beechen Cliff Wy ISLW TW7 6 A4
Beeches Rd CHEAM SM3 39 F5
Beech Gv NWMAL KT3 31 G5
Beechrow KUTN/CMB KT2 22 B4
Beech Wy WHTN TW2 19 H3
Beechwood Av RCH/KEW TW9 7 H4
SUN TW16 26 B1
Beechwood Cl SURB KT6 35 H4
Beeston Wy EBED/NFELT TW14 10 D4
Begonia Pl HPTN TW12 27 H1
Beldham Gdns E/WMO/HCT KT8 28 A5
Belgrade Rd HPTN TW12 28 A3
Belgrave Crs SUN TW16 26 C3
Belgrave Rd BARN SW13 9 E3
HSLWW TW4 11 G1
SUN TW16 26 C3
Belgravia Ms KUT/HW KT1 36 A1
Bel La FELT TW13 19 F3
Bell Dr WAND/EARL SW18 17 F5
Bellevue Rd BARN SW13 9 F5
KUT/HW KT1 2 D7
Bell La TWK TW1 21 F1
Bell Pde HSLW TW3 * 12 A2
Bell Rd E/WMO/HCT KT8 34 C2
HSLW TW3 12 A1
Belmont Av NWMAL KT3 38 B2
Belmont Rd WHTN TW2 20 C2
Beloe Cl PUT/ROE SW15 16 B2
Beltane Dr WIM/MER SW19 25 E3
Belvedere Av WIM/MER SW19 25 F5
Belvedere Cl TEDD TW11 20 D5
Belvedere Dr WIM/MER SW19 25 F5
Belvedere Gv WIM/MER SW19 25 F5
Belvedere Sq WIM/MER SW19 25 F5
Bemish Rd PUT/ROE SW15 17 E1
The Bench RCHPK/HAM TW10 * 21 H3
Bendemeer Rd PUT/ROE SW15 17 E1
Benham Cl CHSGTN KT9 40 D5
Benham Gdns HSLWW TW4 11 G3
Bennet Cl KUT/HW KT1 29 H3
Bennett Cl HSLWW TW4 11 F3
Bennett St CHSWK W4 8 D2
Bensbury Cl PUT/ROE SW15 16 C5
Benson Cl HSLW TW3 11 H2
Bentley Cl WIM/MER SW19 25 H3
Benwell Ct SUN TW16 * 26 B3
Beresford Av BRYLDS KT5 37 E5
TWK TW1 13 H4
Beresford Gdns HSLWW TW4 11 G3
Beresford Rd KUTN/CMB KT2 2 E2
NWMAL KT3 37 F1
Berestede Rd HMSMTH W6 9 E1
Berkeley Cl KUTN/CMB KT2 30 B2
Berkeley Dr E/WMO/HCT KT8 27 G5
Berkeley Gdns ESH/CLAY KT10 44 B1
Berkeley Ms SUN TW16 26 D5
Berkeley Pl WIM/MER SW19 33 E1
Berkeley Rd BARN SW13 9 F4
Berkeley Waye HEST TW5 4 B3
Berkley Cl WHTN TW2 * 20 D3
Bernard Gdns WIM/MER SW19 25 G5
Berry Ct HSLWW TW4 11 G3
Berrylands BRYLDS KT5 36 D2
RYNPK SW20 32 D5
Berrylands Rd BRYLDS KT5 36 C3
Bertram Rd KUTN/CMB KT2 30 D2
Berwick Cl WHTN TW2 19 H1
Berwyn Av HSLW TW3 5 E4
Berwyn Rd RCHPK/HAM TW10 15 E2
Berystede KUTN/CMB KT2 3 J1
Bessant Dr RCH/KEW TW9 8 A3
Bessborough Rd PUT/ROE SW15 24 B1
Betts Wy SURB KT6 35 G5
Beulah Rd WIM/MER SW19 33 G2
Beverley Av HSLWW TW4 11 G2
RYNPK SW20 32 A3
Beverley Cl BARN SW13 9 F5
CHSGTN KT9 40 D3
Beverley Gdns BARN SW13 16 A1
WPK KT4 38 B5
Beverley La KUTN/CMB KT2 31 H2
Beverley Rd BARN SW13 16 A1
CHSWK W4 9 E1
KUT/HW KT1 29 H3
NWMAL KT3 38 B1
SUN TW16 26 A3
WPK KT4 43 H1
Beverley Wy KUTN/CMB KT2 32 A3
RYNPK SW20 32 A3
Beverley Way (Kingston By-Pass)
NWMAL KT3 32 A4
RYNPK SW20 32 A3
RYNPK SW20 32 A3
Bexhill Cl FELT TW13 19 F2
Bexhill Rd MORT/ESHN SW14 15 F1
Bicester Rd RCH/KEW TW9 14 D1
Bideford Cl FELT TW13 19 G3
Bigg's Rw PUT/ROE SW15 17 E1
Billockby Cl CHSGTN KT9 41 G5
Bingley Rd SUN TW16 26 B2
Binns Rd CHSWK W4 8 D1
Birch Cl BTFD TW8 6 C3
HSLW TW3 12 C1
TEDD TW11 21 F5
The Birches HSLWW TW4 * 11 G5
Birchington Rd BRYLDS KT5 36 C4
Birch Rd FELT TW13 19 E5
Birchwood Gv HPTN TW12 27 H1
Bird Wk WHTN TW2 19 G1
Birdwood Cl TEDD TW11 20 D4
Birkenhead Av KUTN/CMB KT2 2 E4
Biscoe Cl HEST TW5 4 D2
Bishops Cl CHSWK W4 8 B1
RCHPK/HAM TW10 22 A3
Bishops Gv HPTN TW12 19 G4
Bishop's Hall KUT/HW KT1 2 B4
Bisley Cl WPK KT4 38 D5
Bittoms Ct KUT/HW KT1 * 2 B6
The Bittoms KUT/HW KT1 2 B6
Blackberry Farm Cl HEST TW5 4 B3
Blackett St PUT/ROE SW15 17 E1
Blackmore's Gv TEDD TW11 29 F1
Blackrurn Wy HSLWW TW4 11 F3
Blackthorn Ct HEST TW5 4 B3
Black's Rd HMSMTH W6 9 H1
Blagdon Rd NWMAL KT3 38 A1
Blagdon Wk TEDD TW11 29 H1
Blakeden Dr ESH/CLAY KT10 44 A1
Blake Ms RCH/KEW TW9 7 H4
Blakemore Gdns BARN SW13 9 G2
Blakes Av NWMAL KT3 38 A2
Blakes La NWMAL KT3 38 A2
Blakes Ter NWMAL KT3 38 B2
Blakewood Cl FELT TW13 18 D4
Blandford Av WHTN TW2 20 A1
Blandford Rd TEDD TW11 20 C5
Blenheim Cl RYNPK SW20 32 D5
Blenheim Gdns KUTN/CMB KT2 3 J1
Blenheim Pl TEDD TW11 21 E5
Blenheim Rd RYNPK SW20 32 D5
Blenheim Wy ISLW TW7 6 B4
Blincoe Cl WIM/MER SW19 25 E2
Bloomfield Rd KUT/HW KT1 36 B1
Blossom Waye HEST TW5 4 B2
Bloxham Crs HPTN TW12 27 G3
Bluefield Cl HPTN TW12 19 H5
Blyth Cl TWK TW1 13 E4
Boar's Head Yd BTFD TW8 7 E3
Boathouse Wk RCH/KEW TW9 7 E4
Bockhampton Rd KUTN/CMB KT2 30 C2
Boddicott Cl WIM/MER SW19 25 F2
Bodicea Ms HSLWW TW4 11 G4
Bodley Cl NWMAL KT3 37 H2
Bodley Rd NWMAL KT3 37 H3
Bodmin St WAND/EARL SW18 25 H1
Bodnant Gdns RYNPK SW20 32 B5
Boileau Rd BARN SW13 9 F3
Boleyn Dr E/WMO/HCT KT8 27 G5
Bolton Cl CHSGTN KT9 41 E5
Bolton Gdns TEDD TW11 29 F1
Bolton Rd CHSGTN KT9 41 E5
CHSWK W4 8 B3
Bond Rd SURB KT6 41 G1
Bonner Hill Rd KUT/HW KT1 3 F6
Bonser Rd TWK TW1 21 E2
Bordon Wk PUT/ROE SW15 16 B5
Borland Rd TEDD TW11 29 G1
Borneo St PUT/ROE SW15 16 D1
Borough Rd ISLW TW7 5 H4
KUTN/CMB KT2 3 G2
Boscombe Rd WIM/MER SW19 33 H3
WPK KT4 38 D5
Boston Gdns CHSWK W4 8 D2
Boston Manor Rd BTFD TW8 6 C1
Boston Park Rd BTFD TW8 * 6 D2
Botsford Rd RYNPK SW20 33 F4
Boucher Cl TEDD TW11 21 E5
Boundaries Rd FELT TW13 18
Boundary Cl KUT/HW KT1 3
NWDGN UB2 4
Bourne Cl ISLW TW7 12
THDIT KT7 40
Bournemouth Rd WIM/MER SW19 33
Bourne Wy HOR/WEW KT19 42
Bowater Gdns SUN TW16 26
Bowfell Rd HMSMTH W6 9
Bowling Green Cl PUT/ROE SW15 16
Bowman Ms WAND/EARL SW18 25
Bowness Crs PUT/ROE SW15 23
Bowness Dr HSLWW TW4 11
Bowsley Ct FELT TW13 18
Bowyers Ct TWK TW1 13
Boyd Cl KUTN/CMB KT2 30
Boyle Farm Rd THDIT KT7 35
Bracken Cl SUN TW16 * 26
WHTN TW2 11
Brackendale Cl HSLW TW3 5
Bracken End ISLW TW7 12
Bracken Gdns BARN SW13 9
Brackenwood SUN TW16 26
Brackley Rd CHSWK W4 8
Brackley Ter CHSWK W4 8
Braddock Cl ISLW TW7 13
Braddon Rd RCH/KEW TW9 14
Bradford Dr HOR/WEW KT19 43
Bradshaw Cl WIM/MER SW19 33
Bradstock Rd EW KT17 43
Braemar Av WIM/MER SW19 25
Braemar Rd BTFD TW8 7
WPK KT4 43
Braeside Av RYNPK SW20 33
Bragg Rd TEDD TW11 28
Braid Cl FELT TW13 19
Brainton Av EBED/NFELT TW14 10
Bramble La HPTN TW12 27
Brambles Cl ISLW TW7 6
The Brambles WIM/MER SW19 * 25
Bramcote Rd PUT/ROE SW15 16
Bramham Gdns CHSGTN KT9 * 41
Bramley Cl WHTN TW2 12
Bramley Wy HSLWW TW4 11
Bramshaw Ri NWMAL KT3 37
Bramwell Cl SUN TW16 27
Brandlehow Rd PUT/ROE SW15 17
Brandon Rd NWDGN UB2 4
Branksome Cl TEDD TW11 20
Branksome Rd WIM/MER SW19 33
Branksome Wy NWMAL KT3 31
Bransby Rd CHSGTN KT9 45
Branstone Rd RCH/KEW TW9 7
Brantwood Av ISLW TW7 13
Brasenose Dr BARN SW13 9
Brassey Cl EBED/NFELT TW14 * 18
Brathway Rd WAND/EARL SW18 17
Braybourne Dr ISLW TW7 6
Breamore Cl PUT/ROE SW15 24
Breamwater Gdns RCHPK/HAM TW10 21
Breasley Cl PUT/ROE SW15 16
Brecon Cl WPK KT4 43
Brende Gdns E/WMO/HCT KT8 34
Brent Lea BTFD TW8 6
Brent Rd BTFD TW8 6
Brentside BTFD TW8 6
Brent Wy BTFD TW8 7
Brewery Mews Centre ISLW TW7 * 13
Brewhouse St PUT/ROE SW15 17
Briar Cl HPTN TW12 19
ISLW TW7 13
Briar Rd WHTN TW2 20
Briar Wk PUT/ROE SW15 16
Briarwood Ct WPK KT4 * 38
Briarwood Rd EW KT17 43
Brick Farm Cl RCH/KEW TW9 8
Brickfield Cl BTFD TW8 6
Bridge Av HMSMTH W6 9
Bridge Gdns E/WMO/HCT KT8 34
Bridgeman Rd TEDD TW11 29
Bridge Pk WAND/EARL SW18 17
Bridge Rd CHSGTN KT9 41
E/WMO/HCT KT8 34
HSLW TW3 12
TWK TW1 13
Bridge St TWK TW1 14
Bridgeview HMSMTH W6 9
Bridge Vls WIM/MER SW19 * 25
Bridge Wy WHTN TW2 12
Bridge Wharf Rd ISLW TW7 13
Bridgewood Rd WPK KT4 43
Bridle Cl HOR/WEW KT19 42
KUT/HW KT1 36
SUN TW16 26
Bridle La TWK TW1 13
Bridle Rd ESH/CLAY KT10 40
Brighton Rd SURB KT6 35
Brinkley Rd WPK KT4 43
Brinsworth Cl WHTN TW2 20
Bristow Rd HSLW TW3 12
Britannia La WHTN TW2 12
Britannia Rd BRYLDS KT5 36
British Gv HMSMTH W6 9
British Grove Pas CHSWK W4 * 9
Broadfields E/WMO/HCT KT8 34
Broadhusrt Cl RCHPK/HAM TW10 14
Broadlands FELT TW13 19
Broadlands Wy NWMAL KT3 38

oad La HPTN TW12 .... 27 G2
oadmead Av WPK KT4 .... 38 B4
oadmead Rd HPTN TW12 .... 27 H1
oad Oak SUN TW16 .... 26 A1
oad Oaks SURB KT6 .... 37 E5
oad St TEDD TW11 .... 29 E1
oad Wk HEST TW5 .... 4 A4
RCH/KEW TW9 .... 9 G4
oadway SURB KT6 .... 37 E5
oadway Av TWK TW1 .... 13 G4
oadway Ct WIM/MER SW19 .... 33 H1
e Broadway THDIT KT7 .... 34 D5
WIM/MER SW19 .... 33 G1
ockenhurst Av WPK KT4 .... 37 H5
ockham Cl WIM/MER SW19 .... 25 C5
ockshot Cl BTFD TW8 .... 7 E2
ompton Cl HSLWW TW3 .... 11 C3
onson Rd RYNPK SW20 .... 33 E4
ook Cl RYNPK SW20 .... 32 C5
ookfield Gdns WAND/EARL SW18.... 17 H3
ook Gdns BARN SW13 .... 16 A4
KUTN/CMB KT2 .... 31 F3
ooklands Pl HPTN TW12 .... 20 A5
ooklands THDIT KT7 .... 35 E5
e Brooklands ISLW TW7 * 5 C4
ook La North BTFD TW8 .... 7 E1
ook Md HOR/WEW KT19 .... 42 D5
ook Rd SURB KT6 .... 41 F1
TWK TW1 .... 13 F4
ook Rd South BTFD TW8 .... 7 E2
ookside Cl FELT TW15 .... 18 B3
ookside Crs WPK KT4 .... 38 B5
ooks La CHSWK W4 .... 7 H2
ooks St KUT/HW KT1 .... 2 C5
ookwood Av BARN SW13 .... 16 A1
ookwood Rd HSLW TW3 .... 5 E5
WAND/EARL SW18 .... 25 C5
oom Cl TEDD TW11 .... 30 A2
oome Rd HPTN TW12 .... 27 C3
oomfield SUN TW16 .... 26 B3
oomfield Rd RCH/KEW TW9 .... 7 G4
SURB KT6 .... 36 C5
TEDD TW11 .... 29 H1
oomhill Rd WAND/EARL SW18.... 17 H4
oom Pk TEDD TW11 .... 2 A1
oom Rd TEDD TW11 .... 21 C5
oom Water TEDD TW11 .... 21 H5
oom Water West TEDD TW11 .... 21 H5
ough Cl HOR/WEW KT19 * 22 A5
oughton Av RCHPK/HAM TW10 .... 21 H4
owells La FELT TW13 .... 18 C2
FELT TW13 .... 18 D2
owning Av WPK KT4 .... 38 C5
owning Cl HPTN TW12 .... 19 G4
owning Wy HEST TW5 .... 4 A4
own's Rd BRYLDS KT5 .... 36 C4
ownlow Rd HOR/WEW KT19 .... 42 B4
unel Wk WHTN TW2 .... 11 H5
unswick Cl THDIT KT7 .... 35 E5
WHTN TW2 .... 20 C3
unswick Rd KUTN/CMB KT2 .... 3 C2
yan Cl SUN TW16 .... 26 A1
yanston Av WHTN TW2 .... 20 A1
yony Wy TWK TW1 .... 12 B1
ckhold Rd WAND/EARL SW18 .... 17 H4
ckingham Av E/WMO/HCT KT8 .... 28 A4
EBED/NFELT TW14 .... 10 C4
ckingham Gdns E/WMO/HCT KT8.... 28 A4
ckingham Rd HPTN TW12 .... 19 G4
KUT/HW KT1 .... 36 C1
RCHPK/HAM TW10 .... 22 A2
ckland Cl CHSGTN KT9 .... 41 C4
cklands Rd TEDD TW11 .... 30 C5
cklands Whf KUT/HW KT1 * 2 B4
ckleigh Av RYNPK SW20 .... 33 C5
llard Rd TEDD TW11 .... 28 D1
lls Aly MORT/ESHN SW14 * 15 C1
lstrode Av HSLW TW3 .... 11 H1
lstrode Gdns HSLW TW3 .... 11 H1
lstrode Rd HSLW TW3 .... 11 H1
rberry Cl NWMAL KT3 .... 31 H4
rden Cl BTFD TW8 .... 7 C3
rdenshott Av RCHPK/HAM TW10...15 E2
rdett Av RYNPK SW20 .... 32 B5
rdett Rd RCH/KEW TW9 .... 7 G3
rford Rd BTFD TW8 * 7 F1
WPK KT4 .... 38 B4
rges Av BARN SW13 .... 9 G3
rgess Cl FELT TW13 .... 19 F4
rghley Av NWMAL KT3 .... 31 H4
rghley Hall Cl WIM/MER SW19 * .. 25 E4
rghley Rd WIM/MER SW19 .... 25 E4
rgh Rd SUN TW16 .... 26 B3
rke Cl PUT/ROE SW15 .... 15 H2
rleigh Pl PUT/ROE SW15 .... 17 F5
rleigh Rd CHEAM SM3 .... 39 F5
rlington Av RCH/KEW TW9 .... 7 H4
rlington Gdns CHSWK W4 .... 8 B1
rlington La CHSWK W4 .... 8 B3
rlington Rd CHSWK W4 * 8 B1
ISLW TW7 ....
NWMAL KT3 .... 38 A1
rnaby Crs CHSWK W4 .... 8 A2
rnaby Gdns CHSWK W4 .... 8 A2
rnell Av RCHPK/HAM TW10 .... 21 H5

Burney Av BRYLDS KT5 .... 36 C2
Burnham St KUTN/CMB KT2 .... 3 G3
Burns Av TWK TW1 .... 13 G4
Burnside Cl TWK TW1 .... 13 H4
Burns Wy HEST TW5 .... 4 A5
Burritt Rd KUT/HW KT1 .... 3 J6
Burr Rd WAND/EARL SW18 .... 25 H1
Burstock Rd PUT/ROE SW15 .... 17 F2
Burston Rd PUT/ROE SW15 .... 17 E3
Burstow Rd RYNPK SW20 .... 33 F3
Burtenshaw Rd THDIT KT7 .... 35 F4
Burton Cl CHSGTN KT9 .... 45 E1
Burton Gdns HEST TW5 .... 4 C4
Burton Rd KUTN/CMB KT2 .... 2 D1
KUTN/CMB KT2 .... 30 B2
Burton's Rd HPTN TW12 .... 20 B4
Burtwell Cl SURB KT6 .... 36 D5
Busch Cl ISLW TW7 .... 6 C4
Bush Cottages WAND/EARL SW18.... 17 H3
Bushey Rd RYNPK SW20 .... 32 D4
Bush Rd RCH/KEW TW9 .... 7 H2
Bushwood Rd RCH/KEW TW9 .... 7 H2
Bushy Park Gdns HPTN TW12 .... 20 C5
TEDD TW11 * 20 C5
Bushy Park Rd TEDD TW11 .... 29 G2
Bushy Rd TEDD TW11 .... 28 D1
Bute Av RCHPK/HAM TW10 .... 22 B2
Bute Gdns RCHPK/HAM TW10 * 22 B3
Butlers Cl HSLW TW4 .... 11 G2
Butterfield Cl TWK TW1 .... 13 E4
Buttermere Cl EBED/NFELT TW14 .. 18 A1
MRDN SM4 .... 39 E3
Buttermere Dr PUT/ROE SW15 .... 17 E1
Butts Crs FELT TW13 .... 19 H3
The Butts BTFD TW8 .... 7 E2
Buxton Dr NWMAL KT3 .... 31 G4
Buxton Rd MORT/ESHN SW14 .... 15 H1
Bychurch End TEDD TW11 * 21 E5
Bye Ways WHTN TW2 .... 20 A3
The Byeways BRYLDS KT5 .... 36 D2
The Byeway MORT/ESHN SW14 .... 15 F1
Byfeld Gdns BARN SW13 .... 9 F4
Byfield Rd ISLW TW7 .... 13 F1
Byron Av NWMAL KT3 .... 38 B2
Byron Cl HPTN TW12 .... 19 G4
Byward Av EBED/NFELT TW14 .... 10 D4
The Byway HOR/WEW KT19 .... 43 E3

C

Cadbury Cl ISLW TW7 .... 6 B4
Cadmer Cl NWMAL KT3 .... 37 H1
Cadogan Cl TEDD TW11 .... 20 D5
Cadogan Rd SURB KT6 .... 36 A2
Caerleon Cl ESH/CLAY KT10 .... 44 C1
Cairngorm Cl TEDD TW11 .... 21 F5
Caldbeck Av WPK KT4 .... 43 G5
California Rd NWMAL KT3 .... 37 F1
Calonne Rd WIM/MER SW19 .... 25 E4
Calverley Rd EW KT17 .... 43 F5
Camac Rd WHTN TW2 .... 20 C1
Cambalt Rd PUT/ROE SW15 .... 17 E3
Camberley Av RYNPK SW20 .... 32 C4
Camborne Ms WAND/EARL SW18 .. 17 H5
Camborne Rd MRDN SM4 .... 39 E2
RYNPK SW20 .... 39 E2
WAND/EARL SW18 .... 17 H5
Camborne Wy HEST TW5 .... 4 D4
Cambria Cl HSLW TW3 .... 11 H2
Cambria Ct EBED/NFELT TW14 .... 10 C5
Cambrian Rd RCHPK/HAM TW10 .. 14 C4
Cambridge Av NWMAL KT3 .... 31 H4
Cambridge Cl HSLWW TW4 .... 11 F2
RYNPK SW20 .... 32 C3
Cambridge Crs TEDD TW11 .... 21 F5
Cambridge Gdns KUT/HW KT1 .... 3 G5
Cambridge Grove Rd KUT/HW KT1.... 3 C5
Cambridge Pk TWK TW1 .... 13 H5
Cambridge Rd BARN SW13 .... 9 E5
HPTN TW12 .... 27 G2
HSLWW TW4 .... 11 F2
KUT/HW KT1 .... 3 G5
NWMAL KT3 .... 37 G1
RCH/KEW TW9 .... 7 H5
RYNPK SW20 .... 32 C3
TEDD TW11 .... 21 F4
TWK TW1 .... 14 A4
Cambridge Rd North CHSWK W4 .. 8 A1
Cambridge Rd South CHSWK W4 .. 8 A1
Camden Av FELT TW15 .... 18 D2
Camel Gv KUTN/CMB KT2 .... 22 A5
Camellia Pl WHTN TW2 .... 12 A5
Camelot Cl WIM/MER SW19 .... 25 H4
Camilla Cl SUN TW16 * 26 A1
Camm Gdns KUT/HW KT1 .... 3 H5
THDIT KT7 .... 34 D4
Campbell Cl WHTN TW2 .... 20 C1
Campbell Rd WHTN TW2 .... 20 C2
Campden Ter CHSWK W4 * 8 D1
Campen Cl WIM/MER SW19 .... 25 F2
Campion Rd ISLW TW7 .... 6 D2
PUT/ROE SW15 .... 16 D2
Camp Rd WIM/MER SW19 .... 24 C5
Camp Vw WIM/MER SW19 .... 24 B5
Camrose Av FELT TW13 .... 18 C4
Camrose Cl MRDN SM4 .... 39 H1

Canbury Av KUTN/CMB KT2 .... 2 E3
Canbury Park Rd KUTN/CMB KT2.... 2 E5
Candler Ms TWK TW1 .... 13 F5
Canford Gdns NWMAL KT3 .... 37 H5
Canford Pl TEDD TW11 .... 29 H1
Cannizaro Rd WIM/MER SW19 .... 32 D1
Cannon Cl HPTN TW12 .... 20 B5
RYNPK SW20 .... 32 D5
Cannon Hill La RYNPK SW20 .... 39 F2
Canterbury Rd FELT TW13 .... 19 F2
Capital Interchange Wy BTFD TW8 .. 7 H1
Cardigan Rd BARN SW13 .... 9 F5
RCHPK/HAM TW10 .... 22 A2
Cardinal Av KUTN/CMB KT2 .... 22 B5
MRDN SM4 .... 39 F3
Cardinal Cl MRDN SM4 .... 39 F3
WPK KT4 .... 43 G3
Cardinal Crs NWMAL KT3 .... 31 F4
Cardinal Pl PUT/ROE SW15 .... 17 E2
Cardinal Rd FELT TW13 .... 18 C1
Cardinal's Wk HPTN TW12 .... 28 B2
Cardington Sq HSLWW TW4 .... 11 E2
Carisbrooke Cl HSLWW TW4 .... 11 E4
Carleton Cl ESH/CLAY KT10 .... 34 C5
Carlingford Rd MRDN SM4 .... 39 E3
Carlisle Cl KUTN/CMB KT2 .... 3 H2
Carlisle Rd HPTN TW12 .... 28 B2
Carlton Av EBED/NFELT TW14 .... 10 D4
Carlton Dr PUT/ROE SW15 .... 17 E3
Carlton Dene EW KT17 * 43 G4
Carlton Park Av RYNPK SW20 .... 32 D5
Carlton Rd MORT/ESHN SW14 .... 15 F1
NWMAL KT3 .... 31 H4
SUN TW16 .... 26 A2
Carlyle Cl E/WMO/HCT KT8 .... 28 A4
Carmalt Gdns PUT/ROE SW15 .... 16 D2
Carmel Wy RCH/KEW TW9 .... 7 H5
Carnegie Cl SURB KT6 .... 41 G3
Carnegie Pl WIM/MER SW19 .... 25 E3
Carnforth Cl HOR/WEW KT19 .... 42 A5
Carnwath Rd FUL/PGN SW6 .... 17 H1
Caroline Cl ISLW TW7 .... 5 C3
Caroline Rd WIM/MER SW19 .... 33 H3
Carrara Whf FUL/PGN SW6 .... 17 F1
Carrick Cl ISLW TW7 .... 6 A5
Carrington Av HSLW TW3 .... 12 A3
Carrington Rd RCHPK/HAM TW10.... 14 D2
Carslake Rd PUT/ROE SW15 .... 16 D4
Carters Yd WAND/EARL SW18 * 17 H3
WAND/EARL SW18 .... 17 H3
Cartwright Wy BARN SW13 .... 9 G3
Carville Crs BTFD TW8 .... 7 F1
Cassilis Rd TWK TW1 .... 13 H4
Cassiobury Av EBED/NFELT TW14 .. 10 A5
Castello Av PUT/ROE SW15 .... 16 D3
Castelnau BARN SW13 .... 9 F3
Castle Cl WIM/MER SW19 .... 25 E5
Castlecombe Dr WIM/MER SW19.... 17 E5
Castlegate RCH/KEW TW9 .... 14 C1
Castle Rd ISLW TW7 .... 6 A5
Castle Rw CHSWK W4 * 8 C1
Castle St KUT/HW KT1 .... 2 C4
Castle Wk SUN TW16 * 26 B2
Castle Wy FELT TW13 .... 18 D4
WIM/MER SW19 .... 24 C3
Castle Yd RCH/KEW TW9 * 14 B2
Catherine Dr RCH/KEW TW9 .... 14 B2
Catherine Gdns HSLW TW3 .... 12 C2
Catherine Rd SURB KT6 .... 36 A2
Catherine Vls RYNPK SW20 * 32 C2
Catherine Wheel Rd BTFD TW8 .... 7 F3
Causeway EBED/NFELT TW14 .... 10 C2
The Causeway CHSGTN KT9 .... 41 G5
ESH/CLAY KT10 .... 44 A1
TEDD TW11 .... 29 E1
WIM/MER SW19 .... 24 D5
Cavalry Crs HSLWW TW4 .... 11 F3
Cavalry Gdns PUT/ROE SW15 .... 17 F3
Cavell Wy HOR/WEW KT19 .... 45 H4
Cavendish Av NWMAL KT3 .... 38 C2
Cavendish Cl SUN TW16 .... 26 A1
Cavendish Ct SUN TW16 .... 26 A1
Cavendish Pde HSLWW TW4 * 4 B5
NWMAL KT3 .... 38 A1
SUN TW16 .... 26 A1
Cavendish Rd CHSWK W4 .... 8 B2
NWMAL KT3 .... 38 A1
SUN TW16 .... 26 A1
Cavendish Ter FELT TW13 * 18 D1
Caverleigh Wy WPK KT4 .... 38 B5
Cave Rd RCHPK/HAM TW10 .... 21 H4
Caversham Rd KUT/HW KT1 .... 2 E4
Caxton Ms BTFD TW8 .... 6 D2
Cecil Cl CHSGTN KT9 .... 41 E3
Cecil Rd HSLW TW3 .... 12 B1
Cedar Av WHTN TW2 .... 12 A5
Cedar Cl KUTN/CMB KT2 .... 23 G4
Cedar Ct WIM/MER SW19 .... 25 E5
Cedarcroft Rd CHSGTN KT9 .... 41 G3
Cedar Hts RCHPK/HAM TW10 .... 22 B1
Cedar Rd E/WMO/HCT KT8 .... 28 D1
TEDD TW11 .... 21 F5
Cedars Cottages PUT/ROE SW15 * .. 16 B4
Cedars Rd BARN SW13 .... 9 F5
CHSWK W4 .... 8 A1
KUT/HW KT1 .... 2 A4
MRDN SM4 .... 39 H1
The Cedars TEDD TW11 .... 29 E1

Cedar Ter RCH/KEW TW9 .... 14 B2
Cedar Wk ESH/CLAY KT10 .... 40 A5
Centaur Ct BTFD TW8 * 7 F1
Central Av HSLW TW3 .... 12 B2
Central Pde SURB KT6 * 36 B3
Central Park Est HSLWW TW4 * 11 E2
Central Rd WPK KT4 .... 43 F1
Central Wy EBED/NFELT TW14 .... 10 C3
The Centre FELT TW13 .... 18 B2
Chadacre Rd EW KT17 .... 43 G4
Chadwick Av WIM/MER SW19 .... 33 H1
Chadwick Cl PUT/ROE SW15 .... 16 A5
TEDD TW11 .... 29 F1
Chadwick Pl SURB KT6 .... 35 H5
Chaffinch Cl SURB KT6 .... 41 H2
Chailey Cl HEST TW5 .... 4 A4
Chalcott Gdns SURB KT6 * 35 H5
Chalfont Ms WAND/EARL SW18 .... 25 C5
Chalgrove Av MRDN SM4 .... 39 H2
Chalky La CHSGTN KT9 .... 45 E2
Challis Rd BTFD TW8 .... 7 E1
Challoners Cl E/WMO/HCT KT8 .... 34 C1
Chalmers Wy EBED/NFELT TW14 .. 10 C3
TWK TW1 .... 13 G2
Chamberlain Gdns HSLW TW3 .... 5 F4
Chamberlain Wy SURB KT6 .... 36 B4
Chancellors St HMSMTH W6 .... 9 H1
Chancellors Whf HMSMTH W6 .... 9 H1
Chancellor's Rd HMSMTH W6 .... 9 H1
Chandler Cl HPTN TW12 .... 27 G5
Chandlers Cl EBED/NFELT TW14 .. 10 A5
Channel Cl HEST TW5 .... 4 D4
Chantry Cl SUN TW16 .... 26 B2
Chantry Rd CHSGTN KT9 .... 41 G4
Chapel Mill Rd KUT/HW KT1 * 3 F7
Chapel Rd HSLW TW3 .... 12 B1
TWK TW1 .... 13 G5
Chapman Sq WIM/MER SW19 .... 24 C2
Chapter Wy HPTN TW12 .... 19 H4
Chara Pl CHSWK W4 .... 8 C2
Charles Babbage Cl CHSGTN KT9.... 44 D1
Charles Rd WIM/MER SW19 .... 33 H3
Charles St BARN SW13 .... 15 H1
HSLW TW3 .... 4 C5
Charleston Cl FELT TW13 .... 18 B3
Charlotte Rd BARN SW13 .... 9 E4
Charlwood Rd PUT/ROE SW15 .... 17 E1
Charlwood Ter PUT/ROE SW15 .... 17 E2
Charminster Av WIM/MER SW19 .. 33 H1
Charminster Rd WPK KT4 .... 39 E5
Charnwood Av WIM/MER SW19 .. 33 H1
Charnwood Cl NWMAL KT3 .... 37 H1
Charter Crs HSLWW TW4 .... 11 F2
Charter Rd KUT/HW KT1 .... 3 J6
Charter Sq KUT/HW KT1 .... 3 K5
Chartfield Av PUT/ROE SW15 .... 16 D3
Chartfield Sq PUT/ROE SW15 .... 17 E3
Chase Ct RYNPK SW20 .... 33 F4
Chase Gdns WHTN TW2 .... 12 C4
Chaseley Ct CHSWK W4 .... 8 A1
Chaseside Av RYNPK SW20 * 32 C2
The Chase SUN TW16 .... 26 C3
Chatham Cl CHEAM SM3 .... 39 G4
Chatham Rd KUT/HW KT1 .... 3 J5
Chatsworth Av RYNPK SW20 .... 33 F5
Chatsworth Cl CHSWK W4 * 8 B2
Chatsworth Crs HSLW TW3 .... 12 C2
Chatsworth Gdns NWMAL KT3 * .. 38 A2
Chatsworth Pl TEDD TW11 .... 21 F4
Chatsworth Rd CHSWK W4 .... 8 B2
Chaucer Av RCH/KEW TW9 .... 7 H5
Cheam Common Rd WPK KT4 .... 43 G5
Cheeseman Cl HPTN TW12 .... 27 F1
Chelsea Cl HPTN TW12 .... 20 B5
WPK KT4 .... 38 B4
Cheltenham Av TWK TW1 .... 13 F5
Cheltenham Cl NWMAL KT3 .... 31 F5
Chelverton Rd PUT/ROE SW15 .... 17 E2
Chelwood Gdns RCH/KEW TW9 .... 7 H5
Chepstow Cl PUT/ROE SW15 .... 17 F3
Cherimoya Gdns E/WMO/HCT KT8.... 28 A5
Cherry Cl MRDN SM4 .... 39 F1
Cherry Crs BTFD TW8 .... 6 C3
Cherry Orchard Gdns
E/WMO/HCT KT8 .... 27 G5
Cherry Orchard Rd E/WMO/HCT KT8.... 27 H5
Cherry Wy HOR/WEW KT19 .... 42 C5
Cherrywood Cl KUTN/CMB KT2 .... 3 G5
Cherrywood Dr PUT/ROE SW15 .... 17 E3
Cherrywood La RYNPK SW20 .... 39 F1
Chertsey La HOR/WEW KT19 .... 45 G5
Chertsey Rd FELT TW13 .... 18 A3
TWK TW1 .... 13 F4
WHTN TW2 .... 20 B1
Chervil Cl FELT TW13 .... 18 B3
Chessington Cl HOR/WEW KT19 .. 42 B5
Chessington Hall Gdns CHSGTN KT9.... 45 E1
Chessington Hill Pk CHSGTN KT9.. 41 H4
Chessington Pde CHSGTN KT9 * .. 41 H5
Chessington Rd CHSGTN KT9 .... 41 H5
HOR/WEW KT19.... 42 A5
Chester Av RCHPK/HAM TW10 .... 14 C4
WHTN TW2 .... 19 G1
Chester Cl BARN SW13 * 16 C1

Chesterfield Dr ESH/CLAY KT10 40 B1
Chesterfield Rd CHSWK W4 8 B2
Chester Rd HSLWW TW4 10 C1
  WIM/MER SW19 32 D1
The Chesters NWMAL KT3 31 H3
Chesterton Cl WAND/EARL SW18 17 H3
Chesterton Ter KUT/HW KT1 3 H3
Chestnut Av BTFD TW8 7 E1
  E/WMO/HCT KT8 29 E5
  ESH/CLAY KT10 34 C4
  HOR/WEW KT19 42 D3
  HPTN TW12 27 H2
  MORT/ESHN SW14 15 C1
  TEDD TW11 29 E2
Chestnut Gv ISLW TW7 13 F2
  NWMAL KT3 31 G5
Chestnut Rd KUTN/CMB KT2 2 C1
  RYNPK SW20 33 E4
  WHTN TW2 20 D2
Chestnut Wy FELT TW13 18 C3
Cheyne Av WHTN TW2 19 C3
Cheyne HI BRYLDS KT5 36 C1
Chichester Cl HPTN TW12 27 G1
Chichester Wy EBED/NFELT TW14 10 D5
Chillingworth Gdns TWK TW1 * 21 E2
Chilmark Gdns NWMAL KT3 38 A3
Chiltern Av WHTN TW2 19 H1
Chiltern Cl WPK KT4 43 H1
Chiltern Dr BRYLDS KT5 37 E2
Chilton Rd RCH/KEW TW9 14 D1
Chilvers Cl WHTN TW2 20 D2
Chisholm Rd RCHPK/HAM TW10 14 C4
Chislehurst Rd RCHPK/HAM TW10 14 B4
Chiswick Br CHSWK W4 8 B5
Chiswick High Rd CHSWK W4 7 H1
Chiswick House Grounds CHSWK W4 * 8 C2
Chiswick La CHSWK W4 8 D1
Chiswick La South CHSWK W4 9 E2
Chiswick Ml CHSWK W4 9 E2
Chiswick Pier CHSWK W4 * 9 E3
Chiswick Quay CHSWK W4 8 B4
Chiswick Sq CHSWK W4 * 8 D2
Chiswick Staithe CHSWK W4 8 B4
  RCH/KEW TW9 8 A4
Chiswick Village CHSWK W4 * 7 H1
Chiswick Whf CHSWK W4 9 E2
Chivenor Gv KUTN/CMB KT2 22 A5
Chobham Gdns WIM/MER SW19 25 G2
Cholmley Rd THDIT KT7 35 G3
Cholmley Ter THDIT KT7 * 35 G4
Cholmley Vls THDIT KT7 * 35 G4
Christabel Cl ISLW TW7 12 D1
Christchurch Av TEDD TW11 21 F5
Christ Church Rd BRYLDS KT5 36 C4
  EPSOM KT18
Christchurch Rd MORT/ESHN SW14 15 E3
Chudleigh Rd WHTN TW2 12 D4
Chumleigh Wk BRYLDS KT5 36 C1
Church Av MORT/ESHN SW14 15 G2
Church Cl HSLW TW3 4 C5
Churchfields E/WMO/HCT KT8 27 H5
Churchfields Av FELT TW13 19 G3
Church Ga FUL/PGN SW6 17 F1
Church HI SURB KT6 36 B2
Churchill Cl EBED/NFELT TW14 18 A1
Churchill Rd HOR/WEW KT19 45 H4
Churchill Wy SUN TW16 18 B5
Church La CHSGTN KT9 41 G5
  TEDD TW11 21 E5
  THDIT KT7 35 G3
  TWK TW1 21 F1
  WIM/MER SW19 33 H3
Church Meadow SURB KT6 40 D1
Church Pth RYNPK SW20 33 G4
  WIM/MER SW19 33 G4
Church Ri CHSGTN KT9 41 G5
Church Rd BARN SW13 9 F5
  E/WMO/HCT KT8 28 C5
  ESH/CLAY KT10 40 A5
  FELT TW13 18 D5
  HEST TW5 4 D3
  ISLW TW7 5 G4
  KUT/HW KT1 2 E4
  RCHPK/HAM TW10 14 B3
  RCHPK/HAM TW10 22 B4
  SURB KT6 35 H5
  TEDD TW11 20 D4
  WIM/MER SW19 33 H3
  WPK KT4 37 H5
Church Rw WAND/EARL SW18 * 17 H3
Church St CHSWK W4 8 D2
  HPTN TW12 28 B3
  HSLW TW3 12 B3
  ISLW TW7 13 G1
  KUT/HW KT1 2 B5
  SUN TW16 26 B5
  TWK TW1 21 F1
Church Ter RCHPK/HAM TW10 14 A3
Churchview Rd WHTN TW2 20 C1
Church Wk BTFD TW8 6 D2
  RYNPK SW20 32 D5
  THDIT KT7 35 E3
Churston Dr MRDN SM4 39 E2
Churton Pl CHSWK W4 * 8 A2
Circle Gdns WIM/MER SW19 33 H5

Clairvale Rd HEST TW5 4 A4
Clandon Cl EW KT17 43 E5
Clandon Ter RYNPK SW20 * 33 E4
Clare Lawn Av MORT/ESHN SW14 15 G3
Claremont Av NWMAL KT3 38 C2
  SUN TW16 26 C5
Claremont Gdns SURB KT6 36 B1
Claremont Gv CHSWK W4 8 D3
Claremont Rd SURB KT6 36 B2
  TEDD TW11 21 E5
  TWK TW1 13 G5
Claremont Ter THDIT KT7 * 35 G4
Claremont Vls KUT/HW KT1 * 3 F5
Clarence Av NWMAL KT3 31 F4
Clarence La PUT/ROE SW15 16 A4
Clarence Rd CHSWK W4 7 H1
  RCH/KEW TW9 7 G4
  TEDD TW11 29 E1
Clarence St KUT/HW KT1 2 B4
  RCH/KEW TW9 14 B2
Clarence Ter HSLW TW3 12 A2
Clarence Vls KUT/HW KT1 * 3 F5
Clarendon Crs WHTN TW2 20 C3
Clarendon Dr PUT/ROE SW15 16 D2
Clare Rd HSLWW TW4 11 G1
Clarkes Av WPK KT4 39 E5
Clark Wy HEST TW5 4 A3
Claudia Pl WIM/MER SW19 25 F1
Clavering Av BARN SW13 9 G2
Clavering Cl TEDD TW11 21 F4
Claygate La ESH/CLAY KT10 40 B1
  THDIT KT7 35 F5
Claymore Cl MRDN SM4 39 H4
Claypole Dr HEST TW5 4 B4
Clayponds La BTFD TW8 7 F1
Clayton Crs BTFD TW8 7 E1
Clayton Rd CHSGTN KT9 40 D5
  ISLW TW7 13 G2
Clearwater Pl SURB KT6 35 H5
Cleaveland Rd SURB KT6 36 A2
Cleeve Wy PUT/ROE SW15 16 A4
Clement Rd WIM/MER SW19 25 F5
Clements Pl BTFD TW8 7 E1
Clevedon Rd KUT/HW KT1 3 G4
  TWK TW1 14 A4
Cleveland Av HPTN TW12 27 G2
Cleveland Gdns BARN SW13 9 F5
  WPK KT4 42 D1
Cleveland Ri MRDN SM4 39 E4
Cleveland Rd BARN SW13 9 E5
  ISLW TW7 13 F2
  NWMAL KT3 37 H1
  WPK KT4 42 D1
Cleves Rd RCHPK/HAM TW10 21 H5
Cleves Wy HPTN TW12 27 G2
  SUN TW16 26 A1
Clifden Rd BTFD TW8 7 E2
  TWK TW1 21 E1
Clifford Av MORT/ESHN SW14 8 B5
  RCH/KEW TW9 15 E1
Clifford Rd HSLWW TW4 11 E1
  RCHPK/HAM TW10 22 A2
Clifton Av FELT TW13 18 D3
Clifton Pde FELT TW13 * 18 D4
Clifton Park Av RYNPK SW20 32 D4
Clifton Pl KUTN/CMB KT2 * 3 G2
Clifton Rd ISLW TW7 5 H5
  KUTN/CMB KT2 3 F2
  TEDD TW11 20 D4
  WIM/MER SW19 33 E1
Clinton Av E/WMO/HCT KT8 34 B1
Clippesby Cl CHSGTN KT9 * 41 G5
Clipstone Rd HSLW TW3 11 H1
Clitherow Rd BTFD TW8 6 C1
Cliveden Rd WIM/MER SW19 33 G3
  TWK TW1 14 A4
Clockhouse Cl WIM/MER SW19 24 D3
Clockhouse Pl PUT/ROE SW15 17 F3
Clock Tower Rd ISLW TW7 13 E1
Cloister Cl TEDD TW11 21 G5
Clonmel Rd TEDD TW11 20 C4
Clonmore St WAND/EARL SW18 25 E1
The Close CHEAM SM3 39 C4
  ISLW TW7 5 C5
  NWMAL KT3 31 F4
  RCH/KEW TW9 15 E1
  SURB KT6 36 B4
Clovelly Rd HSLW TW3 4 D5
Clunbury Av NWDGN UB2 4 C1
Clydesdale Cl ISLW TW7 13 E1
Clydesdale Gdns RCHPK/HAM TW10 14 D2
Clymping Dene EBED/NFELT TW14 10 C5
Coach House La WIM/MER SW19 25 E4
Coalecroft Rd PUT/ROE SW15 16 D2
Cobbett Rd WHTN TW2 19 H1
Cobbler's Wk TEDD TW11 28 D2
Cobb's Rd HSLWW TW4 11 G2
Cobham Av NWMAL KT3 38 B2
Cobham Rd KUT/HW KT1 3 H4
Cochrane Rd WIM/MER SW19 33 F2
Cockcrow HI SURB KT6 * 40 A5
Cocks Crs NWMAL KT3 38 A1
Colborne Wy WPK KT4 43 H2
Coldstream Gdns WAND/EARL SW18 17 G4
Cole Park Gdns TWK TW1 13 F5
Cole Park Rd TWK TW1 13 F5
Cole Rd TWK TW1 13 F4

Coleshill Rd TEDD TW11 28 D1
Colinette Rd PUT/ROE SW15 16 D2
Coliston Rd WAND/EARL SW18 17 H5
College Cl WHTN TW2 20 C1
College Dr THDIT KT7 35 F4
College Gdns NWMAL KT3 38 A2
College Rd ISLW TW7 5 H4
Collier Cl HOR/WEW KT19 41 H5
Collingwood Av BRYLDS KT5 37 F5
Collingwood Cl WHTN TW2 11 H5
Colne Ct HOR/WEW KT19 42 B3
Colne Rd WHTN TW2 20 D1
Colonial Av WHTN TW2 12 B4
Colston Rd MORT/ESHN SW14 15 F2
Columbia Av WPK KT4 38 A4
Colwith Rd HMSMTH W6 9 H2
Colwyn Crs HSLW TW3 5 H4
Combemartin Rd WAND/EARL SW18 17 F5
Commerce Rd BTFD TW8 6 C2
Commondale PUT/ROE SW15 9 H5
Common La ESH/CLAY KT10 44 B1
Common Rd BARN SW13 16 B1
  ESH/CLAY KT10 40 B5
Compass HI RCHPK/HAM TW10 14 A4
Compton Crs CHSGTN KT9 41 F5
  CHSWK W4 8 B2
Compton Rd WIM/MER SW19 33 G1
Concorde Cl HSLW TW3 5 E5
Conifers Cl TEDD TW11 29 G2
Coniston Cl BARN SW13 9 E3
  CHSWK W4 8 A4
  MRDN SM4 39 E3
Coniston Rd WHTN TW2 12 A4
Coniston Wy CHSGTN KT9 41 F2
Connaught Av HSLWW TW4 11 F5
  MORT/ESHN SW14 15 F1
Connaught Rd NWMAL KT3 37 H1
  RCHPK/HAM TW10 * 14 C5
  TEDD TW11 20 C5
Conrad Dr WPK KT4 38 D5
Consfield Av NWMAL KT3 38 B1
Consort Ms ISLW TW7 12 C3
Constable Gdns ISLW TW7 12 C3
Constance Rd WHTN TW2 12 A5
Conway Rd FELT TW13 19 E5
  HSLWW TW4 11 G5
  RYNPK SW20 32 D3
Coombe Bank NWMAL KT3 31 H1
Coombe Cl HSLW TW3 11 H2
Coombe Crs HPTN TW12 27 F2
Coombe End KUTN/CMB KT2 31 G2
Coombefield Cl NWMAL KT3 37 H2
Coombe Gdns NWMAL KT3 38 A1
  RYNPK SW20 32 B4
Coombe Hill Gld KUTN/CMB KT2 31 G3
Coombe Hill Rd KUTN/CMB KT2 31 G3
Coombe House Cha NWMAL KT3 31 G3
Coombe La RYNPK SW20 32 A3
Coombe La West KUTN/CMB KT2 31 K3
  KUTN/CMB KT2 31 H2
  KUTN/CMB KT2 31 H2
Coombe Neville KUTN/CMB KT2 31 F2
Coombe Pk KUTN/CMB KT2 23 F5
Coombe Ridings KUTN/CMB KT2 23 F5
Coombe Ri KUTN/CMB KT2 31 G2
Coombe Rd CHSWK W4 8 D1
  HPTN TW12 27 G1
  KUT/HW KT1 3 H1
  NWMAL KT3 31 H5
Coombe Vls WAND/EARL SW18 17 H5
Coombe Wood Rd KUTN/CMB KT2 23 F5
Copgard Gdns CHSGTN KT9 *
Copperfields SUN TW16 * 26 A1
Copper Mill Dr ISLW TW7 6 A5
Coppice Cl RYNPK SW20 32 D5
Coppice Dr PUT/ROE SW15 16 B4
Coppsfield E/WMO/HCT KT8 27 H5
Copse Gld SURB KT6 36 A4
Copse HI RYNPK SW20 32 B3
Copthall Gdns TWK TW1 21 E1
Corban Rd HSLW TW3 11 H1
Corbiere Ct WIM/MER SW19 33 E1
Corfe Cl HSLWW TW4 19 F1
Corkran Rd SURB KT6 36 A4
Corney Reach Wy CHSWK W4 8 D3
Corney Rd CHSWK W4 8 D2
Cornwall Av ESH/CLAY KT10 44 A1
Cornwall Gv CHSWK W4 8 B1
Cornwall Rd TWK TW1 13 F5
Corporation Av HSLWW TW4 11 F2
Corscombe Cl KUTN/CMB KT2 23 F5
Corsellis Sq TWK TW1 13 G2
Cortis Rd PUT/ROE SW15 16 C4
Cortis Ter PUT/ROE SW15 16 C4
Cotsford Av NWMAL KT3 37 G2
Cotswold Cl ESH/CLAY KT10 40 A1
  KUTN/CMB KT2 31 F1
Cotswold Rd HPTN TW12 27 H1
Cotswold Wy WPK KT4 43 H1
Cottage Gv SURB KT6 36 A3
Cottenham Dr RYNPK SW20 32 C2
Cottenham Park Rd RYNPK SW20 32 B3
  RYNPK SW20 32 C2
Cottenham Pl RYNPK SW20 32 C2
Cotterill Rd SURB KT6 41 G1
Cottimore Rd FELT TW13 19 E3
Cottington Rd FELT TW13 19 E3
Country Wy FELT TW13 18 D5

County Pde BTFD TW8 * 7
Court Cl WHTN TW2 20
Court Cls CHSGTN KT9 41
Court Close Av WHTN TW2 20
Courtenay Rd WPK KT4 43
Court Farm Av HOR/WEW KT19 42
Courthope Rd WIM/MER SW19 25
Courthope Vls WIM/MER SW19 33
Courtlands RCHPK/HAM TW10 14
Courtlands Av HPTN TW12 27
  RCH/KEW TW9 8
Courtlands Dr HOR/WEW KT19 42
Courtlands Rd BRYLDS KT5 36
Court Wy WHTN TW2 20
Coutts Av CHSGTN KT9 41
Coval Gdns MORT/ESHN SW14 15
Coval La MORT/ESHN SW14 15
Coval Rd MORT/ESHN SW14 15
Coverts Rd ESH/CLAY KT10 44
Cowleaze Rd KUTN/CMB KT2 2
Cowley Rd MORT/ESHN SW14 15
Cowper Rd KUTN/CMB KT2 2
Cox La CHSGTN KT9 41
  HOR/WEW KT19 42
Craig Rd RCHPK/HAM TW10 21
Craigwell Av FELT TW13 18
Cranborne Av SURB KT6 41
Cranbrook Dr ESH/CLAY KT10 40
  WHTN TW2 20
Cranbrook Rd CHSWK W4 8
  HSLWW TW4 11
  WIM/MER SW19 33
Crane Av ISLW TW7 13
Cranebank Ms TWK TW1 * 13
Cranebrook WHTN TW2 20
Crane Ct MORT/ESHN SW14 * 15
Cranford Cl WHTN TW2 20
Cranford Wy WHTN TW2 20
Crane Park Rd WHTN TW2 20
Crane Rd WHTN TW2 20
Cranes Dr BRYLDS KT5 36
Cranes Pk BRYLDS KT5 36
Cranes Park Av BRYLDS KT5 36
Cranes Park Crs BRYLDS KT5 36
Craneswater Pk NWDGN UB2 4
Crane Wy WHTN TW2 12
Cranford Cl RYNPK SW20 * 32
Cranford La HEST TW5 4
  HTHAIR TW6 10
Cranleigh Gdns KUTN/CMB KT2 30
Cranleigh Rd ESH/CLAY KT10 34
  FELT TW13 18
  WIM/MER SW19 33
Cranmer Cl MRDN SM4 39
Cranmer Ct HPTN TW12 27
  KUTN/CMB KT2 22
Cranmer Rd HPTN TW12 27
  KUTN/CMB KT2 22
Cranmore Av ISLW TW7 5
Cranston Cl HSLW TW3 4
Cravan Av FELT TW13 18
Craven Rd KUTN/CMB KT2 2
Crawford Cl ISLW TW7 5
Crayke HI CHSGTN KT9 45
Crediton Wy ESH/CLAY KT10 40
Creek Cottages E/WMO/HCT KT8 * 34
Creek Rd E/WMO/HCT KT8 34
Crescent Gdns WIM/MER SW19 25
Crescent Rd KUTN/CMB KT2 30
  RYNPK SW20 33
The Crescent BARN SW13 9
  NWMAL KT3 31
  SURB KT6 36
  WIM/MER SW19 25
Cresswell Rd FELT TW13 19
  TWK TW1 14
Cressys Cnr HSLW TW3 * 12
Creston Wy WPK KT4 39
The Crest BRYLDS KT5 36
Crestway PUT/ROE SW15 16
Crestwood Wy HSLWW TW4 11
Cricketers Cl CHSGTN KT9 41
Crieff Ct TEDD TW11 29
Crispen Rd FELT TW13 19
Crisp Rd HMSMTH W6 9
Crofters Cl ISLW TW7 12
Crofton Av CHSWK W4 8
Crofton Ter RCH/KEW TW9 8
The Croft HEST TW5 4
Croft Wy RCHPK/HAM TW10 21
Cromer Villas Rd WAND/EARL SW18 17
Cromford Rd PUT/ROE SW15 16
Cromford Wy NWMAL KT3 31
Cromwell Av HMSMTH W6 9
  NWMAL KT3 38
Cromwell Cl CHSWK W4 * 8
Cromwell Pl MORT/ESHN SW14 15
Cromwell Rd FELT TW13 19
  HSLW TW3 11
  KUTN/CMB KT2 2
  TEDD TW11 29
  WIM/MER SW19 33
  WPK KT4 42
Cromwell St HSLW TW3 11
Cromwell Ter HSLW TW3 * 11
Crosby Cl FELT TW13 19
Cross Deep TWK TW1 21
Cross Deep Gdns TWK TW1 21

ss Lances Rd *HSLW* TW3 ...12 A2
sslands Av *NWDGN* UB2 ...4 C1
sslands Pde *EBED/NFELT* * ...8 D1
sslands *HOR/WEW* KT19 ...42 C5
ss Rd *FELT* TW13 ...19 F4
  KUTN/CMB KT2 ...3 F1
  WIM/MER SW19 ...33 H2
ss St *BARN* SW13 ...8 D5
  HPTN TW12 ...20 B5
ssway *NWMAL* KT3 ...38 D1
ssways *SUN* TW16 ...26 A3
e Crossways *BRYLDS* KT5 * ...37 E5
  FELT TW5
wn Ar *KUT/HW* KT1 ...2 B5
wn La *MRDN* SM4 ...33 H5
wn Rd *KUTN/CMB* KT2 ...31 F3
  MRDN SM4 ...39 H1
  TWK TW1 ...13 G4
wn Ter *RCH/KEW* TW9 ...4 A2
wntree CI *ISLW* TW7 ...6 A2
wthorne CI *WEW/EARL* SW18 ...17 G5
wther Av *BTFD* TW8 ...7 F1
ylands Dr *SURB* KT6 ...36 B4
ysdale Av *SUN* TW16 ...26 B5
da's CI *HOR/WEW* KT19 ...43 E5
ddington Av *WPK* KT4 ...43 E2
ddington Gld *HOR/WEW* KT19 ...45 H5
sac Rd *BARN* SW13 ...41 F1
mberland CI *RYNPK* SW20 ...33 E2
nberland *CHSGTN* KT9 ...13 C4
nberland Dr *ESH/CLAY* KT10 ...40 B1
mberland House *KUTN/CMB* KT2 ...3 K1
  KUTN/CMB KT2 ...31 F2
mberland Rd *BARN* SW13 ...9 E4
  RCH/KEW TW9 ...7 H4
mbernauld Gdns *SUN* TW16 ...18 A5
mbrae Gdns *SURB* KT6 ...41 E1
nnor Gdns *EW* KT17 ...43 F5
rie Hill CI *WIM/MER* SW19 ...25 C4
tis Rd *HOR/WEW* KT19 ...42 B3
  HSLWW TW4 ...11 C5
sack CI *TWK* TW1 * ...21 E4
clamen CI *HPTN* TW12 ...27 H1
clamen Wy *HOR/WEW* KT19 ...42 B4
gnet Rd *EBED/NFELT* TW14 ...19 F4
e Cygnets *FELT* TW13 ...19 F4
press Av *WHTN* TW2 ...12 B5

D

de Wy *NWDGN* UB2 ...4 C1
ffodil CI *HPTN* TW12 ...27 H1
gmar Rd *KUTN/CMB* KT2 ...3 F2
sy La *FUL/PGN* SW6 ...17 H1
cross Rd *HSLWW* TW4 ...4 B5
e Av *HSLWW* TW4 ...11 F1
le Rd *SUN* TW16 ...26 A2
eside Rd *HOR/WEW* KT19 ...42 C5
e St *CHSWK* W4 ...8 A1
ewood Gdns *WPK* KT4 ...43 G1
meny Crs *HSLW* TW5 ...12 C2
meny Rd *WPK* KT4 ...43 G2
more Av *ESH/CLAY* KT10 ...40 A5
ncer Rd *E/WMO/HCT* KT8 ...34 A1
nebury Av *PUT/ROE* SW15 ...16 A5
nemere St *PUT/ROE* SW15 ...16 D1
nesbury Rd *FELT* TW13 ...18 C1
niel CI *HSLWW* TW4 ...11 C5
n Manson Dr *CHSWK* W4 ...8 A1
rby Crs *SUN* TW16 ...26 D4
rby Gdns *SUN* TW16 ...26 D4
rcy Rd *ISLW* TW7 ...6 D3
rfur St *PUT/ROE* SW15 ...17 E1
rell Rd *RCH/KEW* TW9 ...14 D3
rlaston Rd *WIM/MER* SW19 ...33 E2
rley Dr *NWMAL* KT3 ...31 G4
rtmouth PI *CHSWK* W4 ...8 D2
rwin Rd *EW* A5 ...6 D1
venport CI *TEDD* TW11 * ...29 F1
vid Twigg CI *KUTN/CMB* KT2 ...2 D2
vies Wk *ISLW* TW7 ...5 C4
wes Av *ISLW* TW7 ...13 F5
n CI *HSLW* TW4 ...11 F1
wson Rd *KUT/HW* KT1 ...3 F6
ylesford Av *PUT/ROE* SW15 ...16 B2
acon Rd *KUTN/CMB* KT2 ...2 E5
acons Wk *HPTN* TW12 ...19 H4
altry Rd *PUT/ROE* SW15 ...16 D2
anhill Ct *MORT/ESHN* SW14 * ...15 E2
anhill Rd *MORT/ESHN* SW14 ...15 E2
ar Rd *HPTN* TW12 ...19 H5
  HSLW TW5 ...12 A3
ans CI *CHSWK* W4 ...8 A2
eden CI *KUTN/CMB* KT2 ...22 A5
borah CI *ISLW* TW7 ...5 H4
  Broome Rd *FELT* TW13 ...18 D1
epdale *WIM/MER* SW19 ...25 E4
epwell CI *ISLW* TW7 ...6 B4
erhurst CI *FELT* TW13 ...18 B4
erhurst Crs *HPTN* TW12 ...20 B5
e Rd *RCH/KEW* TW9 ...14 C2
er Park CI *KUTN/CMB* KT2 ...31 E2

Defoe Av *RCH/KEW* TW9 ...7 H3
Delamere Rd *RYNPK* SW20 ...33 E3
Delcombe Av *WPK* KT4 ...38 D5
Dellbow Rd *EBED/NFELT* TW14 ...10 D2
Della La *EW* KT17 ...43 H4
Dell Rd *EW* KT17 ...43 H5
Dells CI *TEDD* TW11 ...29 E1
The Dell *BTFD* TW8 ...6 D2
  EBED/NFELT TW14 ...10 C5
Dell Wk *NWMAL* KT3 ...31 H4
Delta CI *WPK* KT4 ...42 D2
Delta Rd *WPK* KT4 ...42 D2
Dempster CI *SURB* KT6 ...35 H4
Denbigh Gdns *RCHPK/HAM* TW10 ...14 C3
Denbigh Rd *HSLW* TW3 ...5 E5
Dene Av *HSLW* TW3 ...11 G1
Dene Rd *WPK* KT4 ...43 E1
Dene Gdns *THDIT* KT7 ...40 B1
Denehurst Gdns *RCHPK/HAM* TW10 ...14 D2
  WHTN TW2 ...12 C5
Denham Rd *EBED/NFELT* TW14 ...10 D5
Denison Rd *FELT* TW13 ...18 A4
Denleigh Gdns *THDIT* KT7 * ...34 D3
Denman Dr *ESH/CLAY* KT10 ...40 B4
Denmark Av *WIM/MER* SW19 ...33 F2
Denmark Ct *MRDN* SM4 ...39 H2
Denmark Rd *KUT/HW* KT1 ...2 D7
  WHTN TW2 ...20 C3
  WIM/MER SW19 ...33 E1
Dennan Rd *SURB* KT6 ...36 C5
Denning CI *HPTN* TW12 ...27 G1
The Denningtons *WPK* KT4 ...42 D1
Dennis Park Crs *RYNPK* SW20 ...33 H3
Dennis Rd *E/WMO/HCT* KT8 ...34 B1
Denton Rd *TWK* TW1 ...14 A4
Deodar Rd *PUT/ROE* SW15 ...17 F2
Depot Rd *HSLW* TW3 ...12 C1
Derby Rd *BRYLDS* KT5 ...36 D5
  HSLW TW3 ...12 A2
  MORT/ESHN SW14 ...15 E2
  WIM/MER SW19 ...33 H2
Derek Av *HOR/WEW* KT19 ...41 H5
Derek CI *HOR/WEW* KT19 ...42 A4
Derwent Av *PUT/ROE* SW15 ...23 C4
Derwent CI *EBED/NFELT* TW14 ...18 A1
  ESH/CLAY KT10 ...40 A5
Derwent Rd *RYNPK* SW20 ...39 E3
  WHTN TW2 ...12 A4
Devas Rd *RYNPK* SW20 ...32 D3
Devereux La *BARN* SW13 ...9 G3
Devey CI *KUTN/CMB* KT2 ...32 A2
Devon Av *WHTN* TW2 ...20 B1
Devon CI *HOR/WEW* KT19 ...45 H5
Devoncroft Gdns *TWK* TW1 ...13 F5
Devonhurst PI *CHSWK* W4 * ...8 C1
Devonshire Ct *FELT* TW13 * ...18 C2
Devonshire Dr *SURB* KT6 ...36 A5
Devonshire Gdns *CHSWK* W4 ...8 B3
Devonshire Rd *CHSWK* W4 ...8 C1
  FELT TW13 ...19 F3
Devonshire St *CHSWK* W4 ...8 D1
Devon Wy *HEST* TW5 ...40 D3
  HOR/WEW KT19 ...42 A4
Devon Waye *HEST* TW5 ...4 C3
Dewsbury Gdns *WPK* KT4 ...43 F2
Diana Gdns *SURB* KT6 ...41 E1
Dickens CI *RCHPK/HAM* TW10 ...22 B2
Dickenson Rd *FELT* TW13 ...18 D5
Dickerage La *NWMAL* KT3 ...31 F5
Dickerage Rd *KUT/HW* KT1 ...31 F3
  NWMAL KT3 ...31 H4
Dick Turpin Wy *EBED/NFELT* TW14 ...10 A2
Dilton Gdns *PUT/ROE* SW15 ...24 B1
Dimond CI *KUTN/CMB* KT2 ...30 C2
Disraeli Rd *PUT/ROE* SW15 ...17 F2
Distillery La *HMSMTH* W6 ...9 H1
Distillery Rd *HMSMTH* W6 ...9 H1
Ditton CI *THDIT* KT7 ...35 F4
Ditton Grange CI *SURB* KT6 ...36 A5
Ditton Grange Dr *SURB* KT6 ...35 H5
Ditton HI *SURB* KT6 ...35 H5
Ditton Hill Rd *SURB* KT6 ...35 H5
Ditton Lawn *THDIT* KT7 ...35 C5
Ditton Reach *THDIT* KT7 ...35 C3
Ditton Rd *NWDGN* UB2 ...4 C1
  SURB KT6 ...36 B5
Dock Rd *BTFD* TW8 ...7 E3
Dockwell CI *EBED/NFELT* TW14 ...10 B2
Dollary Pde *KUT/HW* KT1 * ...3 J6
Dolphin CI *SURB* KT6 ...36 A2
Dolphin Sq *CHSWK* W4 * ...8 D3
Dolphin St *KUT/HW* KT1 ...2 C4
Dome Buildings *RCH/KEW* TW9 * ...14 A2
Dominion CI *HSLW* TW3 ...5 G5
Donald Woods Gdns *BRYLDS* KT5 ...42 A1
Donnington Rd *WPK* KT4 ...43 F1
Doone CI *TEDD* TW11 ...29 H1
Dora Rd *WIM/MER* SW19 ...25 H5
Dorchester Gv *CHSWK* W4 ...8 D2
Dorchester Ms *TWK* TW1 ...13 H4
Dorchester Rd *WPK* KT4 ...38 D5
Dorien Rd *RYNPK* SW20 ...33 E4
Dorney Wy *HSLWW* TW4 ...11 F3
Dorset Rd *WIM/MER* SW19 ...33 H3
Dorset Wy *WHTN* TW2 ...20 B1
Dorset Waye *HEST* TW5 ...4 D3
Douai Gv *HPTN* TW12 ...28 B3
Douglas Av *NWMAL* KT3 ...38 C1

Douglas Rd *HSLW* TW3 ...12 A1
  KUT/HW KT1 ...3 J5
  SURB KT6 ...41 G1
Dover House Rd *PUT/ROE* SW15 ...16 D2
Dover Park Dr *PUT/ROE* SW15 ...16 C4
Dover Ter *RCH/KEW* TW9 * ...7 H2
Dowdeswell CI *PUT/ROE* SW15 ...15 H2
Downes CI *TWK* TW1 ...13 H4
Downfield *WPK* KT4 ...38 A5
Down Hall Rd *KUT/HW* KT1 ...2 B3
Down PI *HMSMTH* W6 ...9 G1
Down Rd *TEDD* TW11 ...29 G2
Downside *SUN* TW16 ...26 B3
  TWK TW1 ...21 E3
The Downs *RYNPK* SW20 ...33 E2
Downs Vw *WIM/MER* SW19 ...25 H3
Draco Ga *PUT/ROE* SW15 * ...16 D1
Drake Rd *CHSGTN* KT9 ...42 A4
Draper CI *ISLW* TW7 ...5 G5
Drax Av *RYNPK* SW20 ...32 B2
Draycot Rd *BRYLDS* KT5 ...41 G1
Draymans Wy *ISLW* TW7 ...13 E1
Drayton CI *HSLWW* TW4 ...11 G3
The Drive *EBED/NFELT* TW14 ...10 C5
  ESH/CLAY KT10 ...34 B5
  HOR/WEW KT19 ...43 E5
  HSLW TW3 ...5 G4
  KUTN/CMB KT2 ...31 F2
  RYNPK SW20 ...32 D3
  SURB KT6 ...36 B4
Dromore Rd *PUT/ROE* SW15 ...17 F4
Drumaline Rdg *WPK* KT4 ...42 D1
Drummonds PI *RCH/KEW* TW9 ...14 B2
Dryad St *PUT/ROE* SW15 ...17 E1
Dryburgh Rd *PUT/ROE* SW15 ...16 C1
Dudley Dr *MRDN* SM4 ...39 F5
Dudley Rd *KUT/HW* KT1 ...2 E5
  RCH/KEW TW9 ...7 H4
  WIM/MER SW19 ...33 H1
Duke of Cambridge CI *WHTN* TW2 ...12 C4
Duke Rd *CHSWK* W4 ...8 C1
Dukes Av *HSLWW* TW4 ...11 H5
  NWMAL KT3 ...31 H5
  RCHPK/HAM TW10 ...21 H4
Dukes CI *HPTN* TW12 ...19 G5
Dukes Green Av *EBED/NFELT* TW14 ...10 B3
Duke St *RCH/KEW* TW9 ...14 A2
Duke's Av *CHSWK* W4 ...8 C1
Dumbleton CI *KUT/HW* KT1 ...3 J3
Dunbar Rd *NWMAL* KT3 ...37 F1
Duncan Rd *RCH/KEW* TW9 ...14 B1
Dundas Gdns *E/WMO/HCT* KT8 ...28 A5
Dundela Gdns *WPK* KT4 ...43 G3
Dundonald Rd *WIM/MER* SW19 ...33 B2
Dungarvan Av *PUT/ROE* SW15 ...16 B2
Dunleary CI *HSLWW* TW4 ...11 F5
Dunmore Rd *RYNPK* SW20 ...32 D3
Dunmow CI *FELT* TW13 * ...19 F4
Dunsford Wy *PUT/ROE* SW15 ...16 C4
Dunstable Rd *RCH/KEW* TW9 ...14 A2
Dunstall Rd *RYNPK* SW20 ...32 C1
Dunstall Wy *E/WMO/HCT* KT8 ...28 A5
Dunster Av *MRDN* SM4 ...39 E5
Dunton CI *SURB* KT6 ...36 B5
Dupont Rd *RYNPK* SW20 ...33 G4
Durban Rd *CHSGTN* KT9 ...41 F5
Durford Crs *PUT/ROE* SW15 ...24 B1
Durham Av *HEST* TW5 ...4 C2
Durham Rd *EBED/NFELT* TW14 ...10 D5
  RYNPK SW20 ...32 D4
Durham Wharf Dr *BTFD* TW8 ...6 D3
Durlston Rd *KUTN/CMB* KT2 ...30 B1
Durnford Av *WIM/MER* SW19 ...25 H2
Durnsford Rd *WIM/MER* SW19 ...25 H3
Durrington Av *RYNPK* SW20 ...32 D3
Durrington Park Rd *RYNPK* SW20 ...32 D3
Dutch Gdns *KUTN/CMB* KT2 ...31 E1
Dutch Yd *WAND/EARL* SW18 ...17 H4
Dyer's La *PUT/ROE* SW15 ...16 C1
Dynevor Rd *RCHPK/HAM* TW10 ...14 A5
Dysart Av *KUT/HW* KT1 ...21 H5

E

Eagle Rd *HTHAIR* TW6 ...10 A1
Ealing Rd *BTFD* TW8 ...7 F1
Earldom Rd *PUT/ROE* SW15 ...16 D2
Earle Gdns *KUTN/CMB* KT2 ...30 B2
Earl Rd *MORT/ESHN* SW14 ...15 F2
Eastbank Rd *HPTN* TW12 ...20 B5
Eastbourne Gdns *MORT/ESHN* SW14 ...15 F1
Eastbourne Rd *BTFD* TW8 ...7 E1
  CHSWK W4 ...8 B2
  FELT TW13 ...19 E2
Eastbury Gv *CHSWK* W4 ...8 D1
Eastbury Rd *KUTN/CMB* KT2 ...2 E2
Eastern Perimeter Rd *HTHAIR* TW6 ...10 B1
Eastfields Rd *WAND/EARL* SW18 ...17 H2
East La *KUT/HW* KT1 ...2 B6
Eastleigh Wy *EBED/NFELT* TW14 ...18 B1
Eastmont Rd *ESH/CLAY* KT10 ...40 A1
East Rd *KUTN/CMB* KT2 ...2 D2
East Sheen Av *MORT/ESHN* SW14 ...15 G2

East St *BTFD* TW8 ...6 D3
Eastway *MRDN* SM4 ...39 E2
Eaton Dr *KUTN/CMB* KT2 ...3 H1
Eaton Rd *HSLW* TW3 ...12 C2
Ebbisham Rd *WPK* KT4 ...43 H1
Ede CI *HSLW* TW3 ...11 G1
Edenfield Gdns *WPK* KT4 ...43 E2
Edenhurst Av *FUL/PGN* SW6 ...17 G1
Edensor Rd *CHSWK* W4 ...8 D3
Eden St *KUT/HW* KT1 ...2 C5
Edgar Rd *HSLWW* TW4 ...11 G5
Edgecombe CI *KUTN/CMB* KT2 ...31 G2
Edge HI *WIM/MER* SW19 ...33 G2
Edge Hill Ct *WIM/MER* SW19 ...33 G2
Edinburgh Ct *KUT/HW* KT1 * ...2 C2
Edith Gdns *BRYLDS* KT5 ...37 E4
Edmund Gv *FELT* TW13 ...19 G2
Edna Rd *RYNPK* SW20 ...33 E4
Edward CI *HPTN* TW12 ...20 B5
Edward Rd *HPTN* TW12 ...20 B5
Edwin Rd *WHTN* TW2 ...20 D1
Effingham Rd *SURB* KT6 ...35 G4
Egerton Rd *NWMAL* KT3 ...38 A1
  WHTN TW2 ...12 D5
Egliston Ms *PUT/ROE* SW15 ...16 D1
Egliston Rd *PUT/ROE* SW15 ...16 D1
Egmont Av *SURB* KT6 ...36 C5
Egmont Rd *NWMAL* KT3 ...38 A1
  SURB KT6 ...36 C5
Elborough St *WAND/EARL* SW18 ...25 H1
Eldon Av *HEST* TW5 ...4 D3
Eldridge CI *EBED/NFELT* TW14 ...18 A1
Eleanor Gv *BARN* SW13 ...9 E5
Electra Av *HTHAIR* TW6 ...10 A1
Electric Pde *SURB* KT6 ...36 A5
Effin Gv *TEDD* TW11 ...21 E5
Elgar Av *BRYLDS* KT5 ...37 E5
Eliot Gdns *PUT/ROE* SW15 ...16 B2
Elizabeth Cottages *RCH/KEW* TW9 ...7 G4
Elizabeth Gdns *ISLW* TW7 ...13 F2
  SUN TW16 ...26 D5
Elizabeth Wy *FELT* TW13 ...18 D4
Ellenborough PI *PUT/ROE* SW15 ...16 B2
Elleray Rd *TEDD* TW11 ...29 E1
Ellerdine Rd *HSLW* TW3 ...12 B3
Ellerker Gdns *RCHPK/HAM* TW10 ...14 B4
Ellerman Av *WHTN* TW2 ...19 C1
Ellerton Rd *BARN* SW13 ...9 F4
  RYNPK SW20 ...32 B2
  SURB KT6 ...41 G1
Ellesmere Rd *TWK* TW1 ...13 H4
Ellingham Rd *CHSGTN* KT9 ...41 E5
Ellington Rd *FELT* TW13 ...18 A4
  HSLW TW3 ...5 E5
Ellisfield Dr *PUT/ROE* SW15 ...16 A5
Ellison Rd *BARN* SW13 ...9 E5
Elm Bank Gdns *BARN* SW13 ...8 D5
Elmbridge Av *BRYLDS* KT5 ...37 F3
Elmbrook CI *SUN* TW16 ...26 C3
Elm CI *BRYLDS* KT5 ...37 F4
  RYNPK SW20 ...38 D1
  WHTN TW2 ...20 A2
Elm Crs *KUTN/CMB* KT2 ...2
Elmcroft CI *CHSGTN* KT9 * ...41 F2
  EBED/NFELT TW14 ...10 A4
Elmcroft Dr *CHSGTN* KT9 ...41 F2
Elmdene *BRYLDS* KT5 ...37 F5
Elmdon Rd *HSLWW* TW4 ...4 A5
  HTHAIR TW6 ...10 A1
Elm Dr *SUN* TW16 ...26 D4
Elmer Gdns *ISLW* TW7 ...12 C1
Elmer's Dr *TEDD* TW11 ...29 G1
Elmfield Av *TEDD* TW11 ...21 E5
Elm Gdns *ESH/CLAY* KT10 ...40 A5
Elmgate Av *FELT* TW13 ...18 C3
Elm Gv *KUTN/CMB* KT2 ...2 D5
  WIM/MER SW19 ...33 F2
Elm Grove Rd *BARN* SW13 ...9 F5
Elm Rd *CHSGTN* KT9 ...41 F3
  ESH/CLAY KT10 ...40 A5
  EW KT17 ...43 G5
  KUTN/CMB KT2 ...3 F1
  MORT/ESHN SW14 ...15 F1
  NWMAL KT3 ...31 G5
Elm Rd West *CHEAM* SM3 ...39 G4
Elmshaw Rd *PUT/ROE* SW15 ...16 B3
Elmsleigh Rd *WHTN* TW2 ...20 C2
Elmstead CI *HOR/WEW* KT19 ...42 D4
Elmstead Gdns *WPK* KT4 ...43 F2
The Elms *BARN* SW13 ...16 A1
  ESH/CLAY KT10 * ...44 A1
Elmsworth Av *HSLW* TW3 ...5 E5
Elm Tree Av *ESH/CLAY* KT10 ...34 C4
Elmtree Rd *TEDD* TW11 ...20 D5
Elm Wk *RYNPK* SW20 ...38 B1
Elm Wy *HOR/WEW* KT19 ...42 C4
  ...43 H2
Elmwood Av *FELT* TW13 ...18 C3
Elmwood Rd *CHSWK* W4 ...8 B2
Elsenham St *WAND/EARL* SW18 ...25 G1
Elsinore Wy *RCH/KEW* TW9 ...15 E1
Elsrick Av *MRDN* SM4 ...39 H2
Elsworthy *THDIT* KT7 ...34 D3
Elthorne Ct *FELT* TW13 ...18 D1
Elton CI *KUT/HW* KT1 ...29 H1
Elton Rd *KUTN/CMB* KT2 ...3 G2
Elvedon Rd *FELT* TW13 ...18 A5
Ely CI *NWMAL* KT3 ...32 A4

Ely Rd HSLWW TW4	10	D1
Embankment PUT/ROE SW15	17	E1
The Embankment TWK TW1	21	F1
Embercourt Rd THDIT KT7	34	D3
Ember Farm Av E/WMO/HCT KT8	34	C3
Ember Farm Wy E/WMO/HCT KT8	34	C2
Ember Gdns THDIT KT7	34	D4
Ember La ESH/CLAY KT10	34	C4
Emma Ter RYNPK SW20 *	32	D2
Endsleigh Gdns SURB KT6	35	H3
Endway BRYLDS KT5	36	D4
Enfield Rd BTFD TW8	7	E1
Engadine St WAND/EARL SW18	25	G1
England Wy NWMAL KT3	8	B1
Engleheart Dr EBED/NFELT TW14	10	A4
Enmore Gdns MORT/ESHN SW14	15	J3
Enmore Rd PUT/ROE SW15	16	D2
Ennerdale Cl EBED/NFELT TW14	18	A1
Ennerdale Rd RCH/KEW TW9	7	C5
Ennismore Gdns THDIT KT7	34	D3
Enterprise Wy TEDD TW11	21	E5
WAND/EARL SW14	17	H2
Epsom Rd CHEAM SM3 *	39	G4
MRDN SM4	39	G3
Epworth Rd ISLW TW7	6	C3
Ericsson Cl WAND/EARL SW18	17	H3
Erncroft Wy TWK TW1	13	E4
Ernest Gdns CHSWK W4	8	A2
Ernest Rd KUT/HW KT1	3	J3
Ernest Sq KUT/HW KT1	3	J5
Ernle Rd RYNPK SW20	32	C2
Ernshaw Pl PUT/ROE SW15	17	F3
Erpingham Rd PUT/ROE SW15	16	D1
Erridge Rd WIM/MER SW19	33	H4
Errol Gdns NWMAL KT3	38	B1
Esher Rd E/WMO/HCT KT8	34	C2
Esmond St PUT/ROE SW15	17	F2
Essex Av ISLW TW7	12	C1
Essex Cl MRDN SM4	39	E4
Essex Ct BARN SW13	9	E5
Estella Av NWMAL KT3	38	C1
Estridge Cl HSLW TW3	11	H3
Eternit Wk FUL/PGN SW6	9	H4
Evans Gv FELT TW13	19	H2
Evelyn Cl WHTN TW2	12	A5
Evelyn Crs SUN TW16	26	A3
Evelyn Gdns RCH/KEW TW9	14	B2
Evelyn Rd RCH/KEW TW9	14	B1
RCHPK/HAM TW10	21	H5
Evelyn Ter RCH/KEW TW9	14	B1
Evelyn Wy HOR/WEW KT19	45	H4
SUN TW16	26	A3
Evenwood Cl PUT/ROE SW15 *	17	F3
Everatt Cl WAND/EARL SW18 *	17	G4
Everdon Rd BARN SW13	9	F2
The Everglades HSLW TW3 *	12	D2
Eve Rd ISLW TW7	13	F2
Eversfield Rd RCH/KEW TW9	7	G5
Eversley Crs ISLW TW7	5	G4
Eversley Pk WIM/MER SW19	24	C5
Eversley Rd BRYLDS KT5	36	C1
Evesham Ter SURB KT6 *	36	A3
Ewell By-Pass EW KT17	43	H5
Ewell Court Av HOR/WEW KT19	42	D4
Ewell Park Wy EW KT17	43	F5
Ewell Rd SURB KT6	35	G4
SURB KT6	35	J3
Excelsior Cl KUT/HW KT1	3	G5
Exeter Rd FELT TW13	19	J5
Eyot Gdns HMSMTH W6	9	E1

F

Faggs Rd EBED/NFELT TW14	10	A2
EBED/NFELT TW14	10	B2
Fairacre ISLW TW7 *	5	G4
NWMAL KT3	31	H5
Fairacres PUT/ROE SW15	16	C2
Fairdale Gdns PUT/ROE SW15	16	C2
Fairfax Ms PUT/ROE SW15	16	D2
Fairfax Rd TEDD TW11	29	F2
Fairfield Av WHTN TW2	20	A1
Fairfield Cl HOR/WEW KT19	42	D4
Fairfield Cnr KUT/HW KT1 *	2	E5
Fairfield East KUT/HW KT1	2	D4
Fairfield North KUTN/CMB KT2	2	D4
Fairfield Pl KUT/HW KT1	2	D6
Fairfield Rd KUT/HW KT1	2	D5
Fairfield South KUT/HW KT1	2	D6
Fairfield Wy HOR/WEW KT19	42	D4
Fairfield West KUT/HW KT1	2	C5
Fairford Gdns WPK KT4	43	E2
Fairlawn Cl ESH/CLAY KT10	40	A5
FELT TW13	18	D5
KUTN/CMB KT2	31	F1
Fairlawn Rd WIM/MER SW19	33	G2

Fairlawns SUN TW16	26	B5
TWK TW1	13	H4
Fairlight Cl WPK KT4	43	H5
Fairmead BRYLDS KT5	37	E5
Fairmead Cl HEST TW5	4	A3
NWMAL KT3	31	G5
Fair St HSLW TW3	12	B1
Fairway RYNPK SW20	32	D5
Fairway Cl HOR/WEW KT19	42	B3
HSLWW TW4	10	D3
Fairways ISLW TW7 *	5	H5
TEDD TW11	30	A2
The Fairway E/WMO/HCT KT8	28	A5
NWMAL KT3	31	G3
Falcon Cl CHSWK W4	8	A2
Falcon Rd HPTN TW12	27	G2
Falstaff Ms HPTN TW12	20	C5
Fanshawe Rd RCHPK/HAM TW10	21	H4
Fanthorpe St PUT/ROE SW15	16	D1
Fareham Rd EBED/NFELT TW14	10	D5
Farlington Pl PUT/ROE SW15	16	C5
Farlow Rd PUT/ROE SW15	17	E1
Farm Cottages E/WMO/HCT KT8 *	35	F1
Farm Rd HSLWW TW4	19	F1
Farm St WIM/MER SW19 *	17	E5
Farm Wy WPK KT4	43	H2
Farnell Rd ISLW TW7	12	C1
Farnham Gdns RYNPK SW20	32	C4
Farquhar Rd WIM/MER SW19	25	H3
The Farthings KUTN/CMB KT2	3	H1
Fassett Rd KUT/HW KT1	36	B1
Fauconberg Rd CHSWK W4	8	A1
Fawe Park Rd PUT/ROE SW15	17	G2
Fearnley Crs HPTN TW12	19	F5
Fee Farm Rd ESH/CLAY KT10	44	A1
Fellbrook RCHPK/HAM TW10	21	G3
Felsham Ms PUT/ROE SW15 *	17	E1
Felsham Rd PUT/ROE SW15	16	D1
Feltham Av E/WMO/HCT KT8	34	D1
Felthambrook Wy FELT TW13	18	C3
Fendall Rd HOR/WEW KT19	42	B4
Ferguson Av BRYLDS KT5	36	C2
Ferndale Av HSLWW TW4	11	F1
Fernside Av FELT TW13	18	C4
Ferraro Cl HEST TW5	4	D2
Ferry La BARN SW13	9	E2
BTFD TW8	7	F2
BTFD TW8	7	G2
Ferrymoor RCHPK/HAM TW10	21	G3
Ferry Rd BARN SW13	9	F3
E/WMO/HCT KT8	27	H5
TEDD TW11	21	G5
THDIT KT7	35	G3
TWK TW1	21	G1
Ferry Sq BTFD TW8 *	7	F2
Festing Rd PUT/ROE SW15	17	E1
Field Cl CHSGTN KT9	40	D4
E/WMO/HCT KT8	34	A2
Fielden Cl TEDD TW11	21	E4
Fielding Av WHTN TW2	20	B3
Field La BTFD TW8	7	E1
TEDD TW11	21	F5
Field Pl NWMAL KT3	38	A3
Field Rd EBED/NFELT TW14	10	C4
Fife Rd KUT/HW KT1	2	C4
MORT/ESHN SW14	15	F3
Fifth Cross Rd WHTN TW2	20	C2
Filby Rd CHSGTN KT9	41	G5
Finch Dr EBED/NFELT TW14	11	E5
Findon Cl WAND/EARL SW18	17	H4
Finlays Cl CHSGTN KT9	41	H4
Finney La ISLW TW7	6	B4
Fircroft Rd CHSGTN KT9	41	G3
Firdene BRYLDS KT5	37	F5
Fire Bell Aly SURB KT6 *	36	B3
Firebell Ms SURB KT6	36	B3
Fir Gv NWMAL KT3	38	A3
Fir Rd CHEAM SM3	39	G5
FELT TW13	19	E5
Firs Av MORT/ESHN SW14	15	F2
First Av MORT/ESHN SW14	8	D5
First Cl E/WMO/HCT KT8	34	B1
First Cross Rd WHTN TW2	20	D2
Firstway RYNPK SW20	32	D4
Firswood Av HOR/WEW KT19	42	D4
Fir Tree Cl ESH/CLAY KT10	43	E5
Fir Tree Rd HSLWW TW4	11	F1
Fisherdene ESH/CLAY KT10	44	B1
Fisherman Cl RCHPK/HAM TW10	21	H4
Fisk Cl SUN TW16	26	A1
Fitzalan Rd ESH/CLAY KT10	44	A1
Fitzgeorge Av NWMAL KT3	31	G3
Fitzgerald Av MORT/ESHN SW14	15	H1
Fitzgerald Rd MORT/ESHN SW14	15	F1
THDIT KT7	35	F3
Fitzroy Crs CHSWK W4 *	8	A3
Fitzwilliam Av RCH/KEW TW9	7	G5
Fitz Wygram Cl HPTN TW12	20	B5
Fleece Rd SURB KT6	35	H5
Fleetwood Cl CHSGTN KT9	45	E1
Fleetwood Rd KUT/HW KT1	3	K6
Fleetwood Sq KUT/HW KT1	3	K6
Fleming Wy ISLW TW7	13	E1
Fleur Gates WIM/MER SW19	17	E5

Flood La TWK TW1 *	21	F1
Florence Gdns CHSWK W4	8	B2
Florence Rd FELT TW13	18	D1
KUTN/CMB KT2	3	F1
Florian Rd PUT/ROE SW15	17	G2
Floss St PUT/ROE SW15	9	H5
Floyer Cl RCHPK/HAM TW10	14	A5
Fontley Wy PUT/ROE SW15	16	B5
The Footpath PUT/ROE SW15 *	16	B3
Forest Dr SUN TW16	26	A2
Forest Rd CHEAM SM3	39	H5
FELT TW13	18	D2
RCH/KEW TW9	7	H3
Forest Side WPK KT4	38	A5
Forge Dr ESH/CLAY KT10	44	B1
Forge La FELT TW13	19	F5
RCHPK/HAM TW10	22	B1
SUN TW16	26	B5
Forge Ms SUN TW16 *	26	B5
Fortescue Av WHTN TW2	20	B3
The Forum E/WMO/HCT KT8	34	A1
Foster Rd CHSWK W4	8	C1
Foundry Ms HSLW TW3	12	A2
Fountains Av FELT TW13	19	G3
Fountains Cl FELT TW13	19	G3
Fourth Cross Rd WHTN TW2	20	C2
Foxglove La CHSGTN KT9	41	H3
Foxwarren ESH/CLAY KT10	44	A2
Foxwood Cl FELT TW13	18	C3
Frampton Rd HSLWW TW4	11	F3
Francis Av FELT TW13	18	B3
Francis Cl HOR/WEW KT19	42	C2
Francis Gv WIM/MER SW19	33	G2
Francis Rd HSLWW TW4	4	A5
Franklin Cl KUT/HW KT1	3	G6
Franks Av NWMAL KT3	37	F1
Fraser St CHSWK W4	8	D1
French St SUN TW16	26	D4
Frensham Dr PUT/ROE SW15	24	B2
Friars Av PUT/ROE SW15	24	A3
Friars La RCH/KEW TW9	14	A3
Friars Stile Rd RCHPK/HAM TW10	14	B4
Frimley Cl WIM/MER SW19	25	F2
Frimley Rd CHSGTN KT9	41	H4
Fritham Cl NWMAL KT3	37	H3
Frogmore WAND/EARL SW18 *	17	J1
Fromows Cnr CHSWK W4 *	8	B1
Fruen Rd EBED/NFELT TW14	18	A1
Fulham High St FUL/PGN SW6	17	F1
Fullbrooks Av WPK KT4	38	A5
Fullers Av SURB KT6	41	G1
Fullers Wy North SURB KT6	41	G2
Fullers Wy South CHSGTN KT9	41	F3
Fulmar Ct BRYLDS KT5	36	D3
Fulmer Cl HPTN TW12	19	F5
Fulstone Cl HSLWW TW4	11	G2
Fulwell Park Av WHTN TW2	20	B2
Fulwell Rd TEDD TW11	20	C4
Fulwood Gdns TWK TW1	13	E4
Fulwood Wk WIM/MER SW19	24	B5
Furzewood SUN TW16	26	B3

G

Gabriel Cl FELT TW13	19	F4
Gadesden Rd HOR/WEW KT19	42	B5
Gainsborough Cl ESH/CLAY KT10 *	34	D5
Gainsborough Gdns HSLW TW3	12	C3
Gainsborough Rd NWMAL KT3	37	G3
RCH/KEW TW9	7	G5
Galata Rd BARN SW13	9	F3
Gale Cl HPTN TW12	27	F1
Galen Cl HOR/WEW KT19	45	H4
Galgate Cl WIM/MER SW19	25	E1
Galsworthy Rd KUTN/CMB KT2	3	J2
Galveston Rd PUT/ROE SW15	17	G3
Gamlen Rd PUT/ROE SW15	17	E1
Gander Green Crs HPTN TW12	27	H5
Gap Rd WIM/MER SW19	25	H5
Garden Cl HPTN TW12	19	G5
PUT/ROE SW15	16	C5
Garden Ct HPTN TW12	19	G5
Garden Rd RCH/KEW TW9	7	H3
Garden Vls ESH/CLAY KT10 *	44	A1
Gardner Pl EBED/NFELT TW14	10	C3
Garfield Rd TWK TW1	21	F1
Garland Dr HSLW TW3	12	D1
Garrick Cl RCH/KEW TW9	13	H5
Garrick Gdns E/WMO/HCT KT8	27	H5
Garrick Rd RCH/KEW TW9	7	H5
Garrison Cl HSLWW TW4	11	G3
Garrison La CHSGTN KT9	45	F1
Garside Cl HPTN TW12	28	A2
Garth Cl KUTN/CMB KT2	22	C5
MRDN SM4	39	E4
Garth Rd CHSWK W4	8	C1
KUTN/CMB KT2	22	C5
MRDN SM4	39	E5
Garthside KUTN/CMB KT2	22	B5
The Garth HPTN TW12	28	A1
Gartmoor Gdns WIM/MER SW19	25	A1
Gaston Bell Cl RCH/KEW TW9	14	A4
Gatehouse Cl KUTN/CMB KT2	31	F2
The Gateways RCH/KEW TW9 *	14	A2
Gatfield Gv FELT TW13	19	H2
Gatley Av HOR/WEW KT19	42	A4

Gatwick Rd WAND/EARL SW18	43	
Gayfere Rd EW KT17	43	
Geneva Rd KUT/HW KT1	36	
Genoa Av PUT/ROE SW15	16	
George Rd KUTN/CMB KT2	31	
NWMAL KT3		
George St HSLW TW3	4	
RCH/KEW TW9	14	
George Wyver Cl WIM/MER SW19	17	
Georgia Rd NWMAL KT3	37	
Geraldine Rd CHSWK W4	7	
Gerard Av HSLWW TW4	11	
Gerard Rd BARN SW13	9	
Gibbon Rd KUTN/CMB KT2	2	
Gibbon Wk PUT/ROE SW15 *	16	
Gibson Cl CHSGTN KT9	40	
ISLW TW7	12	
Giggs Hill Gdns THDIT KT7	35	
Giggs Hill Rd THDIT KT7	35	
Gilbert St HSLW TW3	12	
Gilders Rd CHSGTN KT9	41	
Gillian Park Rd CHEAM SM3		
Gilliat Ter BRYLDS KT5 *	36	
Gilpin Av MORT/ESHN SW14	15	
Gilpin Crs WHTN TW2		
Gipsy La PUT/ROE SW15		
Girdwood Rd WAND/EARL SW18		
Girling Wy EBED/NFELT TW14	10	
Glade Cl SURB KT6 *		
The Clade EW KT17	43	
Gladioli Cl HPTN TW12	27	
Gladstone Av EBED/NFELT TW14	10	
WHTN TW2	12	
Gladstone Gdns HSLW TW3 *	5	
Gladstone Pl E/WMO/HCT KT8 *	34	
Gladstone Rd KUT/HW KT1	3	
SURB KT6		
WIM/MER SW19	33	
Gladwyn Rd PUT/ROE SW15	17	
Glamorgan Rd KUT/HW KT1	29	
Glasbrook Av WHTN TW2	19	
Glastonbury Rd MRDN SM4	39	
Glazebrook Rd TEDD TW11	29	
Glebe Cl CHSWK W4 *	8	
Glebe Gdns NWMAL KT3	37	
Glebelands E/WMO/HCT KT8	34	
ESH/CLAY KT10		
Glebelands Rd EBED/NFELT TW14	10	
Glebe Rd BARN SW13	9	
Glebe Side TWK TW1	13	
Glebe St CHSWK W4	8	
The Glebe WPK KT4	38	
Glebe Wy FELT TW13		
Glegg Pl PUT/ROE SW15 *	17	
Glen Albyn Rd WIM/MER SW19		
Glenavon Cl ESH/CLAY KT10	40	
Glenbuck Rd SURB KT6		
Glendale Dr WIM/MER SW19	25	
Glendarvon St PUT/ROE SW15	17	
Glendower Gdns MORT/ESHN SW14	15	
Glendower Rd MORT/ESHN SW14	15	
Glenhurst Rd BTFD TW8	7	
Glenmill HPTN TW12	19	
Glen Rd CHSGTN KT9	41	
Glentham Cottages BARN SW13 *	9	
Glentham Gdns BARN SW13	9	
Glentham Rd BARN SW13	9	
The Glen NWDGN UB2	4	
Glenthorne Cl CHEAM SM3	39	
Glenthorne Gdns CHEAM SM3	39	
Glenthorne Rd KUT/HW KT1	36	
Glenthorpe Rd MRDN SM4	39	
Glenville Rd KUTN/CMB KT2	3	
Glenwood Rd EW KT17	43	
HSLW TW3	12	
Gloster Rd NWMAL KT3	37	
Gloucester Cl THDIT KT7 *	35	
Gloucester Ct RCH/KEW TW9 *	14	
Gloucester Rd FELT TW13	18	
HPTN TW12		
HSLWW TW4	11	
KUT/HW KT1		
RCH/KEW TW9	7	
TEDD TW11	20	
Goat Whf BTFD TW8	7	
Godfrey Av WHTN TW2	12	
Godfrey Wy HSLWW TW4	11	
Godstone Rd TWK TW1	13	
Godwin Cl HOR/WEW KT19		
Goldcliff Cl MRDN SM4	39	
Golden Ct RCH/KEW TW9 *	14	
Golf Club Dr KUTN/CMB KT2	31	
Golf Side WHTN TW2	20	
Golf Side Cl NWMAL KT3	31	
Gomer Gdns TEDD TW11	29	
Gomer Pl TEDD TW11		
Gonston Cl WIM/MER SW19	24	
Gonville St FUL/PGN SW6	17	
Goodenough Rd WIM/MER SW19	33	
Gooding Cl NWMAL KT3	37	
Goodwood Cl MRDN SM4	39	
Gordon Av MORT/ESHN SW14	15	
TWK TW1	13	
Gordondale Rd WIM/MER SW19	25	
Gordon Rd BRYLDS KT5		
CHSWK W4		
HSLW TW3	12	

...KUTN/CMB KT2.................................2 E3
...RCH/KEW TW9.................................7 C5
...e Rd RYNPK SW20............................32 D4
...sbury Rd HPTN TW12.........................41 F3
...stling Rd WHTN TW2.........................19 H1
...chic Rd WHTN TW2...........................20 C2
...uld Rd WHTN TW2............................20 D1
...ver Rd ISLW TW7..............................6 A3
...burn Wy E/WMO/HCT KT8......................28 C5
...emesdyke Av
...fton CI HSLWW TW4...........................19 F1
...WPK KT4....................................42 D2
...fton Park Rd WPK KT4.......................42 D1
...fton Rd NWMAL KT3..........................37 H1
...WPK KT4....................................42 C2
...ham Gdns SURB KT6..........................36 B5
...ham Rd HPTN TW12...........................19 H4
...HEST TW5....................................4 C1
...inger Rd ISLW TW7...........................6 A5
...nard Av PUT/ROE SW15.......................16 C3
...ad Av BRYLDS KT5...........................37 E3
...nd Dr RYNPK SW20...........................32 D4
...RYNPK SW20.................................38 D1
...ndison Rd WPK KT4..........................43 H1
...nd Pde MORT/ESHN SW14 *....................15 F2
...SURB KT6 *..................................36 D5
...nd Union Canal Wk
...BTFD TW8.....................................6 D2
...nge Av WHTN TW2............................20 D2
...nge CI E/WMO/HCT KT8.......................34 A1
...HEST TW5....................................4 C1
...nge Park PI RYNPK SW20.....................32 C2
...nge Rd BARN SW13............................9 F4
...CHSGTN KT9.................................41 F3
...CHSWK W4....................................8 A1
...E/WMO/HCT KT8.............................34 A1
...KUT/HW KT1..................................2 C6
...Grange NWMAL KT3 *.........................38 B2
...WIM/MER SW19...............................33 E1
...WPK KT4.....................................42 C3
...ntchester KUT/HW KT1 *......................3 C5
...ntham Rd WHTN TW2..........................20 D3
...nt Wy ISLW TW7..............................6 D3
...nville Av FELT TW13.........................18 B2
...ISLW TW7...................................11 H3
...nville Rd WAND/EARL SW18...................17 G5
...WIM/MER SW19...............................33 H2
...psome CI CHSGTN KT9........................44 D1
...smere Av HSLW TW3..........................12 A4
...vel Rd WHTN TW2............................19 H2
...smere CI EBED/NFELT TW14...................18 A1
...smere Rd WIM/MER SW19......................33 H5
...yham Crs NWMAL KT3.........................37 F1
...yswood Gdns RYNPK SW20.....................32 C4
...at Chertsey Rd CHSWK W4 *....................8 A2
...FELT TW13..................................19 E3
...at South-West Rd
...EBED/NFELT TW14............................10 B1
...at West Rd BTFD TW8..........................6 D1
...BTFD TW8.....................................7 E1
...HEST TW5....................................5 E4
...HMSMTH W6..................................9 F5
...ISLW TW7....................................5 H1
...at West Road Chiswick
...CHSWK W4....................................9 E1
...at West Road Ellesmere Rd
...CHSWK W4....................................8 B2
...at West Road Hogarth La
...CHSWK W4....................................8 C2
...be Ter KUT/HW KT1 *..........................2 C6
...en CI FELT TW13.............................19 F5
...encroft Rd HEST TW5..........................4 C4
...en Dragon La BTFD TW8........................7 F1
...en End CHSGTN KT9...........................41 E3
...enlands HOR/WEW KT19.......................42 A4
...en La CHSGTN KT9............................45 F2
...FELT TW3 *..................................19 F5
...HSLWW TW4..................................10 D2
...NWMAL KT3..................................37 F2
...SUN TW16...................................26 A2
...enlaw Gdns NWMAL KT3.......................38 A4
...enlawn La BTFD TW8...........................7 F2
...en Leas SUN TW16...........................26 A2
...en Leas CI SUN TW16.........................26 A1
...enlink Wk RCH/KEW TW9........................8 A4
...en Man La EBED/NFELT TW14...................10 B2
...enoak Wy WIM/MER SW19......................25 E4
...en Pde HSLW TW3 *...........................12 A4
...enstead Gdns PUT/ROE SW15...................16 B3
...en St SUN TW16..............................26 B3
... Green FELT TW13.............................18 C2
...HEST TW5....................................4 D3
...MRDN SM4...................................39 F1
...NWMAL KT3..................................31 F5
...RCH/KEW TW9.................................14 A3
...WHTN TW2...................................20 D1
...WIM/MER SW19...............................25 E5
...en Wy CHSGTN KT9............................45 G1
...en Wk NWDGN UB2..............................4 D1
...enway RYNPK SW20............................38 D1
... Greenways TWK TW1 *.........................13 F4

The Greenway HSLWW TW4 *....................11 G2
Greenwood CI MRDN SM4.......................39 F1
   THDIT KT7..................................35 F5
Greenwood La HPTN TW12......................20 A5
Greenwood Pk KUTN/CMB KT2...................31 H2
Greenwood Rd ISLW TW7.......................12 D1
   THDIT KT7..................................35 F5
Grena Gdns RCH/KEW TW9......................14 C2
Grena Rd RCH/KEW TW9.........................14 C2
Grenville CI BRYLDS KT5......................37 F5
Grenville Ms WIM/MER SW19...................20 A5
Gresham Rd HPTN TW12.........................27 H1
   HSLW TW3....................................5 F4
Gresham Wy WIM/MER SW19....................25 H5
Gressenhall Rd WAND/EARL SW18...............17 G4
Greville CI TWK TW1..........................13 G5
Greville Rd RCHPK/HAM TW10..................14 C4
Griffin Centre EBED/NFELT TW14 *.............10 C4
Griffin Wy SUN TW16..........................26 B4
Griffiths Rd WIM/MER SW19...................33 H2
Grimwood Rd TWK TW1..........................13 G5
Grosse Wy PUT/ROE SW15......................16 C4
Grosvenor Av MORT/ESHN SW14.................15 H1
Grosvenor Gdns KUTN/CMB KT2.................30 A1
   MORT/ESHN SW14...........................15 H1
Grosvenor HI WIM/MER SW19...................33 F1
Grosvenor Rd BTFD TW8.........................7 E2
   CHSWK W4...................................8 B1
   HSLWW TW4................................11 G1
   RCHPK/HAM TW10..........................14 B3
   TWK TW1...................................13 F5
Grotto Rd TWK TW1...........................21 E2
Grove Av TWK TW1............................21 E1
Grove CI HOR/WEW KT19.......................45 H3
   KUT/HW KT1................................36 C1
Grove Cottages CHSWK W4 *....................8 D2
Grove Ct E/WMO/HCT KT8.......................34 C2
Grove Crs FELT TW13..........................19 F4
   KUT/HW KT1..................................2 C6
Grove End La ESH/CLAY KT10...................34 C5
Grove Footpath BRYLDS KT5....................36 B1
Grove Gdns TEDD TW11........................21 F4
Groveland Wy NWMAL KT3......................37 F2
Grove La KUT/HW KT1..........................36 B1
Groveley Rd SUN TW16.........................18 A5
Grove Park Br CHSWK W4........................8 B8
Grove Park Gdns CHSWK W4.....................8 A3
Grove Park Rd CHSWK W4........................8 A3
Grove Park Ter CHSWK W4.......................8 A3
Grove Rd BARN SW13...........................9 E5
   BTFD TW8....................................6 D1
   E/WMO/HCT KT8............................34 C1
   HSLW TW3...................................11 H2
   ISLW TW7...................................11 H4
   RCHPK/HAM TW10...........................14 C4
   SURB KT6...................................36 A2
   WHTN TW2...................................20 C3
Grove Ter TEDD TW11.........................21 F4
The Grove ISLW TW7............................5 H4
   TEDD TW11.................................21 F4
Grove Wy ESH/CLAY KT10......................34 B4
Guernsey CI HEST TW5..........................4 D4
Guildford Av FELT TW13......................18 A2
Guildford Rd BRYLDS KT5......................36 C2
Gumley Gdns ISLW TW7.........................13 F1
Gunnersbury CI CHSWK W4 *.....................8 A1
Gunnersbury Ms CHSWK W4......................8 A1
Gwalior Rd PUT/ROE SW15.....................17 E2
Gwendolen Av PUT/ROE SW15..................17 E3
Gwynne Whf CHSWK W4..........................9 E2

H

Haddon CI NWMAL KT3.........................38 A2
Hadleigh CI RYNPK SW20......................33 G4
Hadley Gdns CHSWK W4.........................8 C1
   NWDGN UB2..................................4 C1
Haggard Rd TWK TW1.........................13 G5
Hailsham CI SURB KT6.........................36 A4
Haining CI CHSWK W4...........................7 F2
Haldon Rd WAND/EARL SW18...................17 G4
Halford Rd RCHPK/HAM TW10..................14 B3
Haliburton Rd TWK TW1.......................13 F3
Halifax CI TEDD TW11........................28 D1
Hallam Rd BARN SW13.........................16 C1
Hall Ct TEDD TW11...........................21 E5
Hall Farm Dr WHTN TW2.......................12 C5
Hallows Gv SUN TW16.........................18 A5
Hall Rd ISLW TW7.............................12 A4
Hambledon Rd WAND/EARL SW18................17 G5
Hambleton CI WPK KT4.........................43 H1
Ham Common RCHPK/HAM TW10..................22 A3
Ham Croft CI FELT TW13......................18 B3
Ham Farm Rd RCHPK/HAM TW10.................22 A4
Ham Gate Av RCHPK/HAM TW10.................22 B4
Hamilton Av SURB KT6........................41 H1
Hamilton CI FELT TW13.......................29 G1
   TEDD TW11.................................21 F3
Hamilton Crs HSLW TW3.......................12 A3
Hamilton Pde FELT TW13 *....................18 B4
Hamilton PI SUN TW16........................26 C2
Hamilton Rd BTFD TW8.........................7 E2
   WHTN TW2..................................20 D1
Hammersmith Br HMSMTH W6.....................9 G1

Hammersmith Bridge Rd BARN SW13.............9 G2
   HMSMTH W6..................................9 G1
Hammersmith Emb HMSMTH W6 *..................9 H2
Hammersmith Flyover HMSMTH W6...............9 H1
Hammersmith Ter HMSMTH W6 *.................9 F1
Hammond CI HPTN TW12........................27 H3
Hampden Rd KUT/HW KT1.........................3 H6
Hampton CI RYNPK SW20.......................32 D2
Hampton Court Av E/WMO/HCT KT8..............34 C3
Hampton Court Crs
   E/WMO/HCT KT8............................28 C5
Hampton Court Cresent
   E/WMO/HCT KT8............................28 C5
Hampton Court Est THDIT KT7 *...............28 C5
Hampton Court Rd E/WMO/HCT KT8.............28 D5
   E/WMO/HCT KT8............................28 C4
   HPTN TW12.................................28 C4
   KUT/HW KT1................................29 H4
Hampton Court Wy E/WMO/HCT KT8.............34 D1
   THDIT KT7..................................34 D4
Hampton La FELT TW13........................19 F4
Hampton Rd TEDD TW11........................20 C5
   WHTN TW2..................................20 B5
   WPK KT4...................................43 F1
Hampton Rd East EBED/NFELT TW14.............19 G3
Hampton Rd West FELT TW13...................19 F3
Ham Ridings RCHPK/HAM TW10.................22 C5
Ham St RCHPK/HAM TW10......................21 H2
The Ham BTFD TW8.............................6 D3
Handside CI WPK KT4.........................39 E5
Hanford CI WAND/EARL SW18...................25 H1
Hanover Av FELT TW13........................18 B1
Hanover CI RCH/KEW TW9.......................7 H3
Hansler Gv E/WMO/HCT KT8....................34 C2
Hanson CI MORT/ESHN SW14...................15 F1
Hanworth Rd FELT TW13.......................18 C1
   HPTN TW12.................................19 H5
   HSLW TW3..................................12 A1
   HSLWW TW4................................11 G5
   SUN TW16..................................26 B2
Hanworth Ter HSLW TW3......................12 A2
Harbridge Av PUT/ROE SW15...................16 A5
Harcourt CI ISLW TW7.........................13 F1
Harcourt Rd WIM/MER SW19...................33 H2
Harding CI KUTN/CMB KT2......................2 D4
Hardman Rd KUTN/CMB KT2......................2 D4
Hardwicke Av HEST TW5.........................4 D4
Hardwicke Rd RCHPK/HAM TW10................21 H4
Hardwick's Wy WAND/EARL SW18...............17 H4
Hardys Ms E/WMO/HCT KT8.....................34 D1
Harewood Rd ISLW TW7..........................6 A3
Harfield Rd SUN TW16........................27 E4
Harlech Gdns HEST TW5.........................4 A2
Harlequin Av BTFD TW8........................6 A2
Harlequin CI ISLW TW7........................12 D3
Harlequin Rd TEDD TW11 *....................29 E2
Harlington Rd East EBED/NFELT TW14..........10 C5
Harlington Rd West EBED/NFELT TW14..........10 C4
Harpers Yd ISLW TW7 *.........................6 A5
Harris CI HSLW TW3.............................5 F4
Harrow CI CHSGTN KT9........................45 E1
Harrowdene Gdns TEDD TW11..................29 F2
Harte Rd HSLW TW3.............................5 H4
Hartfield Crs WIM/MER SW19..................33 G2
Hartfield Rd CHSGTN KT9.....................41 E4
   WIM/MER SW19.............................33 G2
Hartford Rd HOR/WEW KT19....................41 H5
Hartham CI ISLW TW7...........................6 B4
Hartham Rd ISLW TW7...........................6 A4
Hartington Rd CHSWK W4.......................8 B3
   TWK TW1...................................13 G5
Hartland Rd HPTN TW12.......................20 A4
   ISLW TW7..................................13 F1
   MRDN SM4.................................39 H4
Hartland Wy MRDN SM4.......................39 G4
Harvard HI CHSWK W4...........................8 A1
Harvard Rd CHSWK W4..........................8 A1
   ISLW TW7...................................5 H4
Harvesters CI ISLW TW7......................12 C5
Harvest La THDIT KT7.........................35 E3
Harvest Rd FELT TW13........................18 B4
Harvey Dr HPTN TW12.........................28 A3
Harvey Rd HSLWW TW4........................11 G5
Haslam Av CHEAM SM3........................39 F5
Haslemere CI HPTN TW12.....................19 G5
Hastings Dr SURB KT6........................35 H5
Hatch PI KUTN/CMB KT2........................2 C2
Hatherleigh CI CHSGTN KT9...................41 E4
   MRDN SM4.................................39 H5
Hatherley Rd RCH/KEW TW9.....................7 H3
Hatherop Rd HPTN TW12.......................27 G2
Hatton Cross Est HTHAIR TW6.................10 C5
Hatton Gn EBED/NFELT TW14..................10 A3
Hatton Rd HTHAIR TW6.........................10 A3
Havana Rd WIM/MER SW19.....................25 H3
Haven CI WIM/MER SW19......................25 E3
Haven Ct BRYLDS KT5 *.......................36 C3
Havenswood Ct KUTN/CMB KT2.................31 E1
The Haven RCH/KEW TW9......................14 D1
   SUN TW16.................................26 B4
Haverfield Gdns RCH/KEW TW9..................7 H3
Haverfield Rd BOW E3..........................7 F2
Haverham CI TWK TW1.........................14 A5
Hawkesbury Rd PUT/ROE SW15..................16 C3
Hawkesley CI TWK TW1........................21 E4
Hawkes Rd EBED/NFELT TW14..................10 B5

Hawkewood Rd SUN TW16......................26 B5
Hawkhurst Wy NWMAL KT3.....................37 G2
Hawkins Rd TEDD TW11.......................29 G1
Hawks Rd KUT/HW KT1..........................3 F5
Hawley CI HPTN TW12.........................27 G1
Hawthorn CI HPTN TW12......................19 H5
Hawthorn Hatch BTFD TW8......................6 C3
Hawthorn Rd BTFD TW8.........................6 C3
   FELT TW13.................................18 B1
The Hawthorns EW KT17.......................43 H5
Haycroft Rd SURB KT6........................41 E1
Haydon Park Rd WIM/MER SW19................25 H5
Haygarth PI WIM/MER SW19...................25 E5
Haygreen CI KUTN/CMB KT2...................31 E1
Haylett Gdns KUT/HW KT1 *...................36 A1
Hayling Av FELT TW13........................18 B3
Haymer Gdns WPK KT4.........................43 F2
Haynt Wk RYNPK SW20.........................33 F5
Hayward Gdns PUT/ROE SW15..................16 D4
Hayward Rd THDIT KT7........................35 E5
Hazelbank BRYLDS KT5........................37 F5
Hazelbury CI WIM/MER SW19..................33 H4
Hazel CI BTFD TW8 *...........................6 B1
   WHTN TW2..................................12 B5
Hazelwood Ct SURB KT6.......................36 B3
Hazledene Rd CHSWK W4........................8 B2
Hazlemere Gdns WPK KT4......................38 B5
Hazlewell Rd PUT/ROE SW15..................16 D3
Hazlitt CI FELT TW13........................19 F4
Headley CI CHSGTN KT9......................41 H5
Headway CI RCHPK/HAM TW10.................21 H4
Hearne Rd CHSWK W4...........................7 H1
Heatham Pk WHTN TW2........................13 G5
Heathcote Rd TWK TW1........................13 G4
Heathcroft Av SUN TW16.....................26 A2
Heathdale Av HSLWW TW4.....................11 F1
Heath Dr RYNPK SW20.........................38 D1
Heather CI HPTN TW12........................27 H3
   ISLW TW7..................................12 C3
Heatherdale CI KUTN/CMB KT2................30 D1
Heatherlands SUN TW16......................26 B1
Heathfield Gdns CHSWK W4.....................8 B1
Heathfield North WHTN TW2...................12 D5
Heathfield South WHTN TW2..................13 E5
Heathfield Ter CHSWK W4......................8 B1
Heath Gdns TWK TW1..........................21 E1
Heath Gv SUN TW16...........................26 A2
Heathlands CI SUN TW16.....................26 B4
   TWK TW1...................................21 E2
Heathlands Ct HSLWW TW4....................11 F3
Heathlands Wy HSLWW TW4....................11 F3
Heath Md WIM/MER SW19......................25 E3
Heath RI PUT/ROE SW15......................17 E4
Heath Rd TWK TW1............................13 E2
   TWK TW1...................................21 E1
Heathrow Causeway Centre
   HSLWW TW4................................10 C1
Heathside HSLWW TW4........................11 G5
Heathview Gdns PUT/ROE SW15................16 D5
Heddon CI ISLW TW7..........................13 F2
Hedley Rd WHTN TW2..........................11 H5
Hedgegger Crs BARN SW13......................9 G3
Heights CI RYNPK SW20.......................32 C2
Heldmann CI HSLW TW3........................12 C2
Helen Av EBED/NFELT TW14...................10 C5
Helen CI E/WMO/HCT KT8......................34 A1
Helm CI HOR/WEW KT19.......................45 H5
Helme CI WIM/MER SW19......................25 G5
Hemingford Rd CHEAM SM3....................43 H3
Hemming CI HPTN TW12.......................27 H3
Hemmingsmead HOR/WEW KT19.................42 B5
Hemsby Rd CHSGTN KT9.......................41 G5
Hendon Gv HOR/WEW KT19....................45 H2
Henfield Rd WIM/MER SW19...................33 G3
Henley CI ISLW TW7...........................6 A4
Henley Dr KUTN/CMB KT2......................32 A2
Henley Wy FELT TW13.........................19 E5
Henry Jackson Rd PUT/ROE SW15..............17 E1
Henry Macaulay Av KUTN/CMB KT2..............2 C5
Henry Peters Dr TEDD TW11..................20 D5
Henty CI PUT/ROE SW15.......................16 C3
Henty Wk PUT/ROE SW15......................16 C3
Hepple CI ISLW TW7............................6 C5
Herbert Gdns CHSWK W4........................8 A2
Herbert PI ISLW TW7..........................5 G5
Herbert Rd KUT/HW KT1........................2 E7
   WIM/MER SW19.............................33 G2
Hereford Gdns WHTN TW2 *...................20 B1
Hereford Rd FELT TW13.......................18 C1
Hereford Wy CHSGTN KT9.....................40 D4
Heritage CI SUN TW16.......................26 B3
Herm CI ISLW TW7.............................5 F3
Hermitage CI ESH/CLAY KT10.................34 D1
   RCHPK/HAM TW10..........................14 A3
The Hermitage BARN SW13......................9 E4
   FELT TW13.................................18 A3
   KUT/HW KT1 *.............................36 A1
   NWMAL KT3................................14 A3
Herne Rd SURB KT6...........................41 E1
Heron Ct KUT/HW KT1 *........................2 C7
Heron Rd TWK TW1............................13 F1
Herons PI ISLW TW7..........................13 G1
Heron Wy EBED/NFELT TW14...................10 C5
Hersham CI PUT/ROE SW15....................16 B5
Hershell Ct MORT/ESHN SW14 *...............15 C3
Hertford Av MORT/ESHN SW14.................15 G3
Hester Ter RCH/KEW TW9......................14 D1
Heston Av HEST TW5...........................4 B3
Heston Grange La HEST TW5...................4 C2

Heston Rd HEST TW5....4 D3
Hexham Gdns ISLW TW7....6 B3
Heyford Av RYNPK SW20....33 G5
Heythorp St WAND/EARL SW18....25 G1
Hibernia Gdns HSLW TW3....11 H3
Hibernia Rd HSLW TW3....11 H3
Hidcote Gdns RYNPK SW20....32 C5
Highbury Cl NWMAL KT3....37 F1
Highbury Rd WIM/MER SW19....25 F5
High Cedar Dr RYNPK SW20....32 C2
Highclere Rd NWMAL KT3....31 G5
Highcliffe Dr PUT/ROE SW15....16 A4
High Coombe Pl KUTN/CMB KT2....31 G2
Highcross Wy PUT/ROE SW15....24 B1
Highdown WPK KT4....42 D1
Highdown Rd PUT/ROE SW15....16 C4
High Dr NWMAL KT3....31 F3
High St BTFD TW8....7 E2
  ESH/CLAY KT10....40 A5
  FELT TW13....18 A3
  HPTN TW12....28 A3
  HSLW TW3....12 A1
  KUT/HW KT1....2 B5
  KUT/HW KT1....29 H3
  NWMAL KT3....37 H1
  TEDD TW11....21 F5
  THDIT KT7....35 F3
  WHTN TW2....12 B5
  WIM/MER SW19....25 E5
High Street Ms WIM/MER SW19....25 F5
Hillary Dr ISLW TW7....15 E2
Hillbrow NWMAL KT3....32 A5
Hill Crs BRYLDS KT5....36 C2
  WPK KT4....43 H1
Hill Crest WPK KT4....43 H1
Hillcrest Gdns ESH/CLAY KT10....40 A2
Hillcross Av MRDN SM4....39 F3
Hillersdon Av BARN SW13....9 F5
Hill Field Rd HPTN TW12....27 G2
Hill Gv FELT TW13....19 G2
Hill House Dr HPTN TW12....27 H3
Hillier Pl CHSGTN KT9....41 E5
Hill Ri ESH/CLAY KT10....40 C1
  RCHPK/HAM TW10....14 A3
Hillside WIM/MER SW19....33 E1
Hillside Cl MRDN SM4....39 F1
Hill St RCH/KEW TW9....14 A4
Hill Top CHEAM SM3....39 G4
Hillview RYNPK SW20....33 G2
Hill View Rd ESH/CLAY KT10....44 B1
  TWK TW1....21 G1
Hinchley Cl ESH/CLAY KT10....40 A2
Hinchley Dr ESH/CLAY KT10....40 A2
Hinchley Wy ESH/CLAY KT10....40 B2
Hinton Av HSLW TW4....11 E3
Hobart Pl RCHPK/HAM TW10....14 C5
Hobart Rd WPK KT4....43 H1
Hobbes Wk PUT/ROE SW15....16 C3
Hogarth Gdns HEST TW5....4 D3
Hogarth Ter CHSWK W4 *....8 D2
Hogarth Wy HPTN TW12....28 B3
Hogsmill Wy HOR/WEW KT19....42 B4
Holcombe St HMSMTH W6....9 G1
Holderness Rd ISLW TW7....5 H4
Holland Av RYNPK SW20....32 A3
Holland Gdns BTFD TW8....7 G3
The Hollands WPK KT4....38 A5
Holles Cl HPTN TW12....27 H1
Hollies Cl TWK TW1....21 E2
Hollington Crs NWMAL KT3....38 A3
Holloway St HSLW TW3....12 A1
Hollybank Cl HPTN TW12....19 H5
Holly Bush La HPTN TW12....27 G2
Hollybush Rd KUTN/CMB KT2....30 A2
Holly Cl FELT TW13....19 F5
Holly Farm Rd NWDGN UB2 *....3
Hollyfield Rd BRYLDS KT5....36 C4
Hollygrove Cl HSLW TW3....11 G2
Holly Rd HPTN TW12....28 B1
  HSLW TW3....12 A2
  TWK TW1....21 F1
Hollytree Cl WIM/MER SW19....25 E1
Holman Rd HOR/WEW KT19....42 B4
Holmbush Rd PUT/ROE SW15....17 F4
Holme Ct ISLW TW7....13 F1
Holmesdale Av
  MORT/ESHN SW14....15 E1
Holmesdale Rd RCH/KEW TW9....7 G4
  TEDD TW11....29 H2
Holmes Rd TWK TW1....21 E2
Holm Oak Cl PUT/ROE SW15....17 G4
Holmsley Cl NWMAL KT3....38 A5
Holmwood Rd CHSGTN KT9....41 H5
Holne Cha MRDN SM4....39 H3
Holroyd Rd ESH/CLAY KT10....44 B2
  PUT/ROE SW15....16 D2
Holsworthy Wy CHSGTN KT9....40 D4
The Holt MRDN SM4....39 H1
Holybourne Av PUT/ROE SW15....16 B5
Holyport Rd FUL/PGN SW6....9 H3

Home Ct FELT TW13 *....18 B1
  SURB KT6 *....36 A2
Home Farm Cl THDIT KT7....35 F1
Homefield Rd WIM/MER SW19....33 F1
The Homefield MRDN SM4 *....39 H1
Home Park Ct KUT/HW KT1 *....36 A1
Home Park Rd WIM/MER SW19....25 G3
Home Park Ter KUT/HW KT1 *....2 A4
Home Park Wk KUT/HW KT1....36 A1
Homersham Rd KUT/HW KT1....3 H4
Homewaters Av SUN TW16....26 A3
Homewood Cl HPTN TW12....27 G1
Honeywood Rd ISLW TW7....13 F2
Honnor Gdns ISLW TW7....5 G5
Hood Av MORT/ESHN SW14....15 F3
Hood Rd RYNPK SW20....32 A2
Hook Ri North SURB KT6....41 G2
Hook Ri South CHSGTN KT9....41 G2
  SURB KT6....41 H2
Hook Rd CHSGTN KT9....41 E4
  SURB KT6....41 F1
Hook Underpass (Kingston By-Pass)
  CHSGTN KT9....41 G2
Hope Cl BTFD TW8....7 F1
Hopes Cl HEST TW5....4 D2
Hoppingwood Av NWMAL KT3....31 H5
Hopton Gdns NWMAL KT3....38 B3
Horace Rd KUT/HW KT1....2 E7
Hornbeam Crs BTFD TW8....6 C3
Hornbeam Gdns NWMAL KT3....38 B5
Hornchurch Cl KUTN/CMB KT2....22 A5
Horndean Cl PUT/ROE SW15....24 B1
Horne Wy PUT/ROE SW15....9 H5
Horse Fair KUT/HW KT1....2 A4
Horsley Dr KUTN/CMB KT2....22 A5
Horticultural Pl CHSWK W4....8 C1
Horton La HOR/WEW KT19....45 H4
Hospital Bridge Rd WHTN TW2....20 A1
Hospital Rd HSLW TW3....11 H1
Hotham Cl E/WMO/HCT KT8....27 H5
Hotham Rd PUT/ROE SW15....16 D1
Houblon Rd RCHPK/HAM TW10....14 B3
Houghton Cl HPTN TW12....27 F1
Hounslow Av HSLW TW3....12 A3
Hounslow Centre HSLW TW3 *....12 A1
Hounslow Gdns HSLW TW3....12 A3
Hounslow Rd EBED/NFELT TW14....10 C5
  FELT TW13....19 E3
  WHTN TW2....12 A4
Houston Rd SURB KT6....35 G3
Howard Cl HPTN TW12....28 B2
  SUN TW16....26 A1
Howard Rd ISLW TW7....13 E1
  NWMAL KT3....31 H5
  SURB KT6....36 C3
Howard St THDIT KT7....35 G4
Howard's La PUT/ROE SW15....16 D2
Howgate Rd MORT/ESHN SW14....15 C1
Howsman Rd BARN SW13....9 F2
Howson Ter RCHPK/HAM TW10 *....14 B4
Hubbard Dr CHSGTN KT9....40 D5
Hughenden Rd WPK KT4....38 B4
Hunter Rd RYNPK SW20....32 D3
Hunters Ct RCH/KEW TW9....14 A3
Hunters Rd CHSGTN KT9....41 F2
Huntingdon Gdns CHSWK W4....8 B3
  WPK KT4....43 H2
Huntingfield Rd PUT/ROE SW15....16 B2
Hunting Gate Dr CHSGTN KT9....45 F1
Hunting Gate Ms WHTN TW2 *....20 D1
Huntley Wy RYNPK SW20 *....32 B4
Huntsman Cl FELT TW13....18 C4
Huntsmoor Rd HOR/WEW KT19....42 C4
Hurlingham Gdns FUL/PGN SW6....17 G1
Hurlingham Pk FUL/PGN SW6 *....17 H1
Hurlingham Sq FUL/PGN SW6 *....17 H1
Hurn Court Rd HSLWW TW4....4 A1
Hurstbourne ESH/CLAY KT10....40 A5
Hurst Cl CHSGTN KT9....41 H4
Hurstfield Rd E/WMO/HCT KT8....27 H5
Hurst La E/WMO/HCT KT8....34 B1
Hurst Rd E/WMO/HCT KT8....28 B5
Hussars Cl HSLWW TW4....11 F1
Hyacinth Cl HPTN TW12....27 H1
Hyacinth Rd PUT/ROE SW15....24 B1
Hyde Rd RCHPK/HAM TW10....14 C3
Hyde Wk MRDN SM4....39 H4

I

Ibis La CHSWK W4....8 B4
Ibsley Gdns PUT/ROE SW15....24 B1
Idmiston Rd NWMAL KT3....38 A4
Idmiston Sq WPK KT4....38 A4
Ilex Cl SUN TW16....26 D4
Imber Cross THDIT KT7 *....35 E4
Imber Gv ESH/CLAY KT10....34 C4
Imber Park Rd ESH/CLAY KT10....34 C5
Ingress St CHSWK W4....8 D1
Inner Park Rd WIM/MER SW19....25 E1
Innes Cl RYNPK SW20....33 H4
Innes Gdns PUT/ROE SW15....16 C4
Inveresk Gdns WPK KT4....43 E2
Inverness Rd HSLW TW3....11 H3
  WPK KT4....39 E5
Invicta Cl EBED/NFELT TW14....18 A1

Inwood Av HSLW TW3....12 B1
Inwood Rd HSLW TW3....12 B2
Iris Cl SURB KT6 *....36 C4
Iris Rd HOR/WEW KT19....42 A4
Isabella Ct RCHPK/HAM TW10 *....14 C4
Isabella Pl KUTN/CMB KT2....22 C5
Isis Cl PUT/ROE SW15....16 D2
Islay Gdns HSLWW TW4....11 E3
Ivanhoe Rd HSLWW TW4....11 E1
Ivory Ct FELT TW13....18 B1
Ivybridge Cl TWK TW1....13 F4
Ivy Cl SUN TW16....26 A3
Ivy La HSLWW TW4....11 G2
Ivy Rd HSLW TW3....12 A2
  SURB KT6 *....41 H1

J

Jacaranda Cl NWMAL KT3....31 H5
Jack Good Child Wy
  KUT/HW KT1....3 J6
Jackson Wy HOR/WEW KT19....45 H2
James St HSLW TW3....12 C1
Jasmine Rd HOR/WEW KT19....42 A5
Jasmin Rd HOR/WEW KT19....42 A4
Jeffs Cl HPTN TW12 *....28 A1
Jemmett Cl KUTN/CMB KT2....3 J5
Jenner Wy HOR/WEW KT19....45 H2
Jennings Cl SURB KT6....35 H4
Jephtha Rd WAND/EARL SW18....17 H4
Jersey Rd HEST TW5....5 E3
  HSLW TW3....5 E3
  ISLW TW7....5 E3
Jillian Cl HPTN TW12....27 H2
Jocelyn Rd RCH/KEW TW9....14 B1
Jodrell Cl ISLW TW7....6 B4
John Austin Cl KUTN/CMB KT2....2 E3
Johnsons Dr HPTN TW12....28 B3
John St HSLW TW3....12 B1
Jordans Ms WHTN TW2....20 D2
Jubilee Av WHTN TW2....20 B1
Jubilee Cl KUT/HW KT1....29 H3
Jubilee Vls ESH/CLAY KT10 *....34 D5
Jubilee Wy CHSGTN KT9....42 A2
  EBED/NFELT TW14....18 B1
Juniper Cl CHSGTN KT9....41 G4
Juniper Gdns SUN TW16....26 A1
Justin Cl BTFD TW8....7 E3

K

Keble Cl WPK KT4....38 A5
Keble Pl BARN SW13....9 G2
Keepers Ms TEDD TW11....29 H1
The Keep KUTN/CMB KT2....30 C1
Keevil Dr WIM/MER SW19....17 E5
Kelsall Ms RCH/KEW TW9....8 A4
Kelton Vls KUT/HW KT1 *....3 F5
Kelvedon Cl KUTN/CMB KT2....30 D1
Kelvin Cl HOR/WEW KT19....41 H5
Kelvin Gv CHSGTN KT9....41 G4
Kempton Av SUN TW16....26 C5
Kempton Ct SUN TW16....26 C3
Kempton Pk SUN TW16 *....26 D3
Kempton Rd HPTN TW12....27 G3
Kendal Cl EBED/NFELT TW14....18 A1
Kendall Rd ISLW TW7....6 B5
Kendal Pl PUT/ROE SW15....17 G3
Kendrey Gdns WHTN TW2....12 D4
Kenilworth Av WIM/MER SW19....25 H5
Kenilworth Rd EW KT17....43 F5
Kenley Rd KUT/HW KT1....3 K4
  TWK TW1....13 F4
  WIM/MER SW19....33 H4
Kennet Rd ISLW TW7....13 E1
Kensington Gdns KUT/HW KT1....2 C7
Kent Dr TEDD TW11....20 D5
Kenton Av SUN TW16....26 E4
Kent Rd E/WMO/HCT KT8....34 B1
  KUT/HW KT1....2 B6
  RCH/KEW TW9....7 G3
Kent Wy SURB KT6....41 G2
Kentwode Gn BARN SW13....9 G1
Kenwyn Rd RYNPK SW20....32 D3
Kenyngton Dr SUN TW16....18 B5
Kersfield Rd PUT/ROE SW15....17 E4
Keswick Av PUT/ROE SW15....23 H5
  WIM/MER SW19....33 H4
Keswick Rd PUT/ROE SW15....17 F3
  WHTN TW2....12 D4
Kevin Cl HSLWW TW4....4 A5
Kew Br RCH/KEW TW9....7 H2
Kew Bridge Arches CHSWK W4 *....7 H2
Kew Bridge Ct BTFD TW8....7 H1
Kew Bridge Rd BTFD TW8....7 G1
Kew Foot Rd RCH/KEW TW9....14 B2
Kew Gardens Rd RCH/KEW TW9....7 G3
Kew Gn RCH/KEW TW9....7 G2
Kew Meadow Pth RCH/KEW TW9....7 H4
Kew Riverside Pk RCH/KEW TW9....8 A3

Kew Rd RCH/KEW TW9....7
  RCH/KEW TW9....14
Keywood Dr SUN TW16....26
Kilberry Cl ISLW TW7....5
Killester Gdns WPK KT4....43
Kilmington Rd BARN SW13....9
Kilmorey Gdns TWK TW1....13
Kilmorey Rd TWK TW1....13
Kilnside ESH/CLAY KT10....44
Kimber Rd WAND/EARL SW18....17
King Charles Crs BRYLDS KT5....36
King Charles Wk WIM/MER SW19 *....25
King Charles' Rd BRYLDS KT5....36
King Edward Dr CHSGTN KT9....41
King Edward's Gv TEDD TW11....29
Kingfisher Dr RCHPK/HAM TW10....21
King George Sq RCHPK/HAM TW10....14
King Henry's Reach HMSMTH W6....9
King Henry's Rd KUT/HW KT1....3
Kings Av NWMAL KT3....38
Kingsbridge Rd MRDN SM4....39
Kings Cha E/WMO/HCT KT8....28
Kingsclere Cl PUT/ROE SW15....16
Kingscliffe Gdns WIM/MER SW19....25
Kings Cl THDIT KT7....35
Kingscote Rd NWMAL KT3....31
Kingsdowne Rd SURB KT6....36
Kings Dr BRYLDS KT5....36
Kings Farm Av RCHPK/HAM TW10....14
Kingsgate Rd KUT/HW KT1....2
Kingshill Av WPK KT4....38
Kings Keep KUT/HW KT1 *....36
Kingslawn Cl PUT/ROE SW15....16
Kingsleigh Cl BTFD TW8....7
Kingsley Av HSLW TW3....5
Kingsley Dr WPK KT4....43
Kingsley Rd HSLW TW3....5
Kingsmead RCHPK/HAM TW10....14
Kingsmead Av SUN TW16....26
  SURB KT6....41
  WPK KT4....43
Kingsmead Cl TEDD TW11....29
Kingsmere Cl PUT/ROE SW15....17
Kingsmere Rd WIM/MER SW19....25
Kingsnympton Pk KUTN/CMB KT2....31
Kings Pl CHSWK W4....8
Kings Ride Ga RCHPK/HAM TW10....14
Kings Rd FELT TW13....18
  RCHPK/HAM TW10....14
Kingston Br KUT/HW KT1....2
Kingston By-Pass RYNPK SW20....32
Kingston Cl TEDD TW11....29
Kingston Hall Rd KUT/HW KT1....2
Kingston Hl KUTN/CMB KT2....3
  KUTN/CMB KT2....23
  KUTN/CMB KT2....31
Kingston Hill Pl KUTN/CMB KT2....23
Kingston House Est SURB KT6 *....35
Kingston La TEDD TW11....21
Kingston Ldg NWMAL KT3....37
Kingston Rd BRYLDS KT5....42
  HOR/WEW KT19....42
  NWMAL KT3....37
  PUT/ROE SW15....24
  RYNPK SW20....32
  TEDD TW11....33
  WIM/MER SW19....33
Kingston V PUT/ROE SW15....23
King St RCH/KEW TW9....14
  TWK TW1....21
King Street Pde TWK TW1 *....21
Kingsway MORT/ESHN SW14....15
  NWMAL KT3....38
Kingswood Av HPTN TW12....28
  HSLW TW3....4
Kingswood Cl NWMAL KT3....38
  SURB KT6....36
Kingswood Rd WIM/MER SW19....33
Kingsworthy Cl KUT/HW KT1....3
Kings Yd PUT/ROE SW15 *....17
King's Av HSLW TW3....5
  SUN TW16....18
King's Dr THDIT KT7....35
King's Paddock HPTN TW12....28
King's Pas KUTN/CMB KT2....2
King's Rd KUTN/CMB KT2....2
  MORT/ESHN SW14....15
  SURB KT6....35
  TEDD TW11....20
  TWK TW1....13
  WIM/MER SW19....33
Kinnaird Av CHSWK W4....8
Kinross Av WPK KT4....43
Kinross Cl SUN TW16....18
Kinross Dr SUN TW16....18
Kinsella Gdns WIM/MER SW19....25
Kirby Cl HOR/WEW KT19....43
Kirkees Rd SURB KT6....36
Kirkley Rd WIM/MER SW19....33
Kirrane Cl NWMAL KT3....38
Kitson Rd BARN SW13....9
Kneller Gdns ISLW TW7....12
Kneller Rd NWMAL KT3....37
  WHTN TW2....12
Knevett Ter HSLW TW3....12
Knightwood Crs NWMAL KT3....37
Knight's Pk KUT/HW KT1....
Knight's Pl WHTN TW2....20

ollmead *BRYLDS* KT5 .... 37 F5
olls Cl *WPK* KT4 .... 43 G2
owle Rd *WHTN* TW2 .... 20 D1

L

burnum Crs *SUN* TW16 .... 26 C3
burnum Gv *HSLW* TW3 .... 11 G2
 NWMAL KT3 .... 31 G4
cey Dr *HPTN* TW12 .... 27 G3
dderstile Ride *PUT/ROE* SW15 .... 17 E2
cy Rd *PUT/ROE* SW15 .... 17 E2
dy Booth Rd *KUT/HW* KT1 .... 2 C5
dy Forsdyke Wy *HOR/WEW* KT19 .. 45 H2
dy Harewood Wy *HOR/WEW* KT19 45 H2
dy Hay *WPK* KT4 .... 43 E1
fone Av *FELT* TW13 .... 18 D1
inlock Pl *HSLW* TW3 .... 5 E4
inson St *WAND/EARL* SW18 .... 17 H5
kehurst Rd *HOR/WEW* KT19 .... 42 D6
ke Gdns *RCHPK/HAM* TW10 .... 21 G5
ke Rd *WIM/MER* SW19 .... 25 G5
keside Av *RCH/KEW* TW9 .... 14 D1
mbert Av *RCH/KEW* TW9 .... 14 D1
mbert's Rd *BRYLDS* KT5 .... 36 B2
mbourne Av *WIM/MER* SW19 .... 25 H2
mbourne Gv *KUT/HW* KT1 .... 3 J4
mbton Rd *RCHPK/HAM* TW10 .... 32 D3
mmas Rd *RCHPK/HAM* TW10 .... 21 H4
mpton Av *HSLW* TW3 .... 4 D4
mpton House Cl *WIM/MER* SW19 .. 25 E4
mpton Park Rd *HSLW* TW3 .... 5 E5
mpton Rd *HEST* TW5 .... 5 E5
 HSLW TW3 .... 5 E5
ncaster Av *WIM/MER* SW19 .... 25 E5
ncaster Cl *WPK* KT4 .... 38 C4
ncaster Gdn *KUT/CMB* KT2 .... 22 A5
ncaster Gdns *KUT/CMB* KT2 .... 25 E5
 WIM/MER SW19 .... 25 E5
ncaster Ms *RCHPK/HAM* TW10 .... 14 B4
ncaster Pk *RCHPK/HAM* TW10 .... 14 B4
ncaster Pl *TWK* TW1 .... 13 E5
ncaster Rd *WIM/MER* SW19 .... 25 E5
ncaster Wy *WPK* KT4 .... 38 D4
ncing Rd *FELT* TW13 .... 18 A2
ndford Rd *PUT/ROE* SW15 .... 16 D1
ndgrove Rd *WIM/MER* SW19 .... 25 H5
ndseer Rd *NWMAL* KT3 .... 37 G4
ne Gdns *ESH/CLAY* KT10 .... 40 A1
neway *PUT/ROE* SW15 .... 16 C3
ngbourne Wy *ESH/CLAY* KT10 .... 40 A5
ngdale Cl *MORT/ESHN* SW14 .... 15 G2
ngdon Pk *TEDD* TW11 .... 29 H2
ngdon Pl *MORT/ESHN* SW14 .... 15 F1
ngham Gdns *RCHPK/HAM* TW10 .... 21 H4
ngham House Cl
 RCHPK/HAM TW10 .... 22 A4
ngham Pl *CHSWK* W4 .... 8 D2
ngham Rd *RYNPK* SW20 .... 32 D3
 TEDD TW11 .... 21 G5
nghorn Dr *WHTN* TW2 .... 12 D5
ngley Av *NWMAL* KT3 .... 36 A5
ngley Gv *NWMAL* KT3 .... 31 G4
ngley Rd *ISLW* TW7 .... 7 H4
 SURB KT6 .... 36 B4
 WIM/MER SW19 .... 33 G1
ngridge Ms *HPTN* TW12 .... 27 G3
ngside Av *PUT/ROE* SW15 .... 16 B2
ngston Rd *E/WMO/HCT* KT8 .... 34 B2
ngwood Cha *TEDD* TW11 .... 29 H1
nigan Dr *HSLW* TW3 .... 12 A3
nsbury Av *EBED/NFELT* TW14 .... 10 C4
nsdowne Cl *BRYLDS* KT5 .... 42 A1
 TWK TW1 .... 21 E1
nsdowne Copse *WPK* KT4 * 43 F1
nsdowne Ct *WPK* KT4 .... 43 F1
nsdowne Rd *HSLW* TW3 .... 12 A1
 RYNPK SW20 .... 32 D2
ntern Cl *PUT/ROE* SW15 .... 16 B3
ara Cl *CHSGTN* KT9 .... 45 F1
rch Crs *HOR/WEW* KT19 .... 42 A5
rch Dr *CHSWK* W4 * 9 H1
rches Av *MORT/ESHN* SW14 .... 15 G2
rgewood Av *SURB* KT6 .... 41 H1
rkfield Rd *RCH/KEW* TW9 .... 14 B2
rkspur Rd *WIM/MER* SW19 .... 33 E1
rpent Av *PUT/ROE* SW15 .... 16 D3
tchmere Ct *RCHPK/HAM* TW10 .... 22 B5
tchmere La *KUT/CMB* KT2 .... 30 D1
tchmere Rd *KUT/CMB* KT2 .... 30 B1
teward Rd *BTFD* TW8 .... 7 E2
tham Rd *TWK* TW1 .... 13 E5
timer Cl *WPK* KT4 .... 43 E1
timer Rd *TEDD* TW11 .... 21 E5
ttimer Rd *CHSWK* W4 .... 8 D3
ubin Cl *TWK* TW1 .... 13 G2
uderdale Dr *RCHPK/HAM* TW10 .... 21 E1
urel Av *TWK* TW1 .... 21 E1
urel Gdns *HSLW* TW3 .... 11 F2
urel Rd *BARN* SW13 .... 7 F5
 HPTN TW12 .... 20 C5
 RYNPK SW20 .... 32 B3
uriston Rd *WIM/MER* SW19 .... 25 H5
vender Av *WPK* KT4 .... 43 H2

Lavender Ct *E/WMO/HCT* KT8 .... 28 A5
Lavender Rd *HOR/WEW* KT19 .... 42 A4
Lavenham Rd *WAND/EARL* SW18 .... 25 G2
Laverstoke Gdns *PUT/ROE* SW15 .... 16 A5
Lawford Rd *CHSWK* W4 .... 8 B3
Lawn Cl *NWMAL* KT3 .... 31 H4
Lawn Crs *RCH/KEW* TW9 .... 7 H5
The Lawn *NWDGN* UB2 .... 4 D1
Lawrence Av *NWMAL* KT3 .... 37 G5
Lawrence Pde *ISLW* TW7 * 13 G1
Lawrence Rd *HPTN* TW12 .... 27 G2
 HSLW TW4 .... 10 D2
 RCHPK/HAM TW10 .... 21 H4
Lawson Cl *WIM/MER* SW19 .... 25 E3
Layton Pl *RCH/KEW* TW9 .... 7 H5
Layton Rd *BTFD* TW8 .... 7 H3
 HSLW TW3 .... 12 A2
Layton's La *SUN* TW16 .... 26 A4
Lea Cl *WHTN* TW2 .... 11 G5
Leaf Cl *THDIT* KT7 .... 34 D2
Leafield Rd *RYNPK* SW20 .... 33 G5
Leamington Av *MRDN* SM4 .... 39 G1
Leamington Cl *HSLW* TW3 .... 12 B3
Leas Cl *CHSGTN* KT9 .... 45 G5
Leatherhead Rd *CHSGTN* KT9 .... 44 D4
Lebanon Av *FELT* TW13 .... 19 E5
Lebanon Gdns *WAND/EARL* SW18 .... 17 H4
Lebanon Pk *TWK* TW1 .... 13 G5
Lebanon Rd *WAND/EARL* SW18 .... 17 H4
Leconfield Av *BARN* SW13 .... 16 A1
Leeward Gdns *WIM/MER* SW19 .... 33 F1
Legion Ct *MRDN* SM4 .... 39 H3
Legrace Av *HSLWW* TW4 .... 4 A5
Leicester Cl *WPK* KT4 .... 43 H3
Leigham Dr *ISLW* TW7 .... 7 H5
Leigh Cl *NWMAL* KT3 .... 37 G1
Leigh Pl *FELT* TW13 .... 18 D1
Leigh Rd *HSLW* TW3 .... 12 C2
The Leigh *NWMAL* KT3 .... 31 H1
Leinster Av *MORT/ESHN* SW14 .... 15 F1
Lenelby Rd *SURB* KT6 .... 36 D5
Lenton Ri *RCH/KEW* TW9 .... 14 B1
Leopold Av *WIM/MER* SW19 .... 25 G5
Leopold Rd *WIM/MER* SW19 .... 25 G4
Letchworth Av *EBED/NFELT* TW14 .... 10 A4
Levana Cl *WIM/MER* SW19 .... 25 F1
Lewesdon Cl *WIM/MER* SW19 .... 25 E1
Lewin Rd *MORT/ESHN* SW14 .... 15 G1
Lewis Rd *RCH/KEW* TW9 * 14 A3
Lewiston Cl *WPK* KT4 .... 38 C4
Leybourne Pk *RCH/KEW* TW9 .... 7 H4
Leyfield *WPK* KT4 .... 42 D1
Lichfield Gdns *RCH/KEW* TW9 * 14 B3
Lichfield Rd *HSLWW* TW4 .... 10 D1
 RCH/KEW TW9 .... 7 G4
Lichfield Ter *RCH/KEW* TW9 * 14 B3
Lifford St *PUT/ROE* SW15 .... 17 G2
Lillian Rd *BARN* SW13 .... 9 F2
Lime Crs *SUN* TW16 .... 26 D4
Lime Gv *NWMAL* KT3 .... 31 G5
 TWK TW1 .... 13 E4
Limes Av *BARN* SW13 .... 9 E1
Limes Field Rd *MORT/ESHN* SW14 .... 15 H1
Limes Gdns *WAND/EARL* SW18 .... 17 H4
The Limes *WAND/EARL* SW18 .... 17 H4
Lime Tree Av *ESH/CLAY* KT10 .... 34 C5
 THDIT KT7 .... 34 C5
Lime Tree Rd *HEST* TW5 .... 5 E4
Limpsfield Av *WIM/MER* SW19 .... 25 E3
Lincoln Av *WHTN* TW2 .... 20 B2
 WIM/MER SW19 .... 25 E3
Lincoln Rd *FELT* TW13 .... 19 G3
 NWMAL KT3 .... 31 F5
 WPK KT4 .... 38 C5
Linden Av *HSLW* TW3 .... 12 A3
Linden Cl *THDIT* KT7 .... 35 E4
Linden Cottages *WIM/MER* SW19 * 33 F1
Linden Crs *KUT/HW* KT1 .... 3 F5
Linden Gdns *CHSWK* W4 .... 8 C1
Linden Gv *NWMAL* KT3 .... 31 H5
 TEDD TW11 .... 21 E5
Linden Rd *HPTN* TW12 .... 27 H3
The Lindens *CHSWK* W4 .... 8 B5
Lindisfarne Rd *RYNPK* SW20 .... 32 B2
Lindley Pl *RCH/KEW* TW9 .... 7 H4
Lindsay Cl *CHSGTN* KT9 .... 45 F1
Lindsay Rd *HPTN* TW12 .... 20 A4
 WPK KT4 .... 43 G1
Lindum Rd *TEDD* TW11 .... 29 H2
Lingfield Rd *WIM/MER* SW19 .... 33 E1
 WPK KT4 .... 43 H2
Lingwood Gdns *ISLW* TW7 .... 7 H5
Linkfield *E/WMO/HCT* KT8 .... 27 H5
Linkfield Rd *ISLW* TW7 .... 7 H5
Link Rd *EBED/NFELT* TW14 .... 10 A5
Links Av *MRDN* SM4 .... 39 H1
Linkside *NWMAL* KT3 .... 31 H4
Linksview *CF* HPTN TW12 * 20 C4
Links View Rd *HPTN* TW12 .... 20 C4
The Link *TEDD* TW11 .... 29 E1
Linkway *NWMAL* KT3 .... 38 C1
Link Wy *RCHPK/HAM* TW10 .... 21 G2
Linkway *RYNPK* SW20 .... 32 C5
Linslade Cl *HSLWW* TW4 .... 11 F3
Linstead Wy *WAND/EARL* SW18 .... 17 F5
Lion Av *TWK* TW1 .... 21 E1
Lionel Rd South *BTFD* TW8 .... 7 H1
Lion Gate Gdns *RCH/KEW* TW9 .... 14 C1

Lion Gate Ms *WAND/EARL* SW18 .... 17 H5
Lion Park Av *CHSGTN* KT9 .... 45 H3
Lion Rd *TWK* TW1 .... 21 E1
Lion Wy *BTFD* TW8 .... 7 G1
Lion Wharf Rd *ISLW* TW7 .... 13 G1
Lisbon Av *WHTN* TW2 .... 20 B2
Lismore *WIM/MER* SW19 * 25 G5
Lismore Cl *ISLW* TW7 .... 8 A4
Lissant Cl *SURB* KT6 .... 35 H4
Litchfield Av *MRDN* SM4 .... 39 G4
Littlecombe Cl *PUT/ROE* SW15 .... 17 E4
Littlecote Cl *WIM/MER* SW19 .... 17 E4
Little Ferry Rd *TWK* TW1 * 21 G1
Littlefield Cl *KUT/HW* KT1 .... 2 D5
Little Park Dr *FELT* TW13 .... 19 E2
Little Queens Rd *TEDD* TW11 .... 29 F1
Little St Leonards *MORT/ESHN* SW14 .... 15 F1
Liverpool Rd *KUTN/CMB* KT2 .... 30 D2
Livesey Cl *KUT/HW* KT1 .... 3 E6
Livingstone Rd *HSLW* TW3 .... 12 B2
Lloyd Rd *WPK* KT4 .... 43 H2
Lochaline St *HMSMTH* W6 .... 9 F4
Lockesley Sq *SURB* KT6 * 36 A3
Lock Rd *RCHPK/HAM* TW10 .... 21 H3
Locksmeade Rd *RCHPK/HAM* TW10 .... 21 G4
Lockwood Wy *CHSGTN* KT9 .... 41 H1
Locomotive Dr *EBED/NFELT* TW14 .... 10 B5
Lodge Cl *ISLW* TW7 .... 8 C5
Lofthouse Pl *CHSGTN* KT9 .... 40 D5
Logan Cl *HSLWW* TW4 .... 11 G1
London Rd *EW* KT17 .... 43 G4
 ISLW TW7 .... 5 H5
 KUTN/CMB KT2 .... 2 C2
 MRDN SM4 .... 39 H2
 TWK TW1 .... 21 E2
London Stile *CHSWK* W4 .... 7 H1
Longfellow Rd *WPK* KT4 .... 38 B5
Longford Dr *MORT/ESHN* SW14 .... 15 E3
Longford St *WAND/EARL* SW18 .... 17 H4
Longford Av *EBED/NFELT* TW14 .... 10 A4
Longford Cl *FELT* TW13 .... 19 F3
 HPTN TW12 .... 19 H3
Longford Ct *HOR/WEW* KT19 .... 42 B3
 HPTN TW12 .... 28 A1
Longford Rd *WHTN* TW2 .... 19 H1
Longmead Rd *THDIT* KT7 .... 34 D2
Longstaff Crs *WAND/EARL* SW18 .... 17 H4
Longstaff Rd *WAND/EARL* SW18 .... 17 H4
Long Wk *NWMAL* KT3 .... 31 F5
Longwood Ct *WPK* KT4 .... 43 F1
Longwood Dr *PUT/ROE* SW15 .... 16 B3
Lonsdale Ms *RCH/KEW* TW9 * 7 H4
Lonsdale Rd *BARN* SW13 .... 9 E3
Loraine Rd *CHSWK* W4 .... 8 A2
Lord Chancellor Wk *KUT/CMB* KT2 .... 31 F3
Lord Napier Pl *HMSMTH* W6 .... 9 F1
Lords Cl *FELT* TW13 .... 19 F2
Loring Rd *ISLW* TW7 .... 8 A4
Lorne Rd *RCHPK/HAM* TW10 .... 14 C4
Lovekyn Cl *KUT/CMB* KT2 .... 2 D4
Lovelace Gdns *SURB* KT6 .... 36 A4
Lovelace Rd *SURB* KT6 .... 35 H5
Lovelace Vls *THDIT* KT7 * 35 G4
Love La *MRDN* SM4 .... 39 G4
 SURB KT6 .... 40 D1
Lovell Rd *RCHPK/HAM* TW10 .... 21 H3
Lower Common South
 PUT/ROE SW15 .... 16 C3
Lower Downs Rd *RYNPK* SW20 .... 33 E3
Lower Green Gdns *WPK* KT4 .... 38 B5
Lower Grove Rd *RCHPK/HAM* TW10 .... 14 C4
Lower Hampton Rd *SUN* TW16 .... 27 E4
Lower Ham Rd *KUT/CMB* KT2 .... 30 A1
Lower Kings Rd *KUT/CMB* KT2 .... 2 C2
Lower Marsh La *BRYLDS* KT5 .... 2 C5
Lower Morden La *MRDN* SM4 .... 38 C5
Lower Mortlake Rd *RCH/KEW* TW9 .... 14 B2
Lower Richmond Rd
 MORT/ESHN SW14 .... 15 F1
 PUT/ROE SW15 .... 16 D1
 RCH/KEW TW9 .... 14 D1
Lower Sand Hills *SURB* KT6 .... 35 H4
Lower Sq *ISLW* TW7 .... 13 G1
Lower Sunbury Rd *E/WMO/HCT* KT8 .... 27 G4
 HPTN TW12 .... 27 H4
Lower Teddington Rd *KUT/HW* KT1 .... 2 A3
Lower Wood Rd *ESH/CLAY* KT10 .... 40 B5
Lowther Man *BARN* SW13 * 9 F4
Lowther Rd *BARN* SW13 .... 9 E4
 KUTN/CMB KT2 .... 3 E3
Loxley Rd *HPTN* TW12 .... 19 G4
Ludlow Rd *FELT* TW13 .... 18 B5
Ludovick Wk *PUT/ROE* SW15 .... 15 H2
Lulworth Av *HEST* TW5 .... 5 E4
Luther Ms *TEDD* TW11 .... 21 E5
Luther Rd *TEDD* TW11 .... 21 E5
Luttrell Av *PUT/ROE* SW15 .... 16 D3
Lydney Cl *WIM/MER* SW19 .... 25 F2
Lymington Gdns *HOR/WEW* KT19 .... 42 A5
Lyncroft Gdns *HSLW* TW3 .... 12 B3
Lyndale *THDIT* KT7 .... 34 D4
Lyndale Hampton Court Wy
 ESH/CLAY KT10 .... 34 D4
Lyndhurst Av *BRYLDS* KT5 .... 37 E5
 SUN TW16 .... 26 B5
 WHTN TW2 .... 19 G1
Lyndhurst Dr *NWMAL* KT3 .... 37 H3
Lynmouth Av *MRDN* SM4 .... 39 E4

Lynmouth Gdns *HEST* TW5 .... 4 A4
Lynton Cl *CHSGTN* KT9 .... 41 F3
 ISLW TW7 .... 13 E2
Lynton Rd *NWMAL* KT3 .... 37 G2
Lynwood Dr *WPK* KT4 .... 43 F1
Lynwood Rd *THDIT* KT7 .... 40 A1
Lynwood Ter *WIM/MER* SW19 * 33 G3
Lyric Rd *BARN* SW13 .... 9 E4
Lysander Gdns *SURB* KT6 .... 36 C3
Lysons Wk *PUT/ROE* SW15 * 16 B3
Lytcott Dr *E/WMO/HCT* KT8 .... 27 C5
Lytton Gv *PUT/ROE* SW15 .... 17 E3

M

Macaulay Av *ESH/CLAY* KT10 .... 40 A1
Macbeth St *HMSMTH* W6 .... 9 G1
Macfarlane La *ISLW* TW7 .... 6 A2
Maddison Cl *TEDD* TW11 .... 29 E1
Madrid Rd *BARN* SW13 .... 9 F2
Mafeking Av *BTFD* TW8 .... 7 H2
Magdala Rd *ISLW* TW7 .... 13 F1
Magnolia Cl *KUTN/CMB* KT2 .... 31 E1
Magnolia Rd *CHSWK* W4 .... 8 A2
Magnolia Wy *HOR/WEW* KT19 .... 42 B4
Magnolia Whf *CHSWK* W4 * 8 A2
Maguire Dr *RCHPK/HAM* TW10 .... 21 H4
Main St *FELT* TW13 .... 19 E5
Maitland Cl *HSLW* TW4 .... 11 G1
Malbrook Rd *PUT/ROE* SW15 .... 16 C2
Malcolm Dr *SURB* KT6 .... 36 A5
Malcolm Rd *WIM/MER* SW19 .... 33 F1
Malden Green Av *WPK* KT4 .... 38 A5
Malden Hl *NWMAL* KT3 .... 38 A1
Malden Hill Gdns *NWMAL* KT3 .... 32 A5
Malden Pk *NWMAL* KT3 .... 38 A3
Malden Rd *NWMAL* KT3 .... 38 A1
 WPK KT4 .... 38 A4
Malden Wy *NWMAL* KT3 .... 37 G3
Mallard Cl *WHTN* TW2 .... 11 H5
Mallard Pl *TWK* TW1 .... 21 F3
Mall Rd *HMSMTH* W6 .... 9 G1
The Mall *BTFD* TW8 * 7 F2
 MORT/ESHN SW14 .... 15 F3
 SURB KT6 .... 36 A2
Mall Vls *HMSMTH* W6 * 9 G1
Maltby Rd *CHSGTN* KT9 .... 41 H5
Malthouse Dr *CHSWK* W4 .... 9 E2
 FELT TW13 .... 19 E5
Malting Wy *ISLW* TW7 .... 13 E1
Malvern Cl *SURB* KT6 .... 36 B5
Malvern Dr *FELT* TW13 .... 19 E5
Malvern Rd *HPTN* TW12 .... 27 H3
 SURB KT6 .... 41 F1
Manbre Rd *HMSMTH* W6 .... 9 H1
Mandeville Cl *WIM/MER* SW19 .... 33 F2
Mandeville Dr *SURB* KT6 .... 36 A5
Mandeville Rd *ISLW* TW7 .... 8 B5
Manfred Rd *PUT/ROE* SW15 .... 17 G3
Manning Pl *RCHPK/HAM* TW10 .... 14 C4
Manningtree Cl *WIM/MER* SW19 .... 25 F1
Mann's Cl *ISLW* TW7 .... 13 E3
Manoel Rd *WHTN* TW2 .... 20 B2
Manor Av *HSLWW* TW4 .... 11 E1
Manor Cl *WPK* KT4 .... 37 H5
Manor Ct *KUT/CMB* KT2 * 3 H3
Manor Crs *BRYLDS* KT5 .... 36 D3
 HOR/WEW KT19 .... 45 H5
Manordene Cl *THDIT* KT7 .... 35 F5
Manor Dr *BRYLDS* KT5 .... 36 D3
 ESH/CLAY KT10 .... 40 A2
 FELT TW13 .... 19 E5
 HOR/WEW KT19 .... 42 B5
 SUN TW16 .... 26 B4
Manor Dr North *NWMAL* KT3 .... 37 H5
 WPK KT4 .... 37 H5
The Manor Dr *WPK* KT4 .... 37 H5
Manor Farm Cl *WPK* KT4 .... 37 H5
Manor Gdns *HPTN* TW12 .... 28 A2
 RCH/KEW TW9 .... 14 C2
 RYNPK SW20 .... 33 G4
 SUN TW16 .... 26 B3
Manorgate Rd *KUTN/CMB* KT2 .... 3 G3
Manor Gv *RCH/KEW* TW9 .... 14 D2
Manor House Wy *ISLW* TW7 .... 13 G1
Manor La *FELT* TW13 .... 18 B2
 SUN TW16 .... 26 B4
Manor Pk *RCH/KEW* TW9 .... 14 C2
Manor Pl *EBED/NFELT* TW14 .... 18 B5
Manor Rd *E/WMO/HCT* KT8 .... 34 C1
 RCH/KEW TW9 .... 14 C1
 RYNPK SW20 .... 33 G4
 TEDD TW11 .... 21 G5
 WHTN TW2 .... 20 B2
Manor Rd North *ESH/CLAY* KT10 .... 40 A1
 THDIT KT7 .... 40 A1
Manor Rd South *ESH/CLAY* KT10 .... 40 A3
Manor V *BTFD* TW8 .... 6 D1
Manor Wy *WPK* KT4 .... 37 H5
Mansel Rd *WIM/MER* SW19 .... 33 F1
Mansfield Rd *CHSGTN* KT9 .... 40 D4
Manston Gv *KUTN/CMB* KT2 .... 22 A5
Maple Cl *HPTN* TW12 .... 27 G1
Maple Ct *NWMAL* KT3 .... 31 G5
Maple Gv *BTFD* TW8 .... 7 E3
Maplehurst Cl *KUT/HW* KT1 .... 36 B1

Maple Rd SURB KT6 ...... 36 A2
The Maples ESH/CLAY KT10 * 44 B1
  KUT/HW KT1 * 29 H2
Mapleton Rd WAND/EARL SW18 ...... 17 H4
Maple Wy FELT TW13 ...... 18 B3
Marble Hill Cl TWK TW1 ...... 13 C5
Marble Hill Gdns TWK TW1 ...... 13 C5
Marchmont Rd RCHPK/HAM TW10 ...... 14 C5
March Rd TWK TW1 ...... 13 E5
Marchside Cl HEST TW5 ...... 4 A4
Marfield Cl WPK KT4 ...... 38 B5
Margaret Lockwood Cl KUT/HW KT1 * ... 36 C1
Margin Dr WIM/MER SW19 ...... 25 E4
Marguerite Vls RYNPK SW20 * 32 C2
Maria Theresa Cl NWMAL KT3 ...... 37 G2
Marina Av HSLWW TW4 ...... 38 C3
Marina Wy TEDD TW11 ...... 30 A2
Mariner Gdns RCHPK/HAM TW10 ...... 21 G5
Market Pde FELT TW13 * 19 F2
Market Pl BTFD TW8 ...... 6 D3
  KUT/HW KT1 ...... 2 B4
Market Rd RCH/KEW TW9 ...... 14 D1
Market Ter BTFD TW8 * 7 E2
The Market RCH/KEW TW9 * 14 A3
Markhole Cl HPTN TW12 ...... 27 G2
Marksbury Av RCH/KEW TW9 ...... 14 D1
Mark Ter RYNPK SW20 * 32 C2
The Markway SUN TW16 ...... 26 D4
Marlborogh Rd HEST TW5 ...... 6 C3
Marlborough Rd CHSWK W4 * 8 B1
  FELT TW13 ...... 19 E2
  HPTN TW12 ...... 27 H1
  RCHPK/HAM TW10 ...... 14 B4
Marlingdene Cl HPTN TW12 ...... 27 H1
Marlow Crs TWK TW1 ...... 13 G3
Marmot Rd HSLWW TW4 ...... 11 E1
Marnell Wy HSLWW TW4 ...... 11 E1
Marrick Cl PUT/ROE SW15 ...... 16 B2
Marryat Cl HSLWW TW4 ...... 11 G3
Marryat Pl WIM/MER SW19 ...... 25 F4
Marryat Rd WIM/MER SW19 ...... 25 G3
Marshall Cl HSLWW TW4 ...... 11 G3
Marsh Farm Rd WHTN TW2 ...... 21 E1
Marston Av CHSGTN KT9 ...... 41 F5
Marston Rd TEDD TW11 ...... 21 G5
Martindale MORT/ESHN SW14 ...... 15 F3
Martindale Rd HSLWW TW4 ...... 11 F1
Martineau Dr TWK TW1 ...... 13 E2
Martingales Cl RCHPK/HAM TW10 ...... 22 A3
Martin Gv MRDN SM4 ...... 33 H5
Martin Wy MRDN SM4 ...... 33 H5
Mary Adelaide Cl PUT/ROE SW15 ...... 23 H3
Maryland Wy SUN TW16 ...... 26 B4
Mary Rose Cl HPTN TW12 ...... 27 H5
Mary's Ter TWK TW1 ...... 13 F5
Masefield Rd HPTN TW12 ...... 19 G4
Mason Cl HPTN TW12 ...... 27 G3
  RYNPK SW20 ...... 33 E3
Maswell Park Crs HSLW TW3 ...... 12 B3
Maswell Park Rd HSLW TW3 ...... 12 A3
Matham Rd E/WMO/HCT KT8 ...... 34 C2
Matlock Wy NWMAL KT3 ...... 31 H4
Mauveine Gdns HSLW TW3 ...... 11 H2
Mavis Av HOR/WEW KT19 ...... 42 D4
Mavis Cl HOR/WEW KT19 ...... 42 D4
Mawson Cl RYNPK SW20 ...... 33 F4
Mawson La CHSWK W4 * 9 E2
May Bate Av KUTN/CMB KT2 * 2 B2
Mayberry Pl BRYLDS KT5 ...... 36 C4
May Cl CHSGTN KT9 ...... 41 G5
Maycross Av MRDN SM4 ...... 39 G1
Mayfair Av WHTN TW2 ...... 12 B5
  WPK KT4 ...... 38 B5
Mayfair Cl SURB KT6 ...... 36 B5
Mayfield Cl THDIT KT7 ...... 35 F5
Mayfield Rd WIM/MER SW19 ...... 33 H1
May Rd WHTN TW2 ...... 20 D1
Mayroyd Av SURB KT6 ...... 41 H1
Mays Rd TEDD TW11 ...... 20 C5
Maze Rd RCH/KEW TW9 ...... 7 H3
McCarthy Rd FELT TW13 ...... 19 E5
McDonough Cl CHSGTN KT9 ...... 41 F3
McDougall Ct RCH/KEW TW9 * 7 H5
McKay Rd RYNPK SW20 ...... 32 C2
McKenzie Wy HOR/WEW KT19 ...... 45 H3
Meade Cl CHSWK W4 * 7 H2
Meadlands Dr RCHPK/HAM TW10 ...... 22 A2
Meadowbank BRYLDS KT5 ...... 36 C3
Meadowbank Cl FUL/PGN SW6 ...... 9 H3
Meadow Cl ESH/CLAY KT10 ...... 40 A2
  HSLWW TW4 ...... 11 G5
  RCHPK/HAM TW10 ...... 22 B1
  RYNPK SW20 ...... 33 E5
Meadow Hl NWMAL KT3 ...... 37 H3
Meadow Pl CHSWK W4 * 8 D3
Meadow Rd FELT TW13 ...... 19 E3
Meadows End SUN TW16 ...... 26 B3
Meadowside TWK TW1 ...... 14 A5
Meadowsweet Cl NWMAL KT3 * 31 H5
Meadow Vw CHSGTN KT9 ...... 41 F5
Meadow Waye HEST TW5 ...... 4 B3
Mead Rd RCHPK/HAM TW10 ...... 21 G1
Meadway BRYLDS KT5 ...... 37 F5
  RYNPK SW20 ...... 38 D1
  WHTN TW2 ...... 20 C1
Medcroft Gdns MORT/ESHN SW14 ...... 15 F2
Medfield St PUT/ROE SW15 ...... 16 B5

Melbourne Rd TEDD TW11 ...... 29 H1
  WIM/MER SW19 ...... 33 H3
Melbury Cl ESH/CLAY KT10 ...... 40 C5
Melbourne Gdns RYNPK SW20 ...... 32 C3
Meldone Cl BRYLDS KT5 ...... 37 E3
Melford Cl CHSGTN KT9 ...... 41 G4
Melliss Av RCH/KEW TW9 ...... 8 A4
Melrose Av WHTN TW2 ...... 12 A5
  WIM/MER SW19 ...... 25 G2
Melrose Gdns NWMAL KT3 ...... 31 G5
Melrose Rd BARN SW13 ...... 9 E5
  WAND/EARL SW18 ...... 17 G4
  WIM/MER SW19 ...... 33 H4
Melville Av RYNPK SW20 ...... 32 B2
Melville Rd BARN SW13 ...... 9 F4
Memorial Cl HEST TW5 ...... 4 C2
Memorial Sq KUT/HW KT1 ...... 2 B4
Mendip Cl WPK KT4 ...... 43 H1
Mercer Cl THDIT KT7 ...... 35 E4
Mercier Rd PUT/ROE SW15 ...... 17 F3
Mercury Centre EBED/NFELT TW14 * ... 10 B3
Mercury Rd BTFD TW8 ...... 6 C4
Mere Cl WIM/MER SW19 ...... 17 E5
Meredyth Rd BARN SW13 ...... 9 F3
Mereway Rd WHTN TW2 ...... 20 C1
Merivale Rd PUT/ROE SW15 ...... 17 F2
Merling Cl CHSGTN KT9 ...... 41 E4
Merrilands Rd WPK KT4 ...... 38 D5
Merrilyn Cl ESH/CLAY KT10 ...... 40 B5
Merritt Gdns CHSGTN KT9 ...... 40 D5
Merryweather Ct NWMAL KT3 * 37 H2
Merthyr Ter BARN SW13 ...... 9 G2
Merton Hall Gdns RYNPK SW20 ...... 33 F3
Merton Hall Rd WIM/MER SW19 ...... 33 F3
Merton Rd WAND/EARL SW18 ...... 17 H4
Merton Wy E/WMO/HCT KT8 ...... 34 B1
The Metro Centre ISLW TW7 * 5 H5
The Mews TWK TW1 * 13 G4
Mexfield Rd PUT/ROE SW15 ...... 17 G3
Michaelmas Cl RYNPK SW20 ...... 32 D5
Michelham Gdns TWK TW1 ...... 21 E3
Michelsdale Dr RCH/KEW TW9 ...... 14 B3
Middle Green Cl BRYLDS KT5 ...... 36 C3
Middle La TEDD TW11 ...... 29 E1
Middleton Rd NWMAL KT3 ...... 31 F5
Midmoor Rd WIM/MER SW19 ...... 33 E6
Midsummer Av HSLWW TW4 ...... 11 G2
Midway CHEAM SM3 ...... 39 G4
Miles Pl BRYLDS KT5 * 36 C1
Millais Crs HOR/WEW KT19 ...... 42 D4
Millais Rd NWMAL KT3 ...... 37 H4
Millais Wy HOR/WEW KT19 ...... 42 B3
Millbourne Rd FELT TW13 ...... 19 F4
Miller's Ct CHSWK W4 * 9 F1
Mill Farm Crs HSLWW TW4 ...... 19 F1
Millfield Rd HSLWW TW4 ...... 11 E3
Mill Hl BARN SW13 ...... 16 B1
Mill Hill Rd BARN SW13 ...... 16 C1
Mill Pl KUT/HW KT1 ...... 2 E6
Mill Plat ISLW TW7 ...... 6 B5
Mill Plat Av ISLW TW7 ...... 6 B5
Mill Rd WHTN TW2 ...... 20 B2
Millshot Cl FUL/PGN SW6 ...... 9 H4
Millside Pl ISLW TW7 ...... 6 C5
Mill St KUT/HW KT1 ...... 2 D6
Mill Wy EBED/NFELT TW14 ...... 10 C3
Millwood Rd HSLW TW3 ...... 12 B3
Milner Dr WHTN TW2 ...... 12 C5
Milner Rd KUT/HW KT1 ...... 2 B7
Milnthorpe Rd CHSWK W4 ...... 8 C2
Milton Rd HPTN TW12 ...... 27 H2
  MORT/ESHN SW14 ...... 15 G1
Mina Rd WIM/MER SW19 ...... 33 H3
Minerva Rd KUT/HW KT1 ...... 2 E5
Minimax Cl EBED/NFELT TW14 ...... 10 B4
Minniedale BRYLDS KT5 ...... 36 C2
Minstead Gdns PUT/ROE SW15 ...... 16 A5
Minstead Wy NWMAL KT3 ...... 37 H3
Minstrel Gdns BRYLDS KT5 ...... 36 C1
Missenden Cl EBED/NFELT TW14 ...... 18 A1
Moat Side FELT TW13 ...... 18 D4
The Moat NWMAL KT3 ...... 31 H3
Mogden La ISLW TW7 ...... 13 E3
Mole Abbey Gdns E/WMO/HCT KT8 ... 27 H5
Mole Ct HOR/WEW KT19 ...... 42 B3
Molember Ct E/WMO/HCT KT8 ...... 34 D2
Molember Rd E/WMO/HCT KT8 ...... 34 D2
Molesey Park Av E/WMO/HCT KT8 ...... 34 A2
Molesey Park Cl E/WMO/HCT KT8 ...... 34 A2
Molesey Park Rd E/WMO/HCT KT8 ...... 34 A2
Molesham Cl E/WMO/HCT KT8 ...... 28 A5
Molesham Wy E/WMO/HCT KT8 ...... 34 A1
Monaveen Gdns E/WMO/HCT KT8 ...... 28 A5
Monck's Rw WAND/EARL SW18 * 17 G4
Monkleigh Rd MRDN SM4 ...... 33 F5
Monmouth Av KUT/HW KT1 ...... 29 H2
Mono La FELT TW13 ...... 18 C2
Monroe Dr MORT/ESHN SW14 ...... 15 E3
Monro Pl HOR/WEW KT19 ...... 45 H2
Montague Rd HSLW TW3 ...... 12 A1
  RCHPK/HAM TW10 ...... 14 B4
Montana Rd RYNPK SW20 ...... 32 D3
Montem Rd NWMAL KT3 ...... 37 H1
Montfort Pl WIM/MER SW19 ...... 25 E1
Montolieu Gdns PUT/ROE SW15 ...... 16 C3
Montpelier Rw TWK TW1 ...... 13 G5
Montrose Av WHTN TW2 ...... 12 A5
Montrose Vls HMSMTH W6 * 9 F1

Montserrat Rd PUT/ROE SW15 ...... 17 F2
Moore Cl MORT/ESHN SW14 ...... 15 F1
Moorfield Cl CHSGTN KT9 ...... 41 F4
The Moorings CHSWK W4 * 7 H2
Moorland Cl WHTN TW2 ...... 11 H5
Moor La CHSGTN KT9 ...... 41 G4
Moormead Dr HOR/WEW KT19 ...... 42 D4
Moor Mead Rd TWK TW1 ...... 13 F4
Moor Park Gdns KUTN/CMB KT2 ...... 31 H2
Morden Wy CHEAM SM3 ...... 39 H4
Morecoombe Cl KUTN/CMB KT2 ...... 31 G2
Moresby Av BRYLDS KT5 ...... 37 F4
Moreton Av ISLW TW7 ...... 5 G4
Moreton Rd WPK KT4 ...... 43 H1
Morland Cl HPTN TW12 ...... 19 G5
Morley Rd CHEAM SM3 ...... 39 G5
  TWK TW1 ...... 14 A4
Morningside Rd WPK KT4 ...... 43 H1
Mornington Wk RCHPK/HAM TW10 ...... 21 H5
Morris Gdns WAND/EARL SW18 ...... 17 H5
Morris Rd ISLW TW7 ...... 13 E1
Mortimer Crs WPK KT4 ...... 42 C2
Mortlake High St MORT/ESHN SW14 ... 8 D5
Mortlake Rd MORT/ESHN SW14 ...... 15 E1
  RCH/KEW TW9 ...... 7 H3
Moss Gdns FELT TW13 ...... 18 B2
Mossville Gdns MRDN SM4 ...... 33 G5
Mostyn Rd WIM/MER SW19 ...... 33 G4
Motspur Pk NWMAL KT3 ...... 38 A3
Moulton Av HSLW TW3 ...... 4 B5
Mount Angelus Rd PUT/ROE SW15 ...... 16 A5
Mount Ararat Rd RCHPK/HAM TW10 ... 14 B3
Mountcombe Cl SURB KT6 ...... 36 B4
Mount Ms HPTN TW12 ...... 28 A3
Mount Pleasant Rd NWMAL KT3 ...... 31 F5
Mount Rd CHSGTN KT9 ...... 41 G3
  FELT TW13 ...... 19 F1
  NWMAL KT3 ...... 31 G5
  WIM/MER SW19 ...... 25 H2
The Mount EW KT17 ...... 43 G3
  NWMAL KT3 ...... 31 A5
Mount View Rd ESH/CLAY KT10 ...... 40 C5
Mountwood E/WMO/HCT KT8 ...... 28 A5
Mowbray Rd RCHPK/HAM TW10 ...... 21 H3
Muirdown Av MORT/ESHN SW14 ...... 15 G1
Mulberry Crs BTFD TW8 ...... 6 C3
Mulberry Pl HMSMTH W6 * 9 F1
Mullins Pth MORT/ESHN SW14 ...... 15 G1
Munnings Gdns ISLW TW7 ...... 12 C3
Munster Av HSLWW TW4 ...... 11 F2
Munster Rd TEDD TW11 ...... 29 H1
Murfett Cl WIM/MER SW19 ...... 25 F2
Murray Av HSLW TW3 ...... 12 B3
Murray Rd RCHPK/HAM TW10 ...... 21 G2
  WIM/MER SW19 ...... 33 E1
Musgrave Rd ISLW TW7 ...... 6 A4
Muybridge Rd NWMAL KT3 ...... 31 F4
Myrtle Cl HMSMTH W6 * 9 F1
Myrtle Gv NWMAL KT3 ...... 31 F4
Myrtle Rd HPTN TW12 ...... 28 B1
  HSLW TW3 ...... 12 B1

N

Nallhead Rd FELT TW13 ...... 18 D5
Napier Av FUL/PGN SW6 ...... 17 G1
Napier Rd ISLW TW7 ...... 13 F2
Napoleon Rd TWK TW1 * 13 G5
Naseby Cl ISLW TW7 ...... 5 H4
Nassau Rd BARN SW13 ...... 9 E4
Natalie Ms WHTN TW2 ...... 20 C3
Nell Gwynne Cl HOR/WEW KT19 ...... 45 H3
Nelson Cl EBED/NFELT TW14 * 18 A1
Nelson Gdns HSLW TW3 ...... 11 H4
Nelson Rd NWMAL KT3 ...... 37 G2
  WHTN TW2 ...... 11 H4
Nelson Wk HOR/WEW KT19 ...... 45 H2
Nene Gdns FELT TW13 ...... 19 F5
Nepean St PUT/ROE SW15 ...... 16 B4
Netheravon Rd South CHSWK W4 ...... 9 F1
Netherton Rd TWK TW1 ...... 13 F3
Netley Rd BTFD TW8 ...... 7 F3
Nevada Cl NWMAL KT3 ...... 37 F1
Neville Av NWMAL KT3 ...... 31 G3
Neville Cl HSLW TW3 ...... 4 D5
Neville Gill Cl WAND/EARL SW18 ...... 17 H4
Neville Rd KUT/HW KT1 ...... 3 H4
  RCHPK/HAM TW10 ...... 21 H3
Newbolt Av CHEAM SM3 ...... 43 H4
Newborough Gn NWMAL KT3 ...... 37 G1
Newbury Gdns HOR/WEW KT19 ...... 43 E5
New Cl FELT TW13 ...... 19 F5
Newcombe Gdns HSLWW TW4 ...... 11 G2
Newfield Cl HPTN TW12 ...... 27 H3
Newgate Cl FELT TW13 ...... 19 H5
New Heston Rd HEST TW5 ...... 4 C3
Newhouse Cl NWMAL KT3 ...... 37 G4
New Kelvin Av TEDD TW11 ...... 28 D1
Newlands Av THDIT KT7 ...... 35 E5
Newlands Cl NWDGN UB2 ...... 4 B1
Newlands Wy CHSGTN KT9 ...... 40 D4
Newmans La SURB KT6 ...... 36 A3
Newport Rd BARN SW13 ...... 9 F3
New Rd BTFD TW8 ...... 7 E2
  E/WMO/HCT KT8 ...... 27 H5
  EBED/NFELT TW14 ...... 18 C1

  ESH/CLAY KT10 44
  FELT TW13 19
  HSLW TW3 12
  KUTN/CMB KT2 30
  LHD/OX KT22 44
  RCHPK/HAM TW10 21
Newry Rd TWK TW1 13
Newstead Wy WIM/MER SW19 25
Newton Rd ISLW TW7 6
  WIM/MER SW19 33
Newton's Yd WAND/EARL SW18 17
Nicholes Rd HSLW TW3 11
Nicholson Ms KUT/HW KT1 * 36
Nicol Cl TWK TW1 13
Nigel Fisher Wy CHSGTN KT9 44
Nigel Playfair Av HMSMTH W6 9
Nightingale Cl CHSWK W4 * 8
  HOR/WEW KT19 45
Nightingale Dr HOR/WEW KT19 42
Nightingale La RCHPK/HAM TW10 14
Nightingale Ms KUT/HW KT1 * 2
Nightingale Rd E/WMO/HCT KT8 34
  HPTN TW12 27
Nine Elms Cl EBED/NFELT TW14 18
Niton Rd RCH/KEW TW9 * 8
Noble Cnr HEST TW5 * 4
Norbiton Av KUT/HW KT1 3
Norbiton Common Rd KUT/HW KT1 3
Norbury Av HSLW TW3 12
Norbury Rd FELT TW13 18
Norbury Vls KUT/HW KT1 * 3
Norcutt Rd WHTN TW2 20
Norfolk Cl TWK TW1 * 13
Norfolk Rd FELT TW13 18
Norley V PUT/ROE SW15 24
Norman Av FELT TW13 19
  TWK TW1 13
Normanby Cl PUT/ROE SW15 17
Norman Crs HEST TW5 5
Normanhurst Dr TWK TW1 13
Normansfield Av KUT/HW KT1 29
Normanton Av WAND/EARL SW18 25
Norroy Rd PUT/ROE SW15 17
Norstead Pl PUT/ROE SW15 24
North Av RCH/KEW TW9 7
Northcliffe Cl WPK KT4 42
North Cl MRDN SM4 39
Northcote Av BRYLDS KT5 36
  ISLW TW7 5
Northcote Rd NWMAL KT3 31
  TWK TW1 13
North Dene HSLW TW3 5
North Dr HSLW TW3 5
Northernhay Wk MRDN SM4 39
North Eyot Gdns HMSMTH W6 * 8
Northfield Rd HEST TW5 4
Northfields WAND/EARL SW18 17
North Hyde La NWDGN UB2 4
North La TEDD TW11 29
North Lodge Cl PUT/ROE SW15 * 17
North Pde CHSGTN KT9 41
North Pas WAND/EARL SW18 17
North Pl TEDD TW11 29
North Rd BTFD TW8 7
  RCH/KEW TW9 7
  SURB KT6 36
North St ISLW TW7 13
Northumberland Av ISLW TW7 6
North Verbena Gdns HMSMTH W6 * 9
North Vw WIM/MER SW19 24
Northway MRDN SM4 33
North Weald La KUTN/CMB KT2 22
North Worple Wy MORT/ESHN SW14 ... 15
Norton Av BRYLDS KT5 37
Norwood Cl WHTN TW2 20
Nottingham Rd ISLW TW7 6
Nova Ms CHEAM SM3 33
Nowell Rd BARN SW13 9
Nursery Cl EBED/NFELT TW14 10
  PUT/ROE SW15 17
Nursery Gdns HPTN TW12 19
  HSLWW TW4 11
  SUN TW16 26
Nursery Rd SUN TW16 26
  WIM/MER SW19 33
Nylands Av RCH/KEW TW9 7
Nymans Gdns RYNPK SW20 32

O

Oak Av HEST TW5 5
  HPTN TW12 19
Oakcombe Cl NWMAL KT3 31
Oakcroft Rd CHSGTN KT9 41
Oakcroft Vls CHSGTN KT9 41
Oakdene Av THDIT KT7 35
Oakdene Dr BRYLDS KT5 37
Oakdene Ms CHEAM SM3 39
Oaken Dr ESH/CLAY KT10 40
Oakenshaw Cl SURB KT6 36
Oakfield Cl NWMAL KT3 38
Oakfield Rd WIM/MER SW19 25
Oak Gv SUN TW16 26
Oakhall Dr SUN TW16 18
Oakhill ESH/CLAY KT10 40
Oak Hl SURB KT6 36

k Hill Crs SURB KT6 ....36 B4
k Hill Gv SURB KT6 ....36 B3
khill Pl PUT/ROE SW15................................17 H3
khill Rd PUT/ROE SW15...............................17 C3
k Hill Rd SURB KT6 * 36 B3
khurst Cl TEDD TW11...............................20 D5
khurst Rd HOR/WEW KT19...........................42 B3
kington Cl SUN TW16................................26 D4
kington Dr SUN TW16................................26 D4
klands Av ESH/CLAY KT10.............................34 C5
ISLW TW7...6 A2
klands Dr WHTN TW2.................................12 B5
klands Rd HOR/WEW KT19...........................42 C5
e La ISLW TW7..12 D2
TWK TW1..13 F5
kleigh Av SURB KT6..................................36 D5
kleigh Wy SURB KT6.................................36 D5
kley Cl ISLW TW7.....................................5 G4
k Park Gdns WIM/MER SW19 ....25 E1
ks Av FELT TW13.....................................19 F2
ks Rd NWMAL KT3....................................31 G4
WPK KT4..43 G3
e Oaks CHSGTN KT9.................................40 D2
FELT TW13 * 19 F2
MRDN SM4 ....39 F1
ks Wy SURB KT6......................................41 E1
kway RYNPK SW20...................................38 D1
kwood Av CHSGTN KT9.............................41 G5
HOR/WEW KT19.....................................45 H2
kwood Rd RYNPK SW20.............................32 B3
rsman Pl E/WMO/HCT KT8............................34 B1
servatory Rd MORT/ESHN SW14.....................15 F2
tavia Rd ISLW TW7....................................5 H5
eon Pde ISLW TW7 * 5 H5
ley Pl ISLW TW7......................................5 F2
Mill La HMSMTH W6...................................9 H1
Bridge St KUT/HW KT1................................2 A1
Claygate La ESH/CLAY KT10.........................40 B5
Cote Dr HEST TW5 ....4 D2
Deer Pk RCH/KEW TW9 * 14 C1
Deer Park Gdns RCH/KEW TW9 ......14 C1
Dock Cl RCH/KEW TW9...............................7 H2
Farm Cl HSLWW TW4................................11 G2
Farm Rd HPTN TW12..................................27 C1
field Rd HPTN TW12..................................27 H1
WIM/MER SW19.....................................33 F1
House Cl WIM/MER SW19.............................25 F5
House Gdns TWK TW1 * 13 H4
Kingston Rd WPK KT4................................42 B2
London Rd KUTN/CMB KT2..............................2 D1
Malden La WPK KT4..................................42 D1
Manor Dr ISLW TW7.................................12 B4
Orch SUN TW16......................................26 D4
Palace Yd RCH/KEW TW9............................13 H3
Park Ms HEST TW5 ....4 C3
Pound Cl ISLW TW7 * 5 F2
School Sq THDIT KT7.................................35 E3
Station Gdns TEDD TW11 * 29 F1
ver Cl CHSWK W4.....................................8 A2
ver Rd NWMAL KT3..................................31 H4
slow Av RCHPK/HAM TW10..........................14 B3
slow Gdns THDIT KT7................................34 D5
slow Rd NWMAL KT3................................38 B1
RCHPK/HAM TW10..................................14 B3
slow Wy THDIT KT7..................................34 D5
ossum Wy HSLWW TW4............................10 D1
Orangery RCHPK/HAM TW10........................21 H2
chard Av HEST TW5 ....31 H4
NWMAL KT3...31 H4
THDIT KT7...35 F5
hard Cl HOR/WEW KT19 * 42 A5
RCHPK/HAM TW10..................................14 B3
hard Rd BTFD TW8....................................6 D2
CHSGTN KT9..41 F3
FELT TW13...18 B1
HPTN TW12...27 C2
HSLWW TW4..11 G3
KUT/HW KT1...2 C7
RCH/KEW TW9..14 D1
SUN TW16..26 C2
TWK TW1...13 F3
e Orchard HSLW TW3.................................5 F3
hid Cl CHSGTN KT9..................................44 D1
hid Gdns HSLWW TW4...............................11 G2
nance Cl FELT TW13.................................18 B2
gon Cl WPK KT4.......................................37 F1
ord Gdns TWK TW1...................................21 F2
el Dr BARN SW13......................................9 H2
eans Rd TWK TW1....................................13 G5
ne Rd KUT/HW KT1......................................3 K4
nond Av HPTN TW12..................................28 A3
nond Cl HPTN TW12..................................28 A2
nond Dr HPTN TW12..................................28 A2
nonde Rd MORT/ESHN SW14.........................15 E1
nond Rd RCHPK/HAM TW10.........................14 A3
wood Cl HPTN TW12.................................27 G1
orne Cl FELT TW13....................................19 E5

Osborne Rd HSLW TW3...............................11 G1
KUTN/CMB KT2.......................................30 B2
Osborne Wy CHSGTN KT9...........................41 G4
Osiers Rd WAND/EARL SW18.........................17 H2
Ossier Ms CHSWK W4..................................9 E2
Osterley Av ISLW TW7..................................5 G3
Osterley Crs ISLW TW7.................................5 G3
Osterley La ISLW TW7..................................5 H1
NWDGN UB2...5 H3
Osterley Rd ISLW TW7.................................5 G1
Otterburn Gdns ISLW TW7.............................6 B3
Overdale Av NWMAL KT3.............................31 F4
Overton Cl ISLW TW7..................................6 A4
Oxford Av HEST TW5 ....4 D1
RYNPK SW20...33 F4
Oxford Crs NWMAL KT3.............................37 G3
Oxford Gdns CHSWK W4.............................7 H1
Oxford Rd PUT/ROE SW15...........................17 F2
TEDD TW11...20 C5
Oxford Rd North CHSWK W4..........................8 A1
Oxford Rd South CHSWK W4.........................7 H1
Oxford Rw SUN TW16 * 26 D5
Oxford Wy FELT TW13................................19 E4
Oxleigh Cl NWMAL KT3..............................37 H2

P

Pacific Cl EBED/NFELT TW14...........................18 A1
Paddock Cl WPK KT4.................................37 H5
Paddock Wy PUT/ROE SW15.........................16 D5
Padley Cl CHSGTN KT9.................................41 G4
Padstow Wk EBED/NFELT TW14.....................18 A1
FELT TW13...18 A2
Page Cl HPTN TW12..................................27 F1
Pages Yd CHSWK W4 * 8 D2
Paget Cl HPTN TW12.................................20 C4
Paget La ISLW TW7...................................12 C1
Paget Pl KUTN/CMB KT2 * 31 F1
THDIT KT7...35 E5
Pagoda Av RCH/KEW TW9............................14 C1
Palace Rd E/WMO/HCT KT8..........................28 B5
KUT/HW KT1..36 A1
Palewell Common Dr
MORT/ESHN SW14..................................15 G3
Palewell Pk MORT/ESHN SW14.....................15 G3
Palmer Av CHEAM SM3...............................43 H3
Palmer Cl HEST TW5 ....4 D2
Palmer Crs KUT/HW KT1..............................2 C6
Palmers Rd MORT/ESHN SW14.....................15 F1
Palmerston Gv WIM/MER SW19.....................33 H1
Palmerston Rd HSLW TW3............................5 F4
MORT/ESHN SW14..................................15 F2
WHTN TW2...12 D4
WIM/MER SW19......................................33 H2
Palmers Whf KUT/HW KT1 * 2 A5
Pams Wy HOR/WEW KT19...........................42 C4
Pankhurst Cl ISLW TW7...............................13 E1
Panmuir Rd RYNPK SW20...........................32 C3
The Parade KUT/HW KT1 * 2 D2
RCH/KEW TW9 * 14 D1
SUN TW16..26 A2
Paradise Rd RCH/KEW TW9..........................14 B3
Paragon Gv BRYLDS KT5.............................36 C3
Parbury Ri CHSGTN KT9..............................41 F5
Parfrey St HMSMTH W6...............................9 H1
Park Av HSLW TW3...................................12 A4
MORT/ESHN SW14..................................15 G2
Park Av East EW KT17................................43 F5
Park Av West EW KT17...............................43 F5
Park Cl HPTN TW12...................................28 B3
HSLW TW3...12 B3
KUTN/CMB KT2..2 D1
Park Ct NWMAL KT3.................................37 G1
Park Crs WHTN TW2..................................20 C1
Parkdale Crs WPK KT4................................42 C2
Park Dr MORT/ESHN SW14.........................15 G3
Parke Rd BARN SW13.................................9 F4
Park Farm Rd KUTN/CMB KT2........................30 B2
Parkfield Av FELT TW13.............................18 B3
MORT/ESHN SW14..................................15 F2
Parkfield Crs FELT TW13............................18 B3
Parkfield Pde FELT TW13 * 18 B3
Parkfield Rd FELT TW13.............................18 B3
Parkfields PUT/ROE SW15...........................16 D2
Parkfields Av RYNPK SW20..........................32 C3
Parkfields Rd KUTN/CMB KT2.......................22 C5
Park Gdns KUTN/CMB KT2..........................22 C5
Parkgate Cl KUTN/CMB KT2........................31 E1
Park Gate St HPTN TW12 * 20 B5
Parkgate Gdns MORT/ESHN SW14..................15 G3
Park Hl RCHPK/HAM TW10..........................14 C4
Park House Gdns TWK TW1.........................13 H3
Parkland Gv ISLW TW7.................................6 A4
Parklands BRYLDS KT5..............................36 C2
Parklands Pde HEST TW5 * 4 A5
Parklands Rd MORT/ESHN SW14....................15 F3
Park La RCH/KEW TW9...............................14 A2
RCHPK/HAM TW10..................................14 A2
Parkleys RCHPK/HAM TW10.........................14 A5
Parkleys Pde RCHPK/HAM TW10 * 22 A4
Parkmead PUT/ROE SW15...........................16 C4
Park Pl HPTN TW12..................................28 B3
Park Rd BRYLDS KT5.................................36 D3
CHSWK W4...8 C2
E/WMO/HCT KT8......................................34 B1

FELT TW13...19 E4
HPTN TW12..20 B5
HSLW TW3...12 B3
ISLW TW7..6 A4
KUT/HW KT1..29 H3
KUTN/CMB KT2.......................................22 C5
NWMAL KT3...37 G1
RCHPK/HAM TW10..................................14 C4
SUN TW16...26 C2
TEDD TW11..29 E1
TWK TW1...13 H4
Park Rd North CHSWK W4...........................8 D2
Parkshot RCH/KEW TW9.............................14 A2
Parkside HPTN TW12.................................28 B1
WIM/MER SW19......................................25 E4
Parkside Av WIM/MER SW19.........................25 E5
Parkside Crs BRYLDS KT5............................37 E3
Parkside Gdns WIM/MER SW19.....................25 E5
Parkside Rd HSLW TW3..............................12 A3
Parkstead Rd PUT/ROE SW15.......................16 C3
Park St TEDD TW11..................................28 D1
Park Ter WPK KT4....................................38 B5
Park Vw NWMAL KT3................................32 A5
Park Wy E/WMO/HCT KT8............................34 B5
EBED/NFELT TW14..................................17 H3
Parkway RYNPK SW20...............................39 E1
Parkwood Av ESH/CLAY KT10........................34 B5
Parkwood Gv SUN TW16............................26 B5
Parkwood Rd ISLW TW7...............................6 A4
WIM/MER SW19......................................25 G5
Parr's Pl HPTN TW12.................................28 A5
Parsons Md E/WMO/HCT KT8........................28 B5
Partridge Rd HPTN TW12............................27 G1
Pauline Crs WHTN TW2..............................20 B1
The Pavement TEDD TW11 * 29 C1
WIM/MER SW19......................................33 G1
Paxton Cl RCH/KEW TW9.............................7 G1
Paxton Rd CHSWK W4................................8 D2
Paynesfield Av MORT/ESHN SW14..................15 G1
Peabody Est HMSMTH W6 * 9 H1
Peach Rd FELT TW13.................................18 B1
Pears Rd HSLW TW3..................................12 B1
Pear Tree Cl CHSGTN KT9............................41 H4
Peek Crs WIM/MER SW19...........................25 E5
Pegasus Ct BTFD TW8 * 7 E2
Pegg Rd HEST TW5 ....4 A3
Pelham Rd WIM/MER SW19.........................33 H2
Pemberley Cha HOR/WEW KT19....................42 A5
Pemberley Cl HOR/WEW KT19......................42 A4
Pemberton Rd E/WMO/HCT KT8....................34 B1
Pembridge Av WHTN TW2...........................19 C1
Pembroke Av BRYLDS KT5...........................37 E2
Pembroke Pl ISLW TW7...............................5 H5
Pembury Av WPK KT4................................38 B4
Pembury Rd NWDGN UB2............................4 C1
Pendarves Rd RYNPK SW20.........................32 D3
Penderel Rd HSLW TW3..............................11 H5
The Pennards SUN TW16............................26 D5
Penner Cl WIM/MER SW19...........................25 E3
Penners Gdns SURB KT6............................36 B4
Penney Ms WAND/EARL SW18.......................17 H3
Penrhyn Crs MORT/ESHN SW14....................15 G1
Penrhyn Gdns KUT/HW KT1.........................36 A1
Penrhyn Rd KUT/HW KT1 * 2 C7
KUT/HW KT1..36 B1
Penrith Cl PUT/ROE SW15...........................17 F3
Penrith Rd NWMAL KT3.............................37 C1
Pensford Av RCH/KEW TW9.........................7 H5
Pentelow Gdns EBED/NFELT TW14..................10 B1
Pentlow St PUT/ROE SW15...........................9 H5
Pentney Rd RYNPK SW20............................33 E1
Penwerris Av ISLW TW7...............................5 F3
Pepys Rd RYNPK SW20..............................33 E1
Percival Rd FELT TW13..............................18 A2
MORT/ESHN SW14..................................15 F2
Percival Wy HOR/WEW KT19........................42 B3
Percy Gdns WPK KT4................................37 G5
Percy Rd HPTN TW12................................27 H2
ISLW TW7...13 F2
WHTN TW2...20 A1
Peregrine Wy WIM/MER SW19.......................32 D2
Perkin Cl HSLW TW3.................................12 A2
Perryfield Wy RCHPK/HAM TW10...................21 C2
Perry How WPK KT4..................................38 A5
Perth Cl NWMAL KT3................................32 A4
Petauel Rd TEDD TW11.............................20 D1
Petavel Rd TEDD TW11..............................28 D1
Petersfield Ri PUT/ROE SW15......................16 C4
Petersham Cl RCHPK/HAM TW10...................22 A2
Petersham Rd RCHPK/HAM TW10..................14 A4
Peterstow Cl WIM/MER SW19.......................25 F2
Petley Rd HMSMTH W6................................9 H2
Pettiward Cl PUT/ROE SW15.........................16 D2
Petworth Gdns RYNPK SW20........................32 C5
Pevensey Cl ISLW TW7.................................5 F3
Pevensey Rd FELT TW13.............................19 F1
Peverill Dr TEDD TW11..............................20 C5
Phoenix Cl HOR/WEW KT19..........................42 B3
Phoenix Ct BTFD TW8................................7 E1
Phoenix Pk BTFD TW8 * 7 F1
Phoenix Wy HEST TW5 ....4 A2
Phyllis Av NWMAL KT3..............................38 C2
Pickwick Cl HSLWW TW4............................11 F3
Pier Rd EBED/NFELT TW14............................10 C1
Pigeon La HPTN TW12...............................19 H4
Pilsden Cl WIM/MER SW19 * 25 E1
Pine Gdns BRYLDS KT5...............................36 D3

Pine Gv WIM/MER SW19.............................25 G5
Pinelees Ct MORT/ESHN SW14 * 15 F2
The Pines SUN TW16.................................26 B5
Pine Wk BRYLDS KT5.................................36 D3
Pine Wd SUN TW16..................................26 B5
Pinewood Rd FELT TW13.............................18 C3
Pinkcoat Cl FELT TW13...............................18 C3
Piper Rd KUT/HW KT1..................................3 G6
Pirbright Rd WAND/EARL SW18.....................25 G1
Plane Tree Crs FELT TW13...........................18 C3
Plantagenet Cl WPK KT4.............................42 C3
Playfair St HMSMTH W6 * 9 H1
Pleasance Rd PUT/ROE SW15.......................16 C3
The Pleasance PUT/ROE SW15......................16 C2
Plevna Rd HPTN TW12...............................28 A3
Plough La TEDD TW11 * 21 F5
Ploughmans End ISLW TW7..........................12 C3
Plum Cl FELT TW13..................................18 B1
Point Pleasant WAND/EARL SW18...................17 H2
Point Wharf La BTFD TW8.............................7 E3
Polesden Gdns RYNPK SW20........................32 C4
Pond Wy TEDD TW11...............................29 H1
Ponsonby Rd PUT/ROE SW15.......................16 C5
Poole Court Rd HSLWW TW4...........................4 B5
Poole Rd HOR/WEW KT19...........................42 C5
Pooley Dr MORT/ESHN SW14........................15 F1
Pope's Gv EBED/NFELT TW14........................18 A1
Pope's Av WHTN TW2.................................20 D2
Pope's Gv WHTN TW2................................20 D2
Popham Cl FELT TW13...............................19 E2
Popham Gdns RCH/KEW TW9 * 15 E1
Poplar Cl HOR/WEW KT19...........................42 B5
Poplar Crs HOR/WEW KT19.........................42 B5
Poplar Farm Cl HOR/WEW KT19.....................42 B5
Poplar Gdns NWMAL KT3............................31 G4
Poplar Gv NWMAL KT3...............................31 G5
Poplar Rd CHEAM SM3...............................39 G5
WIM/MER SW19......................................33 H4
Poplar Rd South WIM/MER SW19....................33 H5
Poplar Wy FELT TW13...............................18 B3
Porchester Rd KUT/HW KT1.............................J4
Portinscale Rd PUT/ROE SW15.......................17 F3
Portland Av NWMAL KT3.............................38 A4
Portland Cl WPK KT4.................................38 C4
Portland Rd KUT/HW KT1................................2 D7
KUT/HW KT1..36 B1
Portland Ter RCH/KEW TW9 * 14 A2
Portman Rd MORT/ESHN SW14.....................15 C1
Portman Rd KUT/HW KT1..............................3 F5
Portsmouth Av THDIT KT7............................35 F4
Portsmouth Rd KUT/HW KT1...........................2 B7
PUT/ROE SW15......................................16 C5
Portugal Gdns WHTN TW2 * 20 B2
Post La WHTN TW2...................................20 C1
Potterne Cl WIM/MER SW19..........................17 E5
Potters Gv NWMAL KT3..............................37 F1
Pottery Rd BTFD TW8 * 7 F2
Poulett Gdns TWK TW1..............................21 E2
Pound Cl SURB KT6..................................35 H5
Pound Farm Cl ESH/CLAY KT10......................34 C5
Powder Mill La WHTN TW2..........................19 C1
Powers Ct TWK TW1.................................14 A5
Pownall Gdns HSLW TW3.............................12 A2
Pownall Rd HSLW TW3...............................12 A2
Presburg Rd NWMAL KT3............................37 H2
Preston Cl WHTN TW2...............................20 D3
Preston Dr HOR/WEW KT19.........................42 D5
Preston Rd RYNPK SW20.............................32 B2
Preston Vls KUT/HW KT1 * 3 F5
Prestwick Cl NWDGN UB2.............................4 B1
Priests Br MORT/ESHN SW14.........................15 H1
Primrose Pl ISLW TW7.................................6 A5
Prince George's Av RYNPK SW20....................32 D4
Prince of Wales Ter CHSWK W4......................8 D1
Prince Regent Rd HSLW TW3.........................12 B1
Princes Av SURB KT6................................41 H1
Princes Ms HMSMTH W6 * 9 G1
TWK TW1...11 H2
Princes Rd FELT TW13...............................18 A3
KUTN/CMB KT2..3 G2
RCH/KEW TW9...7 G4
RCHPK/HAM TW10..................................14 C3
TEDD TW11..20 C4
Princes Wy WIM/MER SW19.........................17 E5
Prince's Cl HPTN TW12..............................27 G3
Prince's Rd MORT/ESHN SW14......................15 C1
TEDD TW11..20 C4
WIM/MER SW19......................................33 H1
Prince's St RCH/KEW TW9............................14 B3
Priory Cl HPTN TW12................................27 G3
SUN TW16...26 B2
Priory Gdns BARN SW13.............................16 A1
HPTN TW12...27 G3
Priory La PUT/ROE SW15.............................16 A3
Priory Rd CHSGTN KT9...............................41 F2
HPTN TW12...27 G2
HSLW TW3...12 B3
RCH/KEW TW9...7 H2
Proctors Cl EBED/NFELT TW14.......................18 B1
Promenade Approach Rd CHSWK W4................8 D4
The Promenade CHSWK W4...........................8 D4
Prospect Cl HSLW TW3................................4 C4
Prospect Cottages WAND/EARL SW18..............17 H2
Prospect Crs WHTN TW2.............................12 B4
Prospect Pl CHSWK W4................................8 C1
RYNPK SW20...32 C2
Prospect Rd SURB KT6...............................35 H3
Pulborough Rd WAND/EARL SW18..................17 G5

Pulborough Wy HSLWW TW4 .... 10 D2
Pullman Ct PUT/ROE SW15 .... 16 D4
Pulteney Cl ISLW TW7 .... 13 F1
Pump Aly BTFD TW8 .... 7 E3
Pumping Station Rd CHSWK W4 .... 8 D3
Purbeck Av NWMAL KT3 .... 38 A3
Putney Br PUT/ROE SW15 .... 17 F1
Putney Bridge Ap FUL/PGN SW6 .... 17 F1
Putney Bridge Rd PUT/ROE SW15 .... 17 F2
Putney Common PUT/ROE SW15 .... 16 D1
Putney Ex PUT/ROE SW15 * 17 E2
Putney Heath PUT/ROE SW15 .... 16 C4
Putney Heath La PUT/ROE SW15 .... 17 E4
Putney High St PUT/ROE SW15 .... 17 E4
Putney Hl PUT/ROE SW15 .... 17 E4
Putney Park Av PUT/ROE SW15 .... 16 B2
Putney Park La PUT/ROE SW15 .... 16 C2
Pyne Rd SURB KT6 .... 36 D5
Pyrland Rd RCHPK/HAM TW10 .... 14 C4
Pyrmont Rd CHSWK W4 .... 7 H2

Q

Quadrant Rd RCH/KEW TW9 .... 14 A2
The Quadrant RCH/KEW TW9 .... 14 A3
RYNPK SW20 .... 33 F3
Quakers La ISLW TW7 .... 6 B3
Queen Alexandra's Wy
HOR/WEW KT19 .... 45 H4
Queen Annes Cl WHTN TW2 .... 20 C3
Queen Caroline Est HMSMTH W6 .... 9 H1
Queen Caroline St HMSMTH W6 .... 9 H1
Queen Elizabeth Gdns MRDN SM4 .... 39 H1
Queen Elizabeth Rd KUTN/CMB KT2 .... 2 E3
Queen Elizabeth Wk BARN SW13 .... 9 F4
Queen Mary Av RYNPK SW20 .... 39 E2
Queen Mary Cl SURB KT6 .... 41 H2
Queens Av FELT TW13 .... 18 D4
Queensbridge Pk ISLW TW7 .... 12 D4
Queens Crs RCHPK/HAM TW10 .... 14 C3
Queens Dr BRYLDS KT5 .... 36 D4
Queensgate Gdns PUT/ROE SW15 .... 16 C2
Queens Keep TWK TW1 * 13 H4
Queensmere Cl WIM/MER SW19 .... 25 E2
Queensmere Rd WIM/MER SW19 .... 25 E2
Queens Park Gdns FELT TW13 * 18 A3
Queens Prom KUT/HW KT1 .... 36 A1
Queens Ter ISLW TW7 .... 5 F3
THDIT KT7 .... 35 F3
Queens Wy FELT TW13 .... 18 D4
Queensway SUN TW16 .... 26 C4
Queenswood Av HPTN TW12 .... 28 A1
HSLW TW3 .... 4 C5
Queen's Dr THDIT KT7 .... 35 F3
Queen's Gdns HEST TW5 .... 4 B4
Queen's Pl MRDN SM4 .... 39 H1
Queen's Ride BARN SW13 .... 16 C1
PUT/ROE SW15 .... 16 B2
Queen's Ri RCHPK/HAM TW10 .... 14 C4
Queen's Rd FELT TW13 .... 18 C1
HPTN TW12 .... 20 A4
HSLW TW3 .... 12 A1
KUTN/CMB KT2 .... 3 H1
KUTN/CMB KT2 .... 30 D2
MORT/ESHN SW14 .... 15 A1
NWMAL KT3 .... 38 A1
RCHPK/HAM TW10 .... 14 C4
RCHPK/HAM TW10 .... 22 C1
TEDD TW11 .... 29 E1
THDIT KT7 .... 35 E2
TWK TW1 .... 13 H3
WIM/MER SW19 .... 33 H1
Queen's Ter ISLW TW7 .... 5 F3
Queen's Whf HMSMTH W6 .... 9 H1
Quick Rd CHSWK W4 .... 8 D1
Quintin Av RYNPK SW20 .... 33 F3
Quinton Rd THDIT KT7 .... 35 F5

R

Raby Rd NWMAL KT3 .... 37 G1
Radcliffe Sq PUT/ROE SW15 .... 17 E4
Radius Pk EBED/NFELT TW14 * 10 A2
Radley Cl EBED/NFELT TW14 .... 18 A1
Radnor Gdns TWK TW1 .... 21 E2
Radnor Rd TWK TW1 .... 21 E2
Raeburn Av BRYLDS KT5 .... 37 E3
Raeburn Cl KUT/HW KT1 .... 2 A1
Raglan Cl HSLWW TW4 .... 11 F3
Railshead Rd ISLW TW7 .... 13 F1
Railway Ap TWK TW1 .... 13 F5
Railway Rd TEDD TW11 .... 20 D4
Railway Side BARN SW13 .... 15 H1
Railway Ter FELT TW13 .... 18 A2
Rainville Rd HMSMTH W6 .... 9 H2
Raleigh Dr BRYLDS KT5 .... 37 H3
Raleigh Rd FELT TW13 .... 18 A2
NWDGN UB2 .... 4 C1
RCH/KEW TW9 .... 14 C1
Raleigh Wy FELT TW13 .... 18 D5
Ram Pas KUT/HW KT1 .... 2 B5
Randle Rd RCHPK/HAM TW10 .... 21 H4
Randolph Cl KUTN/CMB KT2 * 23 F5

Ranelagh Av BARN SW13 .... 9 F5
FUL/PGN SW6 .... 17 G1
Ranelagh Dr TWK TW1 .... 13 G2
Ranelagh Gdns CHSWK W4 .... 8 B3
FUL/PGN SW6 .... 17 F1
Rannoch Rd HMSMTH W6 .... 9 H2
Ranyard Cl CHSGTN KT9 .... 41 G2
Raphael Dr THDIT KT7 .... 35 E1
Ravendale Rd SUN TW16 .... 26 A4
Ravenna Rd PUT/ROE SW15 .... 17 E3
Ravens Ait SURB KT6 * 36 A2
Ravensbourne Rd TWK TW1 .... 13 H4
Ravenscar Rd SURB KT6 .... 41 G1
Ravens Cl SURB KT6 .... 36 A3
Ravenscourt SUN TW16 .... 26 A3
Ravensdale Rd HSLWW TW4 .... 11 F1
Ravensfield Gdns HOR/WEW KT19 .... 42 D4
Ravenswood Av SURB KT6 .... 41 G1
Ravenswood Ct KUTN/CMB KT2 * 31 F1
Ravenswood Gdns ISLW TW7 .... 5 H4
Rayleigh Av TEDD TW11 .... 28 D1
Rayleigh Ct KUT/HW KT1 .... 3 G4
Rayleigh Rd WIM/MER SW19 .... 33 G3
Raymond Rd WIM/MER SW19 .... 33 F1
Raymond Wy ESH/CLAY KT10 * 40 B5
Rayner's Rd PUT/ROE SW15 .... 17 F3
Raynes Pk RYNPK SW20 .... 32 D4
Read Cl THDIT KT7 .... 35 F4
Reapers Wy ISLW TW7 .... 12 C3
Reckitt Rd CHSWK W4 .... 8 D1
Rectory Cl RYNPK SW20 .... 32 D4
SURB KT6 .... 35 H5
Rectory Gv HPTN TW12 .... 19 G4
Rectory La SURB KT6 .... 35 H5
Rectory Orch WIM/MER SW19 .... 25 F4
Rectory Rd BARN SW13 .... 9 F5
Redclose Av MRDN SM4 .... 39 H2
Redesdale Gdns ISLW TW7 .... 6 B3
Redfern Av HSLWW TW4 .... 11 H5
Redford Cl FELT TW13 .... 18 A2
Redgate Ter PUT/ROE SW15 .... 17 E4
Redgrave Rd PUT/ROE SW15 .... 17 E1
Red La ESH/CLAY KT10 .... 40 B5
Rediees Cl ISLW TW7 .... 13 F2
Red Lion Ct ISLW TW5 * 12 A1
Red Lion Rd SURB KT6 .... 41 G1
Red Lion Sq WAND/EARL SW18 * 17 H3
Red Lion St RCH/KEW TW9 .... 14 A3
Redway Dr WHTN TW2 .... 12 B5
Regency Ct HPTN TW12 .... 19 G5
Regent Rd BRYLDS KT5 .... 36 C2
Regent St CHSWK W4 .... 7 H1
Rembrandt Ct HOR/WEW KT19 .... 43 E5
Renfrew Rd HSLWW TW4 .... 11 F1
KUTN/CMB KT2 .... 31 E2
Replingham Rd WAND/EARL SW18 .... 25 G1
Restormel Cl HSLW TW3 .... 11 H3
Retreat Rd RCH/KEW TW9 .... 14 A3
The Retreat BRYLDS KT5 .... 36 C3
MORT/ESHN SW14 .... 15 H1
WPK KT4 .... 43 G1
Revell Rd KUT/HW KT1 .... 3 K3
Revelstoke Rd WAND/EARL SW18 .... 25 H2
WIM/MER SW19 .... 25 H4
Reynolds Av CHSGTN KT9 .... 45 F1
Reynolds Pl RCHPK/HAM TW10 .... 14 C4
Reynolds Rd NWMAL KT3 .... 37 G4
Rhodrons Av CHSGTN KT9 .... 41 F4
Ricards Rd WIM/MER SW19 .... 25 G5
Richens Cl HSLW TW3 .... 5 G5
Richlands Av EW KT17 .... 43 H5
Richmond Av RYNPK SW20 .... 33 F3
Richmond Br TWK TW1 .... 14 A3
Richmond Hl RCHPK/HAM TW10 .... 14 B4
Richmond Pde TWK TW1 * 13 H4
Richmond Park Rd KUTN/CMB KT2 .... 2 D2
MORT/ESHN SW14 .... 15 F3
Richmond Rd ISLW TW7 .... 13 F1
KUTN/CMB KT2 .... 22 A5
RYNPK SW20 .... 32 C3
TWK TW1 .... 13 G5
TWK TW1 .... 21 F1
Rickards Cl SURB KT6 .... 41 F1
The Ride BTFD TW8 .... 6 C1
Ridge Rd CHEAM SM3 .... 39 G5
The Ridge BRYLDS KT5 .... 36 D2
WHTN TW2 .... 12 C5
Ridge Wy FELT TW13 .... 19 F3
Ridgeway Rd ISLW TW7 .... 5 H3
Ridgeway Rd North ISLW TW7 .... 5 H3
Ridgway RCHPK/HAM TW10 * 14 B4
WIM/MER SW19 .... 32 D2
Ridgway Gdns WIM/MER SW19 .... 33 E2
Ridgway Pl WIM/MER SW19 .... 33 F1
The Ridings BRYLDS KT5 .... 36 D2
SUN TW16 .... 26 B3
Ringford Rd WAND/EARL SW18 .... 17 G3
Ringway NWDGN UB2 .... 4 A1
Ringwood Gdns PUT/ROE SW15 .... 24 B2
Ringwood Wy HPTN TW12 .... 19 H4
Ripley Gdns MORT/ESHN SW14 .... 15 G1
Ripley Rd HPTN TW12 .... 27 H2
Ripley Wy HOR/WEW KT19 .... 45 H4
Ripon Gdns CHSGTN KT9 .... 41 E4
Risborough Dr WPK KT4 .... 38 B4
River Av THDIT KT7 .... 35 F4

Riverbank E/WMO/HCT KT8 .... 28 D5
River Bank THDIT KT7 .... 35 E2
Riverbank Wy BTFD TW8 .... 6 D2
Riverdale Gdns TWK TW1 .... 13 H3
Riverdale Rd FELT TW13 .... 19 F4
TWK TW1 .... 13 H4
River Gdns EBED/NFELT TW14 .... 10 C3
River La RCHPK/HAM TW10 .... 22 A1
Rivermead E/WMO/HCT KT8 .... 28 B5
KUT/HW KT1 .... 36 A2
Rivermead Cl TEDD TW11 .... 21 G5
River Meads Av WHTN TW2 .... 20 A3
River Reach TEDD TW11 .... 29 H1
Riversdale Rd THDIT KT7 .... 35 F2
Riverside E/WMO/HCT KT8 .... 28 C5
RCH/KEW TW9 .... 14 A3
SUN TW16 .... 26 A5
TWK TW1 .... 21 G1
Riverside Av E/WMO/HCT KT8 .... 34 C2
Riverside Cl KUT/HW KT1 .... 36 A1
Riverside Dr CHSWK W4 .... 8 B3
RCHPK/HAM TW10 .... 21 G3
Riverside Gdns HMSMTH W6 .... 9 G3
The Riverside E/WMO/HCT KT8 .... 28 C5
Riverside Vls SURB KT6 * 35 H5
Riverside Wk ISLW TW7 .... 12 C1
KUT/HW KT1 .... 2 A4
River Ter HMSMTH W6 .... 9 H1
Riverview Gdns BARN SW13 .... 9 G2
River View Gdns TWK TW1 .... 21 E2
Riverview Gv CHSWK W4 .... 8 A2
Riverview Rd CHSWK W4 .... 8 A3
HOR/WEW KT19 .... 42 B3
River Wk SUN TW16 .... 27 E4
River Wy HOR/WEW KT19 .... 42 C4
WHTN TW2 .... 20 A2
Roberts Ct CHSGTN KT9 .... 41 E4
Robin Cl FELT TW13 .... 19 F5
Robin Gv BTFD TW8 .... 6 C2
Robin Hood La PUT/ROE SW15 .... 23 H3
Robin Hood Rd PUT/ROE SW15 .... 23 H3
WIM/MER SW19 .... 24 B5
Robin Hood Wy PUT/ROE SW15 .... 32 A2
RYNPK SW20 .... 32 A2
Robinwood Pl PUT/ROE SW15 .... 24 A3
Rochester Av FELT TW13 .... 18 A2
Rochester Pde FELT TW13 * 18 B3
Rock Av MORT/ESHN SW14 * 15 G1
Rockingham Cl PUT/ROE SW15 .... 16 B2
Rockland Rd PUT/ROE SW15 .... 17 F2
Rocks La BARN SW13 .... 16 B1
Rodney Cl NWMAL KT3 .... 37 H2
Rodney Rd NWMAL KT3 .... 37 H2
WHTN TW2 .... 11 H4
Rodway Rd PUT/ROE SW15 .... 16 B5
Roebuck Cl FELT TW13 .... 18 C4
Roebuck Rd CHSGTN KT9 .... 41 H4
Roedean Crs PUT/ROE SW15 .... 15 H4
Roehampton Ga PUT/ROE SW15 .... 16 B2
Roehampton High St PUT/ROE SW15 .... 16 B5
Roehampton La PUT/ROE SW15 .... 16 B5
Roehampton V PUT/ROE SW15 .... 24 A3
Rokeby Pl RYNPK SW20 .... 32 C2
Roland Wy WPK KT4 .... 43 E1
Rollesby Rd CHSGTN KT9 .... 41 H5
Rollit Crs HSLW TW3 .... 11 H3
Roman Cl EBED/NFELT TW14 .... 10 D3
Romany Gdns CHEAM SM3 .... 39 H4
Romney Cl CHSGTN KT9 .... 41 F3
Romney Rd NWMAL KT3 .... 37 G3
Ronelean Rd SURB KT6 .... 41 G1
Rookeries Cl FELT TW13 .... 18 C5
Rooksmead Rd SUN TW16 .... 26 A4
Rookwood Av NWMAL KT3 .... 38 B1
Rosamond Vls MORT/ESHN SW14 * 15 G2
Rosary Cl HSLW TW3 .... 4 B5
Rosebank EW KT17 .... 43 H4
Rosebank Av NWMAL KT3 .... 32 A4
Rosebery Av NWMAL KT3 .... 38 B1
Rosebery Rd HSLW TW3 .... 12 B3
KUT/HW KT1 .... 3 H5
Rosebery Sq KUT/HW KT1 .... 3 H5
Rosebine Av WHTN TW2 .... 12 C5
Rosecroft Gdns WHTN TW2 .... 20 C1
Rosedale Rd EW KT17 .... 43 F4
RCH/KEW TW9 .... 14 B2
Rosedene Av MRDN SM4 .... 39 H2
Rose End WPK KT4 .... 39 E5
Rose Gdns FELT TW13 .... 18 B2
Roseheath Rd HSLWW TW4 .... 11 G3
Rosehill ESH/CLAY KT10 .... 40 B5
HPTN TW12 .... 27 H3
Roseleigh Cl TWK TW1 .... 14 A4
Rosemary Av E/WMO/HCT KT8 .... 27 H5
HSLWW TW4 .... 4 A5
Rosemary Gdns CHSGTN KT9 .... 41 F3
Rosemary La MORT/ESHN SW14 .... 15 F1
Rosemead Av FELT TW13 .... 18 A2
Rosemont Rd NWMAL KT3 .... 31 F5
RCHPK/HAM TW10 .... 14 B4
Roseville Av HSLW TW3 .... 11 H3
Rosevine Rd RYNPK SW20 .... 32 D3
Rose Wk BRYLDS KT5 .... 37 E2
Rosewood Ct KUTN/CMB KT2 .... 3 G1
Roskell Rd PUT/ROE SW15 .... 17 E1
Rossdale Rd PUT/ROE SW15 .... 16 D2
Rossindel Rd HSLW TW3 .... 11 H3

Rosslyn Av BARN SW13 15
EBED/NFELT TW14 10
Rosslyn Rd TWK TW1 13
Ross Rd WHTN TW2 20
Rostrevor Gdns NWDGN UB2 4
Rostrevor Rd WIM/MER SW19 25
Rothbury Gdns ISLW TW7 6
Rotherwick Cl EBED/NFELT TW14 33
Rotherwood Cl PUT/ROE SW15 17
Rothesay Av RCHPK/HAM TW10 15
RYNPK SW20 39
Rougemont Av MRDN SM4 39
The Roundway ESH/CLAY KT10 40
Rowan Cl NWMAL KT3 31
Rowan Rd BTFD TW8 6
The Rowans SUN TW16 18
Rowan Ter WIM/MER SW19 * 33
Rowden Rd HOR/WEW KT19 42
Rowlls Rd KUT/HW KT1 3
Rowntree Rd WHTN TW2 20
Roxborough Av ISLW TW7 6
Royal Av WPK KT4 43
Royal Cl WIM/MER SW19 25
WPK KT4 43
Royal Oak Ms TEDD TW11 21
Royal Orchard Cl WAND/EARL SW18 17
Royal Rd TEDD TW11 20
Roy Gv HPTN TW12 20
Royston Rd RCHPK/HAM TW10 14
The Roystons BRYLDS KT5 37
Rugby Rd TWK TW1 12
Rumsey Cl HPTN TW12 19
Runnymede Cl WHTN TW2 11
Runnymede Gdns HSLW TW3 11
Runnymede Rd WHTN TW2 11
Ruscombe Wy EBED/NFELT TW14 10
Rushett Cl THDIT KT7 35
Rushett La CHSGTN KT9 45
Rushett Rd THDIT KT7 35
Rushey Cl NWMAL KT3 37
Rushmead RCHPK/HAM TW10 21
Rushmere Ct WPK KT4 43
Rushmere Pl WIM/MER SW19 25
Rushmon Vls NWMAL KT3 * 38
Rusholme Rd PUT/ROE SW15 17
Ruskin Av EBED/NFELT TW14 10
RCH/KEW TW9 7
Ruskin Dr WPK KT4 43
Ruskin Rd ISLW TW7 13
Russell Cl CHSWK W4 8
Russell Gdns RCHPK/HAM TW10 21
Russell Kerr Cl CHSWK W4 * 8
Russell Rd WHTN TW2 11
WIM/MER SW19 33
Rustington Wk CHEAM SM3 39
Ruston Av BRYLDS KT5 37
Rutherwyke Cl EW KT17 43
Rutland Cl CHSGTN KT9 41
MORT/ESHN SW14 15
Rutland Dr MRDN SM4 39
RCHPK/HAM TW10 22
Rutland Gv HMSMTH W6 9
Rutland Rd WHTN TW2 20
Rutlish Rd WIM/MER SW19 33
Ruvigny Gdns PUT/ROE SW15 17
Ruxley Cl HOR/WEW KT19 42
Ruxley Crs ESH/CLAY KT10 44
Ruxley La HOR/WEW KT19 42
Ruxley Ms HOR/WEW KT19 42
Ruxley Rdg ESH/CLAY KT10 44
Ruxley Towers ESH/CLAY KT10 * 44
Ryan Dr BTFD TW8 6
Rydal Gdns HSLW TW3 12
PUT/ROE SW15 23
Ryde Pl TWK TW1 13
Rydon Ms WIM/MER SW19 32
Ryecroft Av WHTN TW2 20
Rye Wk PUT/ROE SW15 17
Ryfold Rd WIM/MER SW19 25
Ryland Cl FELT TW13 18
Rythe Cl CHSGTN KT9 44
Rythe Ct THDIT KT7 35

S

Sable Cl HSLWW TW4 10
Saddlers Ms KUT/HW KT1 29
Sadlers Gate Ms PUT/ROE SW15 16
Sadlers Ride E/WMO/HCT KT8 28
Saffron Wy SURB KT6 36
Sage Yd SURB KT6 * 36
St Agatha's Dr KUTN/CMB KT2 30
St Albans Av FELT TW13 18
St Albans Farm EBED/NFELT TW14 * 10
St Albans Rd KUTN/CMB KT2 30
St Alban's Gdns TEDD TW11 21
St Andrews Cl THDIT KT7 35
ISLW TW7 5
St Andrew's Rd SURB KT6 36
St Andrew's Sq SURB KT6 36
St Anns Rd BARN SW13 * 9
St Anthony's Wy EBED/NFELT TW14 10
St Aubyn's Wk HSLW TW3 11
WIM/MER SW19 33
St Catherines Cl CHSGTN KT9 41
St Catherines Ct FELT TW13 18

hads Cl SURB KT6 ... 35 H4
hristopher's Cl ISLW TW7 ... 5 H4
air Dr WPK KT4 ... 43 G2
unstan's Rd FELT TW13 ... 18 A3
dmund's La WHTN TW2 ... 12 A5
dmunds Sq BARN SW13 ... 9 H2
eorges Sq NWMAL KT3 * ... 31 H5
eorge's Gdns SURB KT6 ... 42 A1
eorge's Industrial Est
  JTN/CMB KT2 ... 22 A5
eorge's Rd FELT TW13 ... 19 E4
UTN/CMB KT2 ... 3 C1
CH/KEW TW9 ... 14 C1
LW TW1 ... 13 G3
IM/MER SW19 ... 33 C1
les Cl HEST TW5 ... 4 B3
elena Ter RCH/KEW TW9 * ... 14 A3
elens THDIT KT7 * ... 34 D4
eliers Av HSLWW TW4 ... 11 H3
lda's Rd BARN SW13 ... 9 G2
ames Rd KUT/HW KT1 * ... 2 B5
ames Sq HMSMTH W6 ... 9 H1
ames St HMSMTH W6 ... 9 H1
ames' Cl NWMAL KT3 ... 38 A2
ames Rd SURB KT6 ... 36 A3
ames's Av HPTN TW12 ... 20 B5
ames's Cottages RCH/KEW TW9 * ... 14 A3
ames's Ct KUT/HW KT1 * ... 2 C7
ames's Rd HPTN TW12 ... 20 B5
ames's Rw CHSGTN KT19 * ... 41 E5
hns Rd NWMAL KT3 ... 31 H5
hn's Ct ISLW TW7 ... 17 E3
hn's Gv BARN SW13 * ... 9 F3
CH/KEW TW9 ... 14 A2
hn's Rd E/WMO/HCT KT8 ... 34 C1
ELT TW13 ... 19 G4
LW TW7 ... 6 A5
JT/HW KT1 ... 29 H3
WIM/MER SW19 ... 33 F2
eonards Rd MORT/ESHN SW14 ... 15 F1
eonard's Gdns HEST TW5 ... 4 B3
eonard's Rd ESH/CLAY KT10 ... 40 A5
URB KT6 ... 36 A3
HDIT KT7 ... 35 F3
eonard's Sq SURB KT6 ... 36 A2
argarets KUTN/CMB KT2 * ... 23 F5
argaret's Rd PUT/ROE SW15 * ... 16 C2
argaret's Ms KUTN/CMB KT2 * ... 23 F5
argaret's Crs PUT/ROE SW15 * ... 16 C3
argaret's Dr TWK TW1 ... 13 G3
argaret's Gv TWK TW1 ... 13 G2
argaret's Rd TWK TW1 ... 13 G2
ark's HI SURB KT6 ... 36 B2
ark's PI WIM/MER SW19 * ... 33 C1
ark's Rd TEDD TW11 ... 29 G2
ary's Rd E/WMO/HCT KT8 ... 34 C2
ary's La TEDD TW11 * ... 29 E1
ary's Ct ISLW TW7 ... 45 C1
ary's Crs ISLW TW7 ... 5 G3
ary's Gv BARN SW13 ... 16 C1
HSWK W4 ... 8 A2
ary's Rd E/WMO/HCT KT8 ... 34 C2
JRB KT6 ... 35 H4
IM/MER SW19 ... 25 F5
PK KT4 ... 42 D1
atthew's Av SURB KT6 ... 36 B5
chaels Cl WPK KT4 ... 43 E1
cholas Rd THDIT KT7 ... 35 E5
auls Rd RCH/KEW TW9 ... 14 C1
aul's Cl CHSGTN KT9 ... 41 E3
SLW TW3 ... 4 B5
aul's Rd BTFD TW8 ... 7 E2
eters Rd KUT/HW KT1 * ... 3 C5
MSMTH W6 * ... 9 F1
VK TW1 ... 13 G3
eter's Sq HMSMTH W6 ... 9 F1
ilip's Av WPK KT4 ... 43 C1
ilip's Rd E/WMO/HCT KT8 ... 34 C2
mon's Av PUT/ROE SW15 ... 16 C5
ephens Gdns TWK TW1 ... 13 H4
ephen's Rd EBED/NFELT TW14 ... 10 A2
eresa's Rd EBED/NFELT TW14 ... 10 A2
omas Cl SURB KT6 ... 36 C5
omas' Rd CHSWK W4 ... 8 B2
ncent Rd WHTN TW2 ... 12 B4
inifred's Rd TEDD TW11 ... 29 C1
mander Cl KUTN/CMB KT2 ... 21 H5
mander Quay KUT/HW KT1 * ... 2 A3
ombe Dr MRDN SM4 ... 39 E5
bury Rd FELT TW13 ... 18 D1
bury Gdns WIM/MER SW19 * ... 33 F2
oury Rd FELT TW13 ... 18 D1
SLWW TW4 ... 10 D1
WMAL KT3 ... 31 C5
CH/KEW TW9 ... 14 B2
IM/MER SW19 ... 33 F2
PK KT4 ... 42 C3
ol SUN TW16 ... 26 C2
ons Rd CHSGTN KT9 ... 41 F5
n Rd PUT/ROE SW15 ... 17 E1
els Ct HMSMTH W6 ... 9 F1
uel Gray Gdns KUTN/CMB KT2 ... 2 B2
ial Rd HSLWW TW4 ... 37 H1
alwood Rd FELT TW13 ... 18 C3
lers Cl HPTN TW12 ... 20 B5

Sandhurst Av BRYLDS KT5 ... 37 E4
Sandon Cl ESH/CLAY KT10 ... 34 C4
Sandpits Rd RCHPK/HAM TW10 ... 22 A2
Sandra Cl HSLW TW3 ... 4 D3
Sandringham Av RYNPK SW20 ... 33 F3
Sandringham Cl WIM/MER SW19 ... 25 E1
Sandringham Ms HPTN TW12 ... 27 G3
Sandringham Rd WPK KT4 ... 43 F2
Sandycombe Rd EBED/NFELT TW14 ... 18 B1
  RCH/KEW TW9 ... 7 H5
Sandycoombe Rd TWK TW1 ... 13 H4
Sandy La RCHPK/HAM TW10 ... 21 H2
  TEDD TW11 ... 29 H2
Sandy Md HOR/WEW KT19 ... 45 H4
Sanger Av CHSGTN KT9 ... 41 G4
Santos Rd WAND/EARL SW18 ... 17 H5
Sark Cl HEST TW5 ... 4 D3
Sarsen Av HSLW TW3 ... 4 D5
Savery Dr SURB KT6 ... 35 H2
Savile Cl NWMAL KT3 ... 37 H2
  THDIT KT7 ... 35 E5
Saville Rd TWK TW1 ... 21 E1
Savill Gdns RYNPK SW20 ... 32 B5
Savona Cl WIM/MER SW19 ... 33 E2
Sawkins Cl WIM/MER SW19 ... 25 E1
Sawyer's HI MORT/ESHN SW14 ... 15 F5
  RCHPK/HAM TW10 ... 14 B5
Saxon Av FELT TW13 ... 19 F2
Saxonbury Av SUN TW16 ... 26 C5
Saxonbury Gdns SURB KT6 ... 35 H5
Saxon Cl SURB KT6 ... 36 A3
Saxon Rd KUTN/CMB KT2 ... 2 C1
Scarth Rd BARN SW13 ... 16 A1
School House La TEDD TW11 ... 29 C2
School La KUT/HW KT1 ... 2 C1
  SURB KT6 ... 36 C5
School Pas KUT/HW KT1 ... 3 F5
School Rd E/WMO/HCT KT8 ... 34 C1
  HPTN TW12 ... 28 B1
  HSLW TW3 ... 12 B1
  KUT/HW KT1 ... 29 H3
School Road Av HPTN TW12 ... 28 B1
Schubert Rd PUT/ROE SW15 ... 17 G3
Scope Wy KUT/HW KT1 ... 36 B1
Scott Cl HOR/WEW KT19 ... 45 E4
Scott Farm Cl THDIT KT7 ... 35 G5
Scott Gdns HEST TW5 ... 4 A5
Scotts Dr HPTN TW12 ... 28 A2
Scotts Farm Rd HOR/WEW KT19 ... 42 B5
Scott Trimmer Wy HSLW TW3 ... 4 B5
Seaforth Av NWMAL KT3 ... 38 C2
Seaforth Gdns HOR/WEW KT19 ... 45 E3
Seaton Cl PUT/ROE SW15 ... 16 C5
  WHTN TW2 ... 12 B4
Seaton Rd WHTN TW2 ... 12 B4
Second Av WHTN/ESHN SW14 ... 15 H1
Second Cl E/WMO/HCT KT8 ... 34 A1
Second Cross Rd WHTN TW2 ... 12 C4
Sedleigh Rd WAND/EARL SW18 ... 17 G4
Seething Wells La SURB KT6 ... 35 H5
Sefton St PUT/ROE SW15 ... 9 H5
Sekhon Ter FELT TW13 ... 19 H4
Selborne Av NWMAL KT3 ... 31 H4
Selbourne Av SURB KT6 ... 41 C1
Selby Cl CHSGTN KT9 ... 45 F1
Selhurst Cl WIM/MER SW19 ... 25 E1
Selkirk Rd WHTN TW2 ... 20 B2
Selsdon Cl SURB KT6 ... 36 B2
Selwood Rd CHEAM SM3 ... 39 C5
  CHSGTN KT9 ... 41 E3
Selwyn Av RCH/KEW TW9 ... 14 C1
Selwyn Cl HSLWW TW4 ... 11 H3
Selwyn Rd NWMAL KT3 ... 37 G2
Seven Kings Wy KUTN/CMB KT2 ... 2 C2
Severn Dr ESH/CLAY KT10 ... 40 B1
Seymour Av MRDN SM4 ... 39 E4
Seymour Cl E/WMO/HCT KT8 ... 34 B1
Seymour Gdns BRYLDS KT5 ... 36 B2
  FELT TW13 ... 18 C4
  TWK TW1 ... 13 G5
Seymour Rd E/WMO/HCT KT8 ... 34 B1
  HPTN TW12 ... 20 B5
  KUT/HW KT1 ... 2 A2
  WAND/EARL SW18 ... 17 C5
  WIM/MER SW19 ... 25 E3
Shacklegate La TEDD TW11 ... 20 D4
Shadbolt Cl WPK KT4 ... 43 E1
Shaef Wy TEDD TW11 ... 29 F2
Shaftesbury Av EBED/NFELT TW14 ... 18 B4
Shaftesbury Rd RCH/KEW TW9 ... 14 B1
Shaftesbury Wy WHTN TW2 ... 20 C4
Shakespeare Av EBED/NFELT TW14 ... 10 B4
Shakespeare Ter RCH/KEW TW9 * ... 14 B3
Shakespeare Wy FELT TW13 ... 18 D4
Shaldon Dr MRDN SM4 ... 39 F2
Shalstone Rd MORT/ESHN SW14 ... 15 E1
Shalston Vls SURB KT6 ... 36 C3
Shannon Cl NWDGN UB2 ... 4 A1
Shannon Commercial Centre
  NWMAL KT3 ... 38 B1
Sharon Cl SURB KT6 ... 35 H5
Sharon Rd CHSWK W4 ... 8 H5
Shawford Rd HOR/WEW KT19 ... 42 C5
Sheaf Cottages THDIT KT7 * ... 34 D5
Sheaths Cottages THDIT KT7 * ... 35 G4
Sheen Common Dr RCHPK/HAM TW10 ... 14 D3
Sheen Court Rd RCHPK/HAM TW10 ... 14 D2
Sheendale Rd RCH/KEW TW9 ... 14 C2

Sheen Gate Gdns MORT/ESHN SW14 ... 15 F2
Sheen La MORT/ESHN SW14 ... 15 F2
Sheen Pk RCH/KEW TW9 ... 14 B2
Sheen Rd RCH/KEW TW9 ... 14 C3
Sheen Wd MORT/ESHN SW14 ... 15 F3
Sheephouse Wy NWMAL KT3 ... 37 G5
Sheep Walk Ms WIM/MER SW19 ... 33 E1
Shelburne Dr HSLWW TW4 ... 11 H4
Shelley Crs HEST TW5 ... 4 A4
Shelson Av FELT TW13 ... 18 A3
Shelson Pde FELT TW13 * ... 18 A3
Shelton Rd WIM/MER SW19 ... 33 H3
Shenley Rd HEST TW5 ... 4 B4
Shepherd Cl FELT TW13 ... 19 F4
Sheppard Cl KUT/HW KT1 ... 36 B1
Sherborne Rd CHSGTN KT9 ... 41 F4
Sherbrooke Wy WPK KT4 ... 38 C4
Shere Cl CHSGTN KT9 ... 41 E4
Sherfield Cl NWMAL KT3 ... 37 E1
Sherfield Gdns PUT/ROE SW15 ... 16 A4
Sheridan Ct HSLWW TW4 ... 11 F3
Sheridan Pl HPTN TW12 ... 28 A3
Sheridan Rd RCHPK/HAM TW10 ... 21 H3
  WIM/MER SW19 ... 33 G3
Sheringham Av WHTN TW2 ... 19 G1
Sherland Rd TWK TW1 ... 21 E1
Sherringham Av FELT TW13 ... 18 B3
Sherwood SURB KT6 ... 41 E1
Sherwood Rd HPTN TW12 ... 20 B5
  WIM/MER SW19 ... 33 G2
Shield Dr BTFD TW8 ... 6 B5
Ship La MORT/ESHN SW14 ... 15 F1
Shire Horse Wy ISLW TW7 ... 12 A3
Shire Ms WHTN TW2 ... 12 B4
The Shires RCHPK/HAM TW10 ... 22 B4
Shirley Cl HSLW TW3 ... 12 B3
Shirley Dr HSLW TW3 ... 12 B3
Shore Cl EBED/NFELT TW14 ... 10 B3
  HPTN TW12 ... 19 F5
Shore Gv FELT TW13 ... 19 H2
Shortlands Rd KUTN/CMB KT2 ... 3 F1
Short Rd CHSWK W4 ... 8 D2
Short Wy WHTN TW2 ... 12 B5
Shottfield Av MORT/ESHN SW14 ... 15 F2
Shrewsbury Av MORT/ESHN SW14 ... 15 F2
Shrewsbury Cl SURB KT6 ... 41 F1
The Shrubbery SURB KT6 * ... 36 B5
Shrubland Av WPK KT4 ... 43 F4
Siddeley Dr HSLWW TW4 ... 11 F1
Sidmouth Av ISLW TW7 ... 5 H5
Sidney Gdns BTFD TW8 ... 7 E2
Sidney Rd TWK TW1 ... 13 F4
Sigrist Sq KUTN/CMB KT2 ... 2 D3
Silverdale Dr SUN TW16 ... 26 C4
Silver Dene PUT/ROE SW15 ... 16 D3
Silvergate HOR/WEW KT19 ... 42 B4
Silverglade CHSGTN KT9 ... 44 D5
Silverhall St ISLW TW7 ... 13 F1
Simpson Rd HSLWW TW4 ... 11 G4
  RCHPK/HAM TW10 ... 21 H4
Simpson Wy SURB KT6 ... 35 H5
Simrose Ct WAND/EARL SW18 ... 17 H3
Sion Rd TWK TW1 ... 21 G1
Sir Abraham Dawes Cottages
  PUT/ROE SW15 * ... 17 F2
Sir Cyril Black Wy WIM/MER SW19 ... 33 G2
Sispara Gdns WAND/EARL SW18 ... 17 G4
Sixth Cross Rd WHTN TW2 ... 20 B3
Skeena HI WAND/EARL SW18 ... 17 F5
Skelgill Rd PUT/ROE SW15 ... 17 G2
Skelwith Rd HMSMTH W6 ... 9 F3
Skerne Rd KUTN/CMB KT2 ... 2 B3
Skerne Wk KUTN/CMB KT2 ... 2 B3
Skinners La HEST TW5 ... 5 E4
Slattery Rd FELT TW13 ... 18 D1
Smallberry Av ISLW TW7 ... 6 A5
Smeaton Rd WAND/EARL SW18 ... 17 H5
Smith St BRYLDS KT5 ... 36 C3
Smithwood Cl WIM/MER SW19 ... 25 H2
Snakey La FELT TW13 ... 18 B4
Snowdrop Cl HPTN TW12 ... 27 H1
Snowy Fielder Waye ISLW TW7 ... 6 C5
Soames Wk NWMAL KT3 ... 31 H3
Soaphouse La BTFD TW8 ... 7 F3
Solna Av PUT/ROE SW15 ... 16 D3
Solway Cl HSLWW TW4 ... 11 F1
Somerset Av CHSGTN KT9 ... 41 G4
  RYNPK SW20 ... 32 C4
Somerset Cl NWMAL KT3 ... 37 H3
Somerset Gdns TEDD TW11 ... 20 D5
Somerset Rd BTFD TW8 ... 6 D2
  KUT/HW KT1 ... 20 D5
  TEDD TW11 ... 20 D5
  WIM/MER SW19 ... 25 E3
Somerset Waye HEST TW5 ... 4 C3
Somerton Av RCH/KEW TW9 ... 15 E1
Somerville Av BARN SW13 ... 9 H2
Sonia Gdns HEST TW5 ... 4 D3
Sonning Gdns HPTN TW12 ... 27 F1
Sopwith Av CHSGTN KT9 ... 41 F4
Sopwith Cl KUTN/CMB KT2 ... 22 C5
Sopwith Wy KUTN/CMB KT2 ... 2 C3
South Av RCH/KEW TW9 * ... 7 H5
South Bank SURB KT6 ... 36 B5
Southbank THDIT KT7 ... 35 C4
South Bank Ter SURB KT6 * ... 36 B5
South Black Lion La HMSMTH W6 ... 9 F1
Southborough Cl SURB KT6 ... 36 A5

Southborough Rd SURB KT6 ... 36 B5
Southborough Road (The Lane)
  SURB KT6 * ... 36 B5
South Cl WHTN TW2 ... 19 H3
Southcote Av BRYLDS KT5 ... 37 E4
  FELT TW13 ... 18 B2
Southdean Gdns WIM/MER SW19 ... 25 G2
Southdown Dr RYNPK SW20 ... 33 G2
Southdown Rd RYNPK SW20 ... 33 E3
Southern Av EBED/NFELT TW14 ... 18 B1
Southey Rd WIM/MER SW19 ... 33 H2
Southfield Gdns TWK TW1 ... 21 E4
Southfields E/WMO/HCT KT8 ... 34 D5
Southfields Ms WAND/EARL SW18 * ... 17 H4
Southfields Rd WAND/EARL SW18 ... 17 H4
Southlands Dr WIM/MER SW19 ... 25 E2
Southland Wy HSLW TW3 ... 12 C3
South La KUT/HW KT1 ... 2 B7
  NWMAL KT3 ... 37 G1
South La West NWMAL KT3 ... 37 G1
Southmead Rd WIM/MER SW19 ... 25 G1
South Park Gv NWMAL KT3 ... 37 F1
South Park Rd WIM/MER SW19 ... 33 H1
South Pl BRYLDS KT5 ... 36 C4
Southridge Pl RYNPK SW20 ... 33 E2
South Rd FELT TW13 ... 19 E5
  HPTN TW12 ... 27 F1
  WIM/MER SW19 ... 20 C3
Southsea Rd KUT/HW KT1 ... 36 B1
Southside Common WIM/MER SW19 ... 33 E1
South St ISLW TW7 ... 13 F1
South Ter SURB KT6 ... 36 B3
South Vale Rd SURB KT6 ... 41 F1
South Vw HOR/WEW KT19 ... 45 H3
Southville Rd THDIT KT7 ... 35 G4
Southway RYNPK SW20 ... 33 E1
South Western Rd TWK TW1 ... 13 F4
Southwood Av KUTN/CMB KT2 ... 3 H5
Southwood Cl WPK KT4 ... 39 E5
Southwood Dr BRYLDS KT5 ... 37 G1
Southwood Gdns ESH/CLAY KT10 ... 40 B2
South Worple Wy MORT/ESHN SW14 ... 15 G1
Space Waye EBED/NFELT TW14 ... 10 C3
Sparks Cl HPTN TW12 ... 27 F1
Sparrow Cl HPTN TW12 ... 27 F1
Sparrow Farm Dr EBED/NFELT TW14 ... 10 D5
Sparrow Farm Rd EW KT17 ... 43 H5
Speart La HEST TW5 ... 4 B3
Speer Rd THDIT KT7 ... 35 E5
Speirs Cl NWMAL KT3 ... 38 A3
Spelthorne Gv SUN TW16 ... 26 A2
Spencer Gdns MORT/ESHN SW14 ... 15 E1
Spencer HI WIM/MER SW19 ... 33 F1
Spencer Hill Rd WIM/MER SW19 ... 33 F2
Spencer House SURB KT6 * ... 36 B2
Spencer Rd CHSWK W4 ... 8 B3
  E/WMO/HCT KT8 ... 34 B1
  ISLW TW7 ... 6 B5
  RYNPK SW20 ... 32 C3
  WHTN TW2 ... 20 D3
Spencer Wk PUT/ROE SW15 ... 17 E2
Spinney Cl NWMAL KT3 ... 37 H2
  WPK KT4 ... 43 E2
The Spinney BARN SW13 * ... 9 G2
  CHEAM SM3 ... 38 A5
  SUN TW16 ... 26 B3
Spreighton Rd E/WMO/HCT KT8 ... 34 B2
Spring Cnr FELT TW13 * ... 18 B5
Spring Cottages SURB KT6 * ... 36 A2
Springfield Av HPTN TW12 ... 28 A1
  RYNPK SW20 ... 33 G5
Springfield Gv SUN TW16 ... 26 B3
Springfield Pl NWMAL KT3 ... 37 F1
Springfield Rd KUT/HW KT1 ... 36 B1
  TEDD TW11 ... 29 H1
  WHTN TW2 ... 19 H1
  WIM/MER SW19 ... 25 G5
Spring Gdns E/WMO/HCT KT8 ... 34 B2
Spring Gv CHSWK W4 ... 7 H1
  HPTN TW12 ... 28 A3
Spring Grove Crs HSLW TW3 ... 5 F4
Spring Grove Rd HSLW TW3 ... 5 F4
  RCHPK/HAM TW10 ... 14 C3
Spring Rd FELT TW13 ... 18 A3
Springvale Av BTFD TW8 ... 7 E1
Springwell Rd HEST TW5 ... 4 A4
Spurfield E/WMO/HCT KT8 ... 28 A5
Spur Rd EBED/NFELT TW14 ... 10 C3
  ISLW TW7 ... 6 B3
The Square HMSMTH W6 ... 9 F1
  RCH/KEW TW9 ... 14 B3
Squires Ct WIM/MER SW19 ... 25 H4
Squirrel Cl HSLWW TW4 ... 11 E5
Squirrels Gn WPK KT4 ... 43 E1
Stable Cl KUTN/CMB KT2 ... 30 C1
Stable Ms TWK TW1 * ... 21 E1
Stafford Pl RCHPK/HAM TW10 ... 14 C5
Stafford Rd NWMAL KT3 ... 31 F5
Stag La PUT/ROE SW15 ... 16 A3
Stags Wy ISLW TW7 ... 6 A3
Staines Rd EBED/NFELT TW14 ... 10 A4
  WHTN TW2 ... 20 B3
Staines Rd East SUN TW16 ... 26 B2
Staines Rd West SUN TW16 ... 26 A2
Stanborough Cl HPTN TW12 ... 27 G1
Stanborough Rd HSLW TW3 ... 12 C1
Stanbridge Rd PUT/ROE SW15 ... 16 D1

Standard Rd *HSLWW* TW4	11	F1
Standen Rd *WAND/EARL* SW18	17	H5
Stanford Cl *HPTN* TW12	27	G1
Stanhope Ter *WHTN* TW2 *	20	B1
Stanley Av *NWMAL* KT3	38	B2
Stanleycroft Cl *ISLW* TW7	5	H4
Stanley Gardens Rd *TEDD* TW11	20	D5
Stanley Rd *HSLW* TW3	12	B2
MORT/ESHN SW14	15	E2
MRDN SM4	39	H1
TEDD TW11	20	D5
WHTN TW2	20	C3
WIM/MER SW19	33	H2
Stanmore Gdns *RCH/KEW* TW9	14	C1
Stanmore Rd *RCH/KEW* TW9	14	C1
Stanton Av *TEDD* TW11	28	D1
Stanton Cl *HOR/WEW* KT19	42	A4
WPK KT4	39	E5
Stanton Rd *BARN* SW13	9	E5
RYNPK SW20	33	E4
Stapleford Cl *KUT/HW* KT1	3	H5
WIM/MER SW19	25	H3
Star And Garter HI *RCHPK/HAM* TW10	22	B1
Star Rd *ISLW* TW7	5	C5
Staten Gdns *TWK* TW1	21	E1
Station Approach Rd *CHSWK* W4	8	B3
Station Av *NWMAL* KT3	31	H5
RCH/KEW TW9	7	H4
Station Cl *HPTN* TW12	28	A3
Station Estate Rd *EBED/NFELT* TW14	18	C1
Station Gdns *CHSWK* W4	8	B3
Station Pde *CHSWK* W4 *	8	B3
EBED/NFELT TW14 *	10	C5
RCH/KEW TW9	7	H4
Station Rd *BARN* SW13	9	E5
CHSGTN KT9	41	F4
HPTN TW12	28	A3
HSLW TW3	12	A2
KUT/HW KT1	2	A2
KUTN/CMB KT2	3	G3
NWMAL KT3	38	C2
SUN TW16	26	B2
TEDD TW11	29	F1
THDIT KT7	35	E4
TWK TW1	21	E1
Station Yd *TWK* TW1	13	F5
Staunton Rd *KUTN/CMB* KT2	30	C2
Staveley Gdns *CHSWK* W4	8	C4
Staveley Rd *CHSWK* W4	8	B2
Steadfast Rd *KUT/HW* KT1	2	B3
Steam Farm La *EBED/NFELT* TW14	10	A2
Steele Rd *ISLW* TW7	13	F2
Steeple Cl *FUL/PGN* SW6	17	F1
WIM/MER SW19	25	F4
Stephenson Rd *WHTN* TW2	11	H5
Sterry Dr *HOR/WEW* KT19	42	D3
THDIT KT7	34	D3
Steve Biko Wy *HSLW* TW3	11	H1
Stevens Cl *HPTN* TW12	27	G1
Stevens' La *ESH/CLAY* KT10	44	B1
Stewart Cl *HPTN* TW12	27	F1
Steyning Wy *HSLWW* TW4	10	D2
Stile Hall Gdns *CHSWK* W4 *	8	A2
Stile Pth *SUN* TW16	26	B5
Stillingfleet Rd *BARN* SW13	9	F3
Stirling Gv *HSLW* TW3	5	F5
Stirling Rd *WHTN* TW2	11	H5
Stirling Wk *BRYLDS* KT5	37	E3
Stockhurst Cl *PUT/ROE* SW15	9	H5
Stoford Cl *WIM/MER* SW19	25	F1
Stoke Rd *KUTN/CMB* KT2	31	F2
Stokesby Rd *CHSGTN* KT9	41	G5
Stonecot Cl *CHEAM* SM3	39	F5
Stonecot HI *CHEAM* SM3	39	F5
Stone Crs *EBED/NFELT* TW14	10	A5
Stonehill Cl *MORT/ESHN* SW14	15	G3
Stonehill Rd *CHSWK* W4	7	H1
MORT/ESHN SW14	15	F3
Stoneleigh Av *WPK* KT4	43	F3
Stoneleigh Broadway *EW* KT17	43	F3
Stoneleigh Crs *HOR/WEW* KT19	43	F3
Stoneleigh Park Rd *HOR/WEW* KT19	43	F3
Stone Pl *WPK* KT4	43	F1
Stormont Wy *CHSGTN* KT9	40	D4
Stoughton Cl *PUT/ROE* SW15	24	B3
Stourhead Cl *WIM/MER* SW19	17	E5
Stourhead Gdns *RYNPK* SW20	32	B5
Stourton Av *FELT* TW13	19	G4
Strachan Pl *RYNPK* SW20	32	D1
Strafford Rd *HSLW* TW3	11	G1
TWK TW1	13	F5
Strand Dr *RCH/KEW* TW9	7	H4
Strand-on-the-Green *CHSWK* W4	7	H2
Stratford Ct *NWMAL* KT3	37	G1
Stratford Rd *PUT/ROE* SW15	17	F4
Strathan Cl *WAND/EARL* SW18	17	E4
Strathearn Av *WHTN* TW2	20	B1
Strathearn Rd *WIM/MER* SW19	25	H1
Strathmore Rd *TEDD* TW11	20	D4
WIM/MER SW19	25	H3

Strathville Rd *WAND/EARL* SW18	25	H2
Stratton Cl *HSLW* TW3	4	C1
WIM/MER SW19	33	G1
Stratton Rd *SUN* TW16	26	A4
WIM/MER SW19	33	H4
Strawberry Hill Rd *TWK* TW1	21	E5
Strawberry V *TWK* TW1	21	E5
Stretton Rd *RCHPK/HAM* TW10	21	H2
Stroud Crs *PUT/ROE* SW15	24	A3
Stroudes Cl *WPK* KT4	38	A4
Stroud Rd *WIM/MER* SW19	25	H3
Stuart Gv *TEDD* TW11	20	D5
Stuart Rd *RCHPK/HAM* TW10	21	G2
WIM/MER SW19	25	H3
Stucley Rd *HEST* TW5	5	F3
Studland Rd *KUTN/CMB* KT2	30	B1
Sudbrook Gdns *RCHPK/HAM* TW10	22	B1
Sudbrook La *RCHPK/HAM* TW10	22	B1
Sudlow Rd *WAND/EARL* SW18	17	H2
Suffolk Cl *BARN* SW13	9	E5
WPK KT4	43	E1
Suffolk Vls *WAND/EARL* SW18 *	17	H5
Sugden Rd *THDIT* KT7	35	F5
Sulivan Rd *FUL/PGN* SW6	17	H1
Sullivan Cl *E/WMO/HCT* KT8	27	H5
Summer Av *E/WMO/HCT* KT8	34	D2
Summer Crossing *THDIT* KT7	35	E2
Summerfield La *SURB* KT6	41	E1
Summer Gdns *E/WMO/HCT* KT8	34	D2
Summerhouse Av *HEST* TW5	4	B4
Summer Rd *E/WMO/HCT* KT8	34	C2
THDIT KT7	35	E2
Summer Trees *SUN* TW16	26	C3
Summerwood Rd *ISLW* TW7	13	E4
TWK TW1	13	E4
Sunbury Av *MORT/ESHN* SW14	15	G2
Sunbury Ct *SUN* TW16	27	E4
Sunbury Court Rd *SUN* TW16	26	D4
Sunbury Cross Centre *SUN* TW16 *	26	A2
Sunbury Rd *FELT* TW13	18	A3
Sunbury Wy *FELT* TW13	18	D5
Sunmead Rd *SUN* TW16	26	B5
Sunna Gdns *SUN* TW16	26	C4
Sunningdale Av *FELT* TW13	19	F2
Sunningdale Cl *SURB* KT6	41	F1
Sunnycroft Rd *HSLW* TW3	5	H5
Sunnymead Rd *PUT/ROE* SW15	16	C3
Sunnyside Pl *WIM/MER* SW19	33	F1
Sunnyside Rd *TEDD* TW11	20	C4
Sunray Av *BRYLDS* KT5	42	A1
Sunrise Cl *FELT* TW13	19	G3
Sunset Rd *WIM/MER* SW19	24	C5
Surbiton Ct *SURB* KT6	35	H5
Surbiton Court Ms *SURB* KT6 *	36	A3
Surbiton Crs *KUT/HW* KT1	36	B1
Surbiton Hall Cl *KUT/HW* KT1	36	B1
Surbiton Hill Pk *BRYLDS* KT5	36	C2
Surbiton Hill Rd *SURB* KT6	36	B1
Surbiton Rd *KUT/HW* KT1	36	A1
Surrey Crs *CHSWK* W4	7	H1
Sury Basin *KUTN/CMB* KT2	2	B2
Sussex Av *ISLW* TW7	12	D1
Sussex Cl *NWMAL* KT3	37	H1
TWK TW1	13	G4
Sussex Gdns *CHSGTN* KT9	41	E5
Sussex Pl *HMSMTH* W6	9	H1
NWMAL KT3	37	H1
Sussex Rd *NWMAL* KT3	37	H1
Sutherland Av *SUN* TW16	26	A4
Sutherland Gdns *MORT/ESHN* SW14	15	H1
SUN TW16	26	A4
WPK KT4	38	C5
Sutherland Gv *TEDD* TW11	20	D5
WAND/EARL SW18	17	G5
Sutherland Rd *CHSWK* W4	8	C2
Sutton Cl *CHSWK* W4 *	8	C2
Sutton Common Rd *CHEAM* SM3	39	G4
Sutton Ct *CHSWK* W4 *	8	B2
Sutton Court Rd *CHSWK* W4	8	B2
Sutton Dene *HSLW* TW3	5	H5
Sutton Hall Rd *HEST* TW5	4	D3
Sutton La *HSLW* TW3	4	C4
Sutton La North *CHSWK* W4	8	B1
Sutton La South *CHSWK* W4	8	B2
Sutton Rd *HEST* TW5	4	D4
Sutton Sq *HEST* TW5	4	C4
Sutton Wy *HEST* TW5	4	C4
Swan Cl *FELT* TW13	19	F4
Swan Island *TWK* TW1 *	21	F3
Swan Pl *BARN* SW13	9	E5
Swan Rd *FELT* TW13	19	F3
Swanscombe Rd *CHSWK* W4	8	C1
Swan St *ISLW* TW7	13	G1
Swanton Gdns *WIM/MER* SW19	25	E1
Swanwick Cl *PUT/ROE* SW15	16	A5
Swift Rd *FELT* TW13	19	E4
Swinburne Rd *PUT/ROE* SW15	16	B2
Swinfield Cl *FELT* TW13	18	D5
Sycamore Cl *FELT* TW13	18	B3
Sycamore Gv *NWMAL* KT3	31	H5
Sycamore Rd *WIM/MER* SW19	32	D1
Sycamore Wy *TEDD* TW11	29	H1
Sydney Rd *EBED/NFELT* TW14	18	B1
RCH/KEW TW9	14	B2
RYNPK SW20	33	E4
TEDD TW11	21	E5
Sydney Ter *ESH/CLAY* KT10 *	40	A5
Sylvan Gdns *SURB* KT6	36	A4

Syon Gate Wy *BTFD* TW8	6	B3
Syon La *ISLW* TW7	6	A2
Syon Pk *ISLW* TW7 *	13	G1
Syon Park Gdns *ISLW* TW7	6	A3

T

Tabor Gv *WIM/MER* SW19	33	F2
Tachbrook Rd *EBED/NFELT* TW14	10	A5
Tadworth Av *NWMAL* KT3	38	A1
Talbot Rd *ISLW* TW7	13	F2
WHTN TW2	20	D1
Tallow Rd *BTFD* TW8	6	D2
Talma Gdns *WHTN* TW2	12	D5
Tamesis Gdns *WPK* KT4	42	D1
Tamian Wy *HSLWW* TW4	10	D2
Tangier Rd *RCHPK/HAM* TW10	14	D2
Tanglewood Wy *FELT* TW13	18	C3
Tangley Gv *PUT/ROE* SW15	16	A5
Tangley Park Rd *HPTN* TW12 *	19	G5
Tangmere Gv *KUTN/CMB* KT2	22	A5
Tankerton Rd *SURB* KT6	41	G1
Tapping Cl *KUTN/CMB* KT2	3	C1
Taunton Av *HSLW* TW3	12	D1
RYNPK SW20	32	C4
Taunton Cl *CHEAM* SM3	39	H5
Tawny Cl *FELT* TW13	18	B3
Tayben Av *WHTN* TW2	12	D4
Taylor Av *RCH/KEW* TW9	8	A5
Taylor Cl *HOR/WEW* KT19	45	H4
HPTN TW12	20	B5
HSLW TW3	5	F4
Taylors Ct *FELT* TW13	18	B2
Tealing Dr *HOR/WEW* KT19	42	D3
Teck Cl *ISLW* TW7	13	G5
Tedder Cl *CHSGTN* KT9	40	D4
Teddington Pk *TEDD* TW11	21	E5
Teddington Park Rd *TEDD* TW11	21	E4
Teesdale Av *ISLW* TW7	6	B4
Teesdale Gdns *ISLW* TW7	6	B4
Telegraph La *ESH/CLAY* KT10	40	A3
Telegraph Rd *PUT/ROE* SW15	16	C5
Telford Rd *WHTN* TW2	11	H5
Temeraire Pl *BTFD* TW8	7	G1
Templar Pl *HPTN* TW12	27	H2
Templecombe Wy *MRDN* SM4	39	F2
Temple Rd *HSLW* TW3	12	A2
RCH/KEW TW9	7	G5
Temple Sheen Rd		
MORT/ESHN SW14	15	F2
Tennyson Av *NWMAL* KT3	38	C2
TWK TW1	21	E1
Tennyson Cl *EBED/NFELT* TW14	10	A4
Tennyson Rd *HSLW* TW3	5	F5
Terrace Gdns *BARN* SW13	9	E5
Terrace La *RCHPK/HAM* TW10	14	B4
The Terrace *BARN* SW13	8	D5
Terrace Vls *HMSMTH* W6 *	9	F1
Terrac St *RCH/KEW* TW9	14	A4
Thackeray Cl *ISLW* TW7	6	B5
WIM/MER SW19	33	E2
Thames Bank *MORT/ESHN* SW14	15	E1
Thames Cl *HPTN* TW12	28	A4
Thames Down Link *BRYLDS* KT5	37	F2
HOR/WEW KT19	42	B3
NWMAL KT3	37	G5
WPK KT4	42	C2
Thames Eyot *TWK* TW1 *	21	F2
Thamesgate Cl *RCHPK/HAM* TW10	21	H4
Thameside *TEDD* TW11	30	A2
Thameside Centre *BTFD* TW8 *	7	G2
Thames Meadow *E/WMO/HCT* KT8	27	H5
Thames Pth *BARN* SW13	9	E1
BTFD TW8	7	F3
ISLW TW7	6	D5
SUN TW16	26	D5
Thames Pl *PUT/ROE* SW15	17	E1
Thamespoint *TEDD* TW11 *	30	A2
Thames Reach *KUT/HW* KT1 *	2	A2
Thames Rd *CHSWK* W4	7	H2
ISLW TW7	6	B3
Thames Side *KUT/HW* KT1	2	A2
THDIT KT7	35	G3
Thames St *HPTN* TW12	28	A4
KUT/HW KT1	2	B4
SUN TW16	26	C5
Thamesvale Cl *HSLW* TW3	4	D5
Thames Village *CHSWK* W4	8	B4
Thatchers Wy *ISLW* TW7	12	C5
The Beverly *MRDN* SM4	39	E5
The Green *WIM/MER* SW19	25	E5
Thelma Gv *TEDD* TW11	29	F1
Thetford Rd *NWMAL* KT3	37	G2
Third Cl *E/WMO/HCT* KT8	34	A1
Third Cross Rd *WHTN* TW2	20	C2
Thistledene *THDIT* KT7	34	D3
Thistleworth Cl *ISLW* TW7	6	A3
Thompson Av *RCH/KEW* TW9	15	E1
Thompson Cl *CHEAM* SM3	39	H5
Thompson Rd *HSLW* TW3	12	A3
Thorkhill Gdns *THDIT* KT7	35	F5
Thorkhill Rd *THDIT* KT7	35	G5
Thornbury Av *ISLW* TW7	5	G3
Thornbury Rd *ISLW* TW7	5	G3
Thorncliffe Rd *NWDGN* UB2	4	C1
Thorndon Gdns *HOR/WEW* KT19	42	D3

Thorne Cl *ESH/CLAY* KT10	44
Thorne St *BARN* SW13	15
Thornhill Av *SURB* KT6	41
Thornhill Rd *SURB* KT6	41
Thornton HI *WIM/MER* SW19	33
Thornton Rd *MORT/ESHN* SW14	15
WIM/MER SW19	33
Thorpe Rd *KUTN/CMB* KT2	30
Thrigby Rd *CHSGTN* KT9	41
Thurleston Av *MRDN* SM4	39
Thursley Gdns *WIM/MER* SW19	25
Thurstan Rd *RYNPK* SW20	32
Tibbets Cl *WIM/MER* SW19	25
Tibbet's Ride *PUT/ROE* SW15	17
Tideswell Rd *PUT/ROE* SW15	16
Tideway Cl *RCHPK/HAM* TW10	21
Tildesley Rd *PUT/ROE* SW15	16
Tilford Gdns *WIM/MER* SW19	25
Tilley Rd *FELT* TW13	18
Timbercroft *HOR/WEW* KT19	42
Tintern Cl *PUT/ROE* SW15	17
Titan Ct *BTFD* TW8	7
Tithe Barn Cl *KUTN/CMB* KT2	3
Tiverton Rd *HSLW* TW3	5
Tiverton Wy *CHSGTN* KT9	40
Tivoli Rd *HSLW* TW3	4
Toad La *HSLWW* TW4	11
Toby Wy *SURB* KT6	42
Toland Sq *PUT/ROE* SW15	16
Tolson Rd *ISLW* TW7	13
Tolverne Rd *RYNPK* SW20	32
Tolworth Broadway *SURB* KT6	36
Tolworth Cl *SURB* KT6	37
Tolworth Park Rd *SURB* KT6	41
Tolworth Ri North	
(Kingston By-Pass) *BRYLDS* KT5	37
Tolworth Ri South	
NWMAL KT3	37
Tolworth Rd *SURB* KT6	41
Tolworth Underpass	
(Kingston By-Pass) *SURB* KT6	41
Tomlinson Cl *CHSWK* W4	8
Tonfield Rd *CHEAM* SM3	39
Topiary Sq *RCH/KEW* TW9	14
Torrington Wy *MRDN* SM4	39
Torwood Rd *PUT/ROE* SW15	16
Tower Gdns *ESH/CLAY* KT10	44
Tower Ri *RCH/KEW* TW9	14
Tower Rd *TWK* TW1	21
Towers Pl *RCH/KEW* TW9	14
Towfield Rd *FELT* TW13	19
Town End Pde *KUT/HW* KT1 *	6
Town Field Wy *ISLW* TW7	6
Townhall Av *CHSWK* W4	8
Town Meadow *BTFD* TW8	7
Townmead Rd *RCH/KEW* TW9	14
Townshend Rd *RCH/KEW* TW9	14
Townshend Ter *RCH/KEW* TW9	14
Town Whf *ISLW* TW7 *	13
Toynbee Rd *RYNPK* SW20	33
Trafalgar Av *WPK* KT4	43
Trafalgar Rd *WHTN* TW2	20
Tranmere Rd *WHTN* TW2	12
Transport Av *BTFD* TW8	6
Traps La *NWMAL* KT3	31
Treaty Centre *HSLW* TW3 *	12
Tree Cl *RCHPK/HAM* TW10	14
Treen Av *BARN* SW13	15
Tregaron Gdns *NWMAL* KT3	37
Trehern Rd *MORT/ESHN* SW14	15
Trematon Pl *TEDD* TW11	29
Trentham St *WAND/EARL* SW18	25
Trent Wy *WPK* KT4	43
Treville St *PUT/ROE* SW15	16
Trevithick Cl *EBED/NFELT* TW14	18
Trevor Cl *ISLW* TW7	13
Trevor Rd *WIM/MER* SW19	33
Trewenna Dr *CHSGTN* KT9	41
Trewince Rd *RYNPK* SW20	33
The Triangle *KUT/HW* KT1 *	3
Trinity Church Rd *BARN* SW13	9
Trinity Cl *HSLWW* TW4	11
Trinity Pde *HSLW* TW3 *	12
Trinity Rd *RCH/KEW* TW9 *	14
WIM/MER SW19	33
Trotter Wy *HOR/WEW* KT19	45
Trowlock Av *TEDD* TW11	29
Trowlock Wy *TEDD* TW11	29
Trystings Cl *ESH/CLAY* KT10	40
Tudor Av *HPTN* TW12	27
WPK KT4	43
Tudor Cl *CHSGTN* KT9	41
HPTN TW12	27
Tudor Dr *KUTN/CMB* KT2	22
MRDN SM4	38
Tudor Gdns *BARN* SW13	15
TWK TW1	21
Tudor Rd *HPTN* TW12	27
HSLW TW3	12
KUTN/CMB KT2	3
Tufton Gdns *E/WMO/HCT* KT8	28
Tulip Cl *HPTN* TW12	27
Tunworth Crs *PUT/ROE* SW15	16
Turner Av *WHTN* TW2	20
Turner Rd *NWMAL* KT3	37
Turnpike Wy *ISLW* TW7	6
Turpin Rd *EBED/NFELT* TW14	10

Winchilsea Crs E/WMO/HCT KT8 ....28 B4
Windermere Rd PUT/ROE SW15........23 H4
Windham Rd RCH/KEW TW9 ....14 C1
Windlesham Gv WIM/MER SW19........25 E1
Windmill Cl SURB KT6.....................35 H5
Windmill La SURB KT6...................35 G4
Windmill Ri KUTN/CMB KT2............31 E2
Windmill Rd HPTN TW12..................20 A5
　WIM/MER SW19.........................24 C3
Windrush NWMAL KT3.....................37 E1
Windrush Cl CHSWK W4 * 8 B5
Windsor Av E/WMO/HCT KT8............27 H5
　NWMAL KT3................................37 F2
Windsor Rd KUTN/CMB KT2..............2 C1
　RCH/KEW TW9............................7 G5
　SUN TW16.................................26 B2
　TEDD TW11................................20 C5
　WPK KT4...................................43 F1
Windy Ridge Cl WIM/MER SW19........25 E5
Winery La KUT/HW KT1..................2 E6
Winery Cl CHSGTN KT9...................44 D1
Wingfield Rd KUTN/CMB KT2............30 C1
Wingrave Rd HMSMTH W6...............9 H2
Winifred Rd HPTN TW12..................19 H4
　WIM/MER SW19..........................33 H3
Winslow Rd HMSMTH W6.................9 H2
Winslow Wy FELT TW13....................19 E3
Winston House SURB KT6 * 36 B2
Winter Box Wk RCHPK/HAM TW10.....14 C3
Winterfold Cl WIM/MER SW19...........25 F2
Winters Rd THDIT KT7......................35 G4
Winthorpe Rd PUT/ROE SW15...........17 F2
Witham Rd ISLW TW7.......................5 G4
Withycombe Rd WIM/MER SW19........17 E5
Wittering Cl KUTN/CMB KT2.............22 A5
Wivenhoe Ct HSLW TW3..................11 G2
Woffington Cl TEDD TW11................29 H2
Woking Cl PUT/ROE SW15...............16 A2
Wolseley Av WAND/EARL SW18.........25 E2
Wolseley Gdns CHSWK W4................8 A2
Wolsey Av THDIT KT7......................35 E2

Wolsey Cl HSLW TW3.....................12 B2
　KUTN/CMB KT2............................3 K3
　RYNPK SW20..............................32 C2
　WPK KT4...................................43 F3
Wolsey Crs MRDN SM4.....................39 G4
Wolsey Dr KUTN/CMB KT2...............22 B5
Wolsey Rd E/WMO/HCT KT8.............34 C1
　HPTN TW12................................28 A1
　SUN TW16.................................26 A2
Wolsey Wy CHSGTN KT9.................41 H4
Wolverton Av KUTN/CMB KT2............3 H2
Wonford Cl KUTN/CMB KT2..............31 H3
Woodall Cl CHSGTN KT9..................44 D1
Woodberry Cl SUN TW16................26 B1
Woodbine Cl WHTN TW2..................20 C2
Woodbine La WPK KT4.....................43 G2
Woodbines Av KUT/HW KT1..............2 B7
Woodborough Rd PUT/ROE SW15......16 C2
Woodbourne Dr ESH/CLAY KT10.......40 A5
Woodcote Cl KUTN/CMB KT2............22 C5
Woodfield Gdns NWMAL KT3............38 A2
Woodfield Rd THDIT KT7..................40 A1
Woodgate Av CHSGTN KT9...............41 E4
Woodhayes Rd WIM/MER SW19.........32 D1
Woodland Cl HOR/WEW KT19 * 42 D5
Woodland Gdns ISLW TW7................12 D1
Woodlands RYNPK SW20..................38 D1
Woodlands Av NWMAL KT3...............31 F3
　WPK KT4...................................43 E1
Woodlands Cl ESH/CLAY KT10..........44 A1
Woodlands Dr SUN TW16.................16 D4
Woodlands Gv ISLW TW7..................5 H5
Woodlands Rd BARN SW13..............16 A1
　ISLW TW7..................................12 D1
　SURB KT6.................................36 A4
The Woodlands ISLW TW7................6 A5
Woodlands Wy PUT/ROE SW15..........17 G3
Woodland Wk HOR/WEW KT19..........41 H5
Woodland Wy BRYLDS KT5...............42 A1
　MRDN SM4.................................39 G1
Wood La ISLW TW7..........................5 H2

Woodlawn Cl PUT/ROE SW15...........17 G3
Woodlawn Crs WHTN TW2................20 A2
Woodlawn Dr FELT TW13.................19 E2
Woodman Ms WIM/MER SW19..........25 G5
Woodside WIM/MER SW19...............25 G5
Woodside Av ESH/CLAY KT10...........34 D4
Woodside Cl BRYLDS KT5.................37 F4
Woodside Rd KUTN/CMB KT2.............3 G4
　NWMAL KT3................................31 G4
Woodspring Rd WIM/MER SW19........25 F2
Woodstock Av CHEAM SM3...............39 G4
Woodstock Cl SUN TW16.................26 A1
Woodstock La North SURB KT6..........40 D1
Woodstock La South CHSGTN KT9......40 D2
　ESH/CLAY KT10..........................40 C4
Woodstock Ri CHEAM SM3...............39 G5
Woodstock La WPK KT4....................43 F4
Wood St CHSWK W4.........................8 D1
　KUT/HW KT1..............................2 B4
Woodthorpe Rd PUT/ROE SW15.......16 C2
Woodview CHSGTN KT9.....................44 D4
Woodview Cl PUT/ROE SW15............23 G4
Woodville Cl TEDD TW11..................21 F4
Woodville Gdns SURB KT6 * 36 A4
Woodville Rd MRDN SM4..................39 H1
　RCHPK/HAM TW10.......................21 G3
Woodward Cl ESH/CLAY KT10...........40 A5
Wool Rd RYNPK SW20.....................32 C1
Worcester Gdns WPK KT4................42 D2
Worcester Park Rd WPK KT4.............42 B2
Worcester Rd WIM/MER SW19..........25 G5
Wordsworth Dr CHEAM SM3..............43 H3
Wordsworth Rd HPTN TW12.............19 G4
Worlidge St HMSMTH W6...................9 H1
Worple Av ISLW TW7.......................13 F5
　WIM/MER SW19..........................33 E2
Worple Rd ISLW TW7......................13 F2
　RYNPK SW20..............................32 D4
　WIM/MER SW19..........................33 F2
Worple Road Ms WIM/MER SW19......33 C1
Worple St MORT/ESHN SW14............15 C1

Worple Wy RCHPK/HAM TW10.........14
Worthing Rd HEST TW5....................4
Worthington Rd SURB KT6................36
Worton Gdns ISLW TW7....................5
Worton Rd ISLW TW7.......................13
Worton Wy ISLW TW7.......................5
Wraysbury Cl HSLWW TW4...............11
Wrights Aly WIM/MER SW19.............32
Wyatt Cl FELT TW13........................19
Wyatt Dr BARN SW13.......................9
Wychwood Cl SUN TW16.................26
Wydell Cl MRDN SM4........................38
Wyke Cl ISLW TW7..........................6
Wyke Rd RYNPK SW20......................32
Wymond St PUT/ROE SW15.............16
Wyndham Crs HSLWW TW4...............11
Wyndham Rd KUTN/CMB KT2...........30
Wyvern Est NWMAL KT3 * 32

Y

Yale Cl HSLWW TW4........................11
Yenston Cl MRDN SM4.....................39
Yeovilton Pl KUTN/CMB KT2............22
Yew Tree Cl WPK KT4.......................37
Yew Tree Wk HSLWW TW4................11
York Av MORT/ESHN SW14..............15
York Pde BTFD TW8 *........................7
York Rd BTFD TW8...........................7
　HSLW TW3.................................12
　KUTN/CMB KT2...........................3
　RCHPK/HAM TW10.......................14
　TEDD TW11................................20
York Wy CHSGTN KT9......................45
　FELT TW13................................19

Abbey Primary School
　MRDN SM4..................................39 H4
Abbotsbury Primary School
　MRDN SM4..................................39 H2
ABC Cinema
　PUT/ROE SW15...........................17 F1
Acorn Medical Centre
　TWK TW1...................................21 F1
Acre Road Health Clinic
　KUTN/CMB KT2............................2 E1
Airedale Physiotherapy Clinic
　CHSWK W4..................................9 E1
Albany Park Canoe & Sailing Club
　KUTN/CMB KT2...........................30 A1
Albemarle Primary School
　WIM/MER SW19...........................25 F2
Alexandra Infant School
　KUTN/CMB KT2............................3 G1
Alexandra Junior School
　HSLW TW3..................................5 E5
The All England Lawn Tennis
　& Croquet Club
　WIM/MER SW19...........................25 E3
All Saints CE Primary School
　PUT/ROE SW15...........................16 D1
The Alton School
　PUT/ROE SW15...........................16 A5
Amida Golf
　FELT TW13................................19 H3
The Andrew Ewing
　Primary School
　HEST TW5..................................4 C3
Apex Retail Park
　FELT TW13................................19 G3
Aragon Primary School
　MRDN SM4.................................39 F4
Archdeacon Cambridge's
　CE Primary School
　WHTN TW2.................................20 D2
Arndale Health Centre
　WAND/EARL SW18.......................17 H4
Ashcroft Technology Academy
　PUT/ROE SW15...........................17 G3
Ashton House School
　ISLW TW7...................................5 G4
Asquith Court School
　HPTN TW12................................28 A3
Assembly Rooms
　SURB KT6.................................36 B1
Aston Clinic
　NWMAL KT3...............................37 H1
Athelstan House School
　HPTN TW12................................27 H3
Atkinson Morley Hospital
　RYNPK SW20..............................32 C2
Auriol Junior School
　HOR/WEW KT19..........................43 E3

Back Care Clinic
　WPK KT4...................................38 B5
Barn Elms Athletics Track
　BARN SW13.................................9 G5
Barn Elms Sports Centre
　BARN SW13.................................9 H4
Barn Elms Water Sports Centre
　PUT/ROE SW15...........................9 H5
Barnes Hospital
　MORT/ESHN SW14.......................15 H1
Barnes Primary School
　BARN SW13...............................15 H1
Barnes Sports Club
　BARN SW13.................................9 G4
Barwell Business Park
　CHSGTN KT9..............................45 E1
Beauclerc Infant School
　SUN TW16.................................26 D5
The Beavers Comm Primary School
　HSLWW TW4...............................10 D1
Bective House Clinic
　PUT/ROE SW15...........................17 G2
Bedelsford Special School
　KUT/HW KT1................................2 C7
The Bentall Shopping Centre
　KUT/HW KT1................................2 A4
Berkeley Primary School
　HEST TW5...................................4 A2
Best Western Lodge Hotel
　PUT/ROE SW15...........................17 G3
Best Western Master Robert Hotel
　HEST TW5...................................4 C4
Beverley School
　NWMAL KT3................................38 B2
Beverley Trading Estate
　MRDN SM4.................................39 E4
Bingham Hotel
　TWK TW1...................................14 A4
Bishop Gilpin Primary School
　WIM/MER SW19...........................25 G5
Bishop Perrin CE Primary School
　WHTN TW2.................................12 A5
Bishop Wand CE Secondary School
　SUN TW16.................................26 A4
Blossom House School
　RYNPK SW20..............................32 D2
The Blue School
　ISLW TW7..................................13 F1
Brandlehow Primary School
　PUT/ROE SW15...........................17 G2
Brentford Business Centre
　BTFD TW8....................................6 D3
Brentford County Court
　BTFD TW8....................................7 E3
Brentford FC London Broncos RLFC
　(Griffin Park)
　BTFD TW8....................................7 E2

Brentford Fountain Leisure Centre
　BTFD TW8....................................7 G1
Brentford Health Centre
　BTFD TW8....................................6 D2
Brentford School for Girls
　BTFD TW8....................................7 E2
Brentwaters Business Park
　BTFD TW8....................................6 D3
Brewery Mews Business Centre
　ISLW TW7..................................13 E1
Broadway Shopping Centre
　HMSMTH W6................................9 H1
Brookfield Primary School
　CHEAM SM3................................39 F5
Brook Lane Business Centre
　BTFD TW8....................................7 E1
Broomfield House School
　RCH/KEW TW9..............................7 G4
Brunel University
　ISLW TW7....................................5 H3
　TWK TW1...................................13 G2
Brunel University
　(Osterley Campus) Track
　ISLW TW7....................................5 H3
Buckingham Primary School
　HPTN TW12................................19 G5
Buckland Infant School
　CHSGTN KT9..............................41 G4
Burlington Infant School
　NWMAL KT3................................38 A1
Cambridge Park Bowling
　& Sports Club
　TWK TW1...................................13 H4
Campion House College
　ISLW TW7....................................5 G3
Canbury 2000 Business Park
　KUTN/CMB KT2............................2 D3
Canbury Business Centre
　KUTN/CMB KT2............................2 D3
Canbury Medical Centre
　KUTN/CMB KT2............................2 E2
Canbury School
　KUTN/CMB KT2...........................31 E1
Cannizaro House Hotel
　WIM/MER SW19...........................32 D1
Cardinal Road Infant School
　FELT TW13.................................18 C1
Carlisle Infant School
　HPTN TW12................................28 A1
The Carlton Mitre Hotel
　E/WMO/HCT KT8.........................28 D5
The Cassel Hospital
　RCHPK/HAM TW10.......................22 A4
Casualty Plus Clinic
　BTFD TW8....................................6 D1
Cavendish Primary School
　CHSWK W4...................................8 D3

Centaurs Business Centre
　ISLW TW7....................................6
Centaurs RFC
　ISLW TW7....................................6
Centre Court Shopping Centre
　WIM/MER SW19...........................33
Charrington Bowl
　SURB KT6..................................42
Chartfield School
　PUT/ROE SW15...........................16
Chase Bridge Primary School
　WHTN TW2.................................12
Chatsworth J & I School
　HSLW TW3.................................12
Cheam Common J & I School
　WPK KT4...................................43
Chennestone Community School
　SUN TW16.................................26
Chessington Cricket Club
　CHSGTN KT9..............................44
Chessington Community College
　& Sports Centre
　CHSGTN KT9..............................45
Chessington Golf Club
　CHSGTN KT9..............................45
Chessington World of Adventures
　CHSGTN KT9..............................44
Chiswick Community School
　CHSWK W4...................................8
Chiswick House
　CHSWK W4...................................8
Christ Church CE Infant School
　NWMAL KT3................................31
Christ Church CE Junior School
　NWMAL KT3................................31
Christ Church CE Primary School
　BRYLDS KT5...............................36
Christs School
　RCHPK/HAM TW10.......................14
Chrysanthemum Clinic
　CHSWK W4...................................4
Churchill College
　RYNPK SW20...............................32
The Churchill Medical Centre
　KUTN/CMB KT2............................2
Cineworld
　FELT TW13.................................18
Civil Service Sports Ground
　CHSWK W4...................................4
Clarendon Special School
　HPTN TW12................................20
The Clinic
　RCHPK/HAM TW10.......................14
Colet Court
　BARN SW13.................................9
Collis Primary School
　TEDD TW11................................20

...ombe Girls School
NWMAL KT3 ....31 C4
...ombe Hill Golf Club
KUTN/CMB KT2 ....31 C2
...ombe Hill J & I School
NWMAL KT3 ....31 C3
...ombe Wood Golf Club
....3 K1
...rinthian Casuals FC
SURB KT6 ....41 H2
...ddington Cemetery
WPK KT4 ....43 C1
...ddington CP School
WPK KT4 ....43 E2
...rell Primary School
RCH/KEW TW9 ....14 D1
...nmead School
HPTN TW12 ....27 H2
...utsche Schule
RCHPK/HAM TW10 ....22 A1
...ana Fountain
E/WMO/HCT KT8 ....29 E4
...ckwell's Industrial Estate
EBED/NFELT TW14 ....10 C3
...nhead (Wimbledon College
Preparatory School)
WIM/MER SW19 ....33 E2
...rchester Primary School
WPK KT4 ....38 D5
...uglas Bader Foundation
PUT/ROE SW15 ....16 B4
...ndonald Primary School
WIM/MER SW19 ....33 C2
...sart School
KUTN/CMB KT2 ....22 A4
SURB KT6 ....36 B4
...ing Road Trading Estate
BTFD TW8 ....7 E1
...st Molesey Cricket Club
E/WMO/HCT KT8 ....28 B5
...st Sheen Cemetery
RCHPK/HAM TW10 ....14 D3
...st Sheen Primary School
MORT/ESHN SW14 ....15 H2
...en Walk Shopping Centre
KUT/HW KT1 ....2 C5
...ngham Primary School
CHSGTN KT9 ....45 E1
...ott School
PUT/ROE SW15 ....16 D4
...bassy of the Holy See
WIM/MER SW19 ....24 D3
...berhurst School
ESH/CLAY KT10 ....34 C4
...ber Sports Club
ESH/CLAY KT10 ....34 B5
...som & Ewell High School
HOR/WEW KT19 ....42 B5
...her College
THDIT KT7 ....34 D4
...olution House
RCH/KEW TW9 ....7 F5
...vell Athletics Track
HOR/WEW KT19 ....42 C4
...irfield Trade Park
KUT/HW KT1 ....3 F7
...rnell House Medical Centre
HSLW TW3 ....5 E4
...tham Airparcs Leisure Centre
FELT TW13 ....19 E2
...tham Athletics Arena
EBED/NFELT TW14 ....10 B5
...thambrook Industrial Estate
FELT TW13 ....18 C3
...tham Community College
FELT TW13 ....18 D2
...tham Hill Infant School
FELT TW13 ....18 A3
...tham Hill Junior School
FELT TW13 ....18 A3
...tham & Hounslow Borough FC
EBED/NFELT TW14 ....10 B5
...tham Superbowl
FELT TW13 ....18 C2
...m House Cinema
RCH/KEW TW9 ....14 A3
...e Ways Business Centre
FELT TW13 ....18 C3
...e Foot Clinic
WIM/MER SW19 ....33 F1
...rge Lane Primary School
FELT TW13 ....27 F1
...eehold Industrial Centre
HSLWW TW4 ....10 D3
...lham FC (Craven Cottage)
PUT/ROE SW15 ....9 H4
...ller Smith & Turner Sports Club
CHSWK W4 ....8 D4
...lwell Golf Club
HPTN TW12 ....20 C4
...flac Sports Ground Pavilion
SUN TW16 ....26 B3
...e Garth Road Industrial Centre
MRDN SM4 ....38 D4
...een Lecky Health Centre
PUT/ROE SW15 ....17 E2
...nlyn Medical Centre
E/WMO/HCT KT8 ....34 B2

Glenthorne High School
CHEAM SM3 ....39 H5
Gosbury Hill Health Centre
CHSGTN KT9 ....41 F3
Granard Primary School
PUT/ROE SW15 ....16 C4
Grand Avenue Primary School
BRYLDS KT5 ....37 F4
Grasshoppers RFC
ISLW TW7 ....6 A2
Grassroots School
HPTN TW12 ....27 H3
Great West Trading Estate
BTFD TW8 ....6 C2
Green Dragon Primary School
BTFD TW8 ....7 F1
Green Lane Primary School
WPK KT4 ....38 C4
Greenmead Primary School
PUT/ROE SW15 ....16 C3
The Green School for Girls
ISLW TW7 ....6 B3
Grey Court School
RCHPK/HAM TW10 ....22 A3
Grist Memorial Sports Club
E/WMO/HCT KT8 ....34 D2
Grove House (Froebel College)
PUT/ROE SW15 ....16 A4
Grove Park Primary School
CHSWK W4 ....8 B2
Grove Road Primary School
HSLW TW3 ....11 H2
The Groves Medical Centre
NWMAL KT3 ....31 H5
Gumley House Convent School
ISLW TW7 ....13 F1
Gunnersbury Catholic School
BTFD TW8 ....6 D1
Hall Grove Wimbledon
RYNPK SW20 ....33 E3
Hall School Wimbledon
Junior Department
RYNPK SW20 ....24 B3
Ham Health Clinic
RCHPK/HAM TW10 ....21 H3
Ham House (NT)
RCHPK/HAM TW10 ....21 H1
Hammersmith Apollo
HMSMTH W6 ....9 H1
Hammersmith Industrial Estate
HMSMTH W6 ....9 H2
Hammersmith New Cemetery
RCH/KEW TW9 ....8 A5
Ham & Petersham CC
RCHPK/HAM TW10 ....22 A4
Hampton Cemetery
HPTN TW12 ....27 H2
Hampton Community College
HPTN TW12 ....19 H5
Hampton Court House School
E/WMO/HCT KT8 ....28 D4
Hampton Court Palace
E/WMO/HCT KT8 ....29 E5
Hampton Court Palace Golf Club
SURB KT6 ....35 H2
Hampton Farm Industrial Estate
FELT TW13 ....19 F3
Hampton FC
HPTN TW12 ....28 A3
Hampton Hill Junior School
HPTN TW12 ....20 B5
Hampton Infant School
HPTN TW12 ....27 G2
Hampton Junior School
HPTN TW12 ....27 H3
The Hampton Medical Centre
HPTN TW12 ....27 H2
Hampton Open Air Pool
HPTN TW12 ....28 B2
Hampton School
HPTN TW12 ....19 H5
Hampton Wick Infants School
TEDD TW11 ....29 H2
Hanworth Trading Estate
FELT TW13 ....19 F3
Harrodian School
BARN SW13 ....9 E3
Haslemere Industrial Estate
EBED/NFELT TW14 ....10 B3
Hatfield Primary School
MRDN SM4 ....39 F3
Hawkedale GM School
SUN TW16 ....26 A5
The Hawker Centre
KUTN/CMB KT2 ....22 A5
Hawkins Clinic
PUT/ROE SW15 ....17 E2
RYNPK SW20 ....32 A3
Health & Vitality Osteopathic Clinic
HOR/WEW KT19 ....42 C4
Heath Business Centre
HSLW TW3 ....12 B2
Heathfield Primary School
WHTN TW2 ....19 H1
The Heathland School
HSLWW TW4 ....11 G4
Heathmere Primary School
PUT/ROE SW15 ....24 B1

Heathrow International Trading Estate
HSLWW TW4 ....10 C1
Helston Court Business Centre
WIM/MER SW19 ....24 C5
Heston Community School
HEST TW5 ....4 D3
Heston Community Sports Hall
HEST TW5 ....4 D3
Heston Industrial Mall
HEST TW5 ....4 C3
Heston Infant School
HEST TW5 ....4 D3
Heston Junior School
HEST TW5 ....4 D3
Heston Park CC
HEST TW5 ....4 C2
Heston Swimming Baths
HEST TW5 ....4 C2
Hillcroft College
SURB KT6 ....36 B3
Hillcross Primary School
MRDN SM4 ....39 G1
Hinchley Wood Primary School
ESH/CLAY KT10 ....40 B1
Hinchley Wood School
& Sixth Form Centre
ESH/CLAY KT10 ....40 B1
Hogarth Business Park
CHSWK W4 ....8 D2
Hogarth's House
CHSWK W4 ....8 C2
Holborn College Independent School
HMSMTH W6 ....9 H1
The Hollyfield School
SURB KT6 ....36 B2
Hollymount Primary School
RYNPK SW20 ....32 D3
Holy Cross Preparatory School
KUTN/CMB KT2 ....31 F2
Holy Cross RC Convent School
NWMAL KT3 ....37 G1
Holy Trinity CE Primary School
RCHPK/HAM TW10 ....14 D2
Holy Trinity Primary School
WIM/MER SW19 ....33 H1
Hook Rise South Industrial Park
CHSGTN KT9 ....41 G2
Horton Country Park
HOR/WEW KT19 ....45 H2
Hotham Primary School
PUT/ROE SW15 ....17 E2
Hounslow Business Park
HSLW TW3 ....11 H2
Hounslow Cricket Club
HSLW TW3 ....4 C5
Hounslow Cemetery
HSLWW TW4 ....11 G5
Hounslow College
Independent School
FELT TW13 ....19 E4
Hounslow Heath Golf Club
HSLWW TW4 ....11 E3
Hounslow Heath Infant School
HSLWW TW4 ....11 F1
Hounslow Heath Junior School
HSLWW TW4 ....11 F1
Hounslow Manor School
HSLW TW3 ....12 A1
Hounslow Manor Sports Hall
HSLW TW3 ....12 A1
Hounslow Town Primary School
HSLW TW3 ....12 B1
Hurlingham Business Park
FUL/PGN SW6 ....17 H1
Hurlingham & Chelsea
Secondary School
FUL/PGN SW6 ....17 H1
Hurlingham House
FUL/PGN SW6 ....17 G1
Hurlingham Private School
PUT/ROE SW15 ....17 G2
Hurst Park Primary School
E/WMO/HCT KT8 ....27 H5
Ibstock Place School
PUT/ROE SW15 ....15 H4
Imber Court Trading Estate
E/WMO/HCT KT8 ....34 C3
Innkeepers Lodge
CHEAM SM3 ....39 H5
Inwood Business Centre
HSLW TW3 ....12 A2
The Islamic Grammar School
WAND/EARL SW18 ....17 G5
Isleworth Cemetery
ISLW TW7 ....6 B5
Isleworth Recreation Centre
ISLW TW7 ....13 E2
Isleworth & Syon School for Boys
ISLW TW7 ....5 H3
Isleworth Town Primary School
ISLW TW7 ....6 A5
Ivybridge Primary School
TWK TW1 ....13 E4
Ivybridge Retail Park
ISLW TW7 ....13 E3
Jack & Jill School
HPTN TW12 ....27 H1
WHTN TW2 ....20 D2

John Nightingale School
E/WMO/HCT KT8 ....27 G5
John Paul II RC School
WIM/MER SW19 ....17 E5
Joseph Hood Primary School
RYNPK SW20 ....33 F4
Jurys Inn Hotel
HTHAIR TW6 ....10 A1
Kempton Park Racecourse
SUN TW16 ....26 C2
Kenyngton Manor Primary School
SUN TW16 ....18 B5
Kew Bridge Steam Museum
BTFD TW8 ....7 G1
Kew College
RCH/KEW TW9 ....7 H3
Kew Gardens (Royal Botanic Gardens)
BTFD TW8 ....7 F4
Kew Palace
RCH/KEW TW9 ....7 F3
Kew Retail Park
RCH/KEW TW9 ....8 A4
Kew Riverside Primary School
RCH/KEW TW9 ....8 A5
King Athelstan Primary School
KUT/HW KT1 ....2 E6
The Kingfisher Sports Centre
KUT/HW KT1 ....2 D5
Kings College School
WIM/MER SW19 ....32 D1
Kingsgate Business Centre
KUTN/CMB KT2 ....2 C2
Kings House School
RCHPK/HAM TW10 ....14 C3
Kingsmeadow Athletics Centre
KUT/HW KT1 ....3 H7
Kingston Business Centre
CHSGTN KT9 ....41 F2
Kingston Cemetery
KUT/HW KT1 ....3 G6
Kingston College
of Further Education
KUT/HW KT1 ....2 B6
Kingston College Theatre
KUT/HW KT1 ....2 B6
Kingston Crematorium
KUT/HW KT1 ....3 G7
Kingston Crown Court
KUT/HW KT1 ....2 B6
Kingston Grammar School
KUT/HW KT1 ....2 E4
Kingston Hospital
KUTN/CMB KT2 ....3 J2
Kingstonian FC
KUT/HW KT1 ....3 J7
Kingston University
BRYLDS KT5 ....36 D2
KUT/HW KT1 ....2 D7
KUTN/CMB KT2 ....23 G5
KUTN/CMB KT2 ....31 G2
PUT/ROE SW15 ....24 A2
Kingsway Business Park
HPTN TW12 ....27 G3
Knollmead Primary School
BRYLDS KT5 ....42 B1
The Lady Eleanor Holles School
HPTN TW12 ....20 A5
Lampton School
HSLW TW3 ....4 D4
Langdon Down Centre
TEDD TW11 ....29 H2
Latchmere J & I School
KUTN/CMB KT2 ....30 C1
The Latymer Preparatory School
HMSMTH W6 ....9 F1
Lazards Sports Club
SUN TW16 ....26 C3
Leigh Close Industrial Estate
NWMAL KT3 ....37 G1
Linden Bridge School
WPK KT4 ....42 D2
Linden Lodge School
WIM/MER SW19 ....25 F1
Lindon Bennett School
FELT TW13 ....19 E5
Linley House School
BRYLDS KT5 ....36 C3
Liongate Hotel
E/WMO/HCT KT8 ....29 E5
Lion House School
PUT/ROE SW15 ....17 E2
Little Eden & Eden High School
FELT TW13 ....19 E4
London Butterfly House
ISLW TW7 ....6 C4
London Cornish RFC
PUT/ROE SW15 ....24 A3
London Irish RFC
SUN TW16 ....26 B3
London School of Economics
Sports Club
NWMAL KT3 ....37 G3
London Scottish Golf Club
WIM/MER SW19 ....24 C3
London Welsh FC
RCH/KEW TW9 ....14 B1
London Wetland Centre
BARN SW13 ....9 G4

Long Ditton County Infant School
SURB KT6 .... 35 H5

Longford Community School
EBED/NFELT TW14 .... 10 A5

Longford Industrial Estate
HPTN TW12 .... 28 A1

Lovelace Primary School
CHSGTN KT9 .... 40 D4

Lowther Primary School
BARN SW13 .... 9 F2

The Malden Centre
NWMAL KT3 .... 38 A1

Malden Golf Club
NWMAL KT3 .... 31 H4

Malden Manor Primary School
NWMAL KT3 .... 37 H4

Malden Parochial Primary School
WPK KT4 .... 37 H5

The Mall School
WHTN TW2 .... 20 C3

Manor Drive Health Centre
WPK KT4 .... 38 A5

Maple Grove Business Centre
HSLWW TW3 .... 10 D2

Maple Industrial Estate
FELT TW13 .... 18 B2

Maple Infant School
SURB KT6 .... 36 A2

Marble Hill House
TWK TW1 .... 13 H5

Marlborough Primary School
ISLW TW7 .... 6 B4

Marlborough Trading Estate
RCH/KEW TW9 .... 8 A4

Marshgate Primary School
RCHPK/HAM TW10 .... 14 C3

Marymount International School
KUTN/CMB KT2 .... 31 F2

Mary Wallace Theatre
TWK TW1 .... 21 F1

Maswell Park Health Centre
HSLW TW3 .... 12 B3

The Mead Infant School
WPK KT4 .... 43 E2

Meadlands Primary School
RCHPK/HAM TW10 .... 21 H4

Megabowl
KUT/HW KT1 .... 2 D4

Merlin School
PUT/ROE SW15 .... 17 E3

Merton Adult College
RYNPK SW20 .... 33 F5

Merton College
MRDN SM4 .... 39 G3

Merton Park Primary School
WIM/MER SW19 .... 33 G4

Merton Road Industrial Estate
WAND/EARL SW18 .... 17 H5

Metro Industrial Centre
ISLW TW7 .... 5 H5

Metropolitan Police FC
E/WMO/HCT KT8 .... 34 C3

Mill Farm Business Park
HSLWW TW4 .... 11 F5

Molesey Lock
E/WMO/HCT KT8 .... 28 D5

Moor Lane Junior School
CHSGTN KT9 .... 41 G4

Morden Cemetery
MRDN SM4 .... 38 D3

Morden First School
MRDN SM4 .... 39 H2

Morden Park Pool
MRDN SM4 .... 39 G2

Mortlake Cemetery
MORT/ESHN SW14 .... 15 H1

Mortlake Crematorium
RCH/KEW TW9 .... 8 A5

Mount Medical Centre
FELT TW13 .... 19 F2

The Mount Primary School
NWMAL KT3 .... 3 K6

Murky Puddle Theatre
NWMAL KT3 .... 32 A5

Museum of Richmond
TWK TW1 .... 14 A3

**Museum of Rugby
& Twickenham Stadium Tours**
WHTN TW2 .... 12 D4

Musical Museum
BTFD TW8 .... 7 F2

The National Archives
RCH/KEW TW9 .... 8 A3

National Physical Laboratory
TEDD TW11 .... 28 D1

**NEC Harlequins RFC
(Twickenham Stoop Stadium)**
WHTN TW2 .... 12 D5

Nelson Hospital
RYNPK SW20 .... 33 G4

Nelson Primary School
WHTN TW2 .... 12 A4

New Brentford Cemetery
HSLW TW3 .... 4 C5

New Chiswick Pool
CHSWK W4 .... 8 D3

Newland House School
TWK TW1 .... 21 E4

New Victoria Hospital
KUTN/CMB KT2 .... 31 H3

Nonsuch House Hotel
EW KT17 .... 43 H4

Nonsuch Primary School
EW KT17 .... 43 G4

North East Surrey Crematorium
NWMAL KT3 .... 38 D3

North Feltham Trading Estate
EBED/NFELT TW14 .... 10 C2

**Northfields Prospect
Business Centre**
PUT/ROE SW15 .... 17 C2

The Norwegian School
WIM/MER SW19 .... 32 D2

Norwood Green Infant School
NWDGN UB2 .... 4 B1

Norwood Green Junior School
NWDGN UB2 .... 4 B1

Oak Hill Health Centre
SURB KT6 .... 36 B3

Oaklands School
ISLW TW7 .... 12 C1

Oak Lane Cemetery
TWK TW1 .... 13 F5

Oak Lane Medical Centre
TWK TW1 .... 13 G5

Odeon Cinema
KUT/HW KT1 .... 2 D4
RCH/KEW TW9 .... 14 A3
WIM/MER SW19 .... 33 H2

Old Barnes Cemetery
BARN SW13 .... 9 G5

Oldfield House Special School
HPTN TW12 .... 27 C3

Old Tiffinians Sports Ground
E/WMO/HCT KT8 .... 34 D2

Old Vicarage School
RCHPK/HAM TW10 .... 14 B4

Orange Tree Theatre
RCH/KEW TW9 .... 14 B2

The Orchard Junior School
HSLWW TW4 .... 11 H2

The Orchard School
E/WMO/HCT KT8 .... 34 C2

Oriel Primary School
FELT TW13 .... 19 F3

Orleans House Gallery
TWK TW1 .... 21 G1

Orleans Infant School
TWK TW1 .... 13 G5

Osier Industrial Estate
WAND/EARL SW18 .... 17 H2

Osterley Park & House (NT)
ISLW TW7 .... 5 F2

**Our Lady Immaculate RC
Primary School**
BRYLDS KT5 .... 37 E5

**Our Lady of Victorys
RC Primary School**
PUT/ROE SW15 .... 17 E5

**Our Lady Queen of Heaven
RC Primary School**
WIM/MER SW19 .... 17 E5

**Our Lady & St Johns
RC Primary School**
BTFD TW8 .... 6 D1

Paddock School
PUT/ROE SW15 .... 16 A1

Palm House
RCH/KEW TW9 .... 7 G4

Park Hill School
KUTN/CMB KT2 .... 3 H1

Parkside Hospital
WIM/MER SW19 .... 25 E3

**The Patrick Doody Clinic
& Health Centre**
WIM/MER SW19 .... 33 H2

Pattinson Clinic
RCH/KEW TW9 .... 14 A3

The Paul Robeson Theatre
HSLW TW3 .... 12 A1

Pavilion Restaurant
RCH/KEW TW9 .... 7 F5

Pelham Primary School
WIM/MER SW19 .... 33 H2

The Petersham Hotel
RCHPK/HAM TW10 .... 14 B5

Pools in the Park
RCH/KEW TW9 .... 14 A2

Poplar Primary School
WIM/MER SW19 .... 33 H5

The Pountney Clinic
HSLW TW3 .... 11 H1

Premier Inn
BTFD TW8 .... 7 F2
CHSGTN KT9 .... 44 D3
FUL/PGN SW6 .... 17 F1
HOR/WEW KT19 .... 42 D4
WHTN TW2 .... 20 B1

Princess of Wales Conservatory
RCH/KEW TW9 .... 7 G3

Prospect House School
PUT/ROE SW15 .... 17 E5

Putney Animal Hospital
PUT/ROE SW15 .... 17 E2

Putney Arts Theatre
PUT/ROE SW15 .... 17 E2

**Putney Exchange
Shopping Centre**
PUT/ROE SW15 .... 17 E2

Putney High School
PUT/ROE SW15 .... 17 E3

Putney Leisure Centre
PUT/ROE SW15 .... 16 D2

Putney Lower Common Cemetery
BARN SW13 .... 9 G5

Putneymead Medical Centre
PUT/ROE SW15 .... 16 D2

Putney Park School
PUT/ROE SW15 .... 16 C2

Putney School of Art
PUT/ROE SW15 .... 17 F2

Putney Town Social & Bowls Club
PUT/ROE SW15 .... 9 H5

Putney Vale Cemetery
PUT/ROE SW15 .... 24 B2

Putney Vale Crematorium
PUT/ROE SW15 .... 24 B2

Queen Charlotte's Cottage
RCH/KEW TW9 .... 7 E5

Queen Mary's University Hospital
PUT/ROE SW15 .... 16 B4

The Queens CE Primary School
RCH/KEW TW9 .... 7 G3

Queens Manor Primary School
FUL/PGN SW6 .... 9 H3

Queens Medical Centre
RCHPK/HAM TW10 .... 14 C3

Rainbow Industrial Estate
RYNPK SW20 .... 32 C4

Raynes Park High School
RYNPK SW20 .... 32 C5

Raynes Park Sports Ground
RYNPK SW20 .... 32 B4

Raynes Park Vale FC
RYNPK SW20 .... 39 E2

Red Lion Business Park
SURB KT6 .... 41 G1

Rewards Centre
HSLW TW3 .... 12 B1

Reynard Mills Trading Estate
BTFD TW8 .... 6 D1

Ricards Lodge High School
WIM/MER SW19 .... 25 G4

**Richmond Park
National Nature Reserve**
RCHPK/HAM TW10 .... 23 H2

**Richmond Adult
& Community College**
RCH/KEW TW9 .... 14 A2

**Richmond American International
University**
RCHPK/HAM TW10 .... 14 B4

The Richmond Clinic
RCH/KEW TW9 .... 14 C2

Richmond Community College
TWK TW1 .... 21 E1

Richmond FC
RCH/KEW TW9 .... 14 A2

Richmond Gate Hotel
RCHPK/HAM TW10 .... 14 B5

The Richmond Golf Club
RCHPK/HAM TW10 .... 22 B2

**The Richmond Green
Medical Centre**
RCH/KEW TW9 .... 14 A3

Richmond Hill Hotel
RCHPK/HAM TW10 .... 14 B5

Richmond House School
HPTN TW12 .... 19 G5

Richmond Magistrates Court
RCH/KEW TW9 .... 14 A2

Richmond Park Golf Club
PUT/ROE SW15 .... 15 H5

Richmond Road Medical Centre
KUTN/CMB KT2 .... 2 C1

Richmond Theatre
RCH/KEW TW9 .... 14 A2

Richmond upon Thames College
WHTN TW2 .... 12 D5

River Gardens Business Centre
EBED/NFELT TW14 .... 10 C2

Riversdale Primary School
WAND/EARL SW18 .... 25 H1

Riverside Quarter
WAND/EARL SW18 .... 17 H2

Riverside Studios Cinema
BARN SW13 .... 9 G1

Riverview CE Primary School
HOR/WEW KT19 .... 42 B3

Robin Hood Primary School
KUTN/CMB KT2 .... 23 G5

The Roche School
WAND/EARL SW18 .... 17 H3

Roehampton Church School
PUT/ROE SW15 .... 16 C5

The Roehampton Priory Hospital
PUT/ROE SW15 .... 16 A2

Roehampton Recreation Centre
PUT/ROE SW15 .... 16 A5

Roehampton University
PUT/ROE SW15 .... 17 F4

**Roehampton University
(Digby Stuart College)**
PUT/ROE SW15 .... 16 A3

**Roehampton University
(Froebel College)**
PUT/ROE SW15 16

**Roehampton University
(Southlands College)**
PUT/ROE SW15 16

Rokeby School
KUTN/CMB KT2 31

Ronald Rose Primary School
WIM/MER SW19 17

Rosary RC Infant School
HEST TW5 4

Roselands Clinic
NWMAL KT3 37

Rose of Kingston (Kingston Theatre)
KUT/HW KT1 2

Rosslyn Park RFC
PUT/ROE SW15 16

The Rotunda
KUT/HW KT1 2

Rowan Preparatory School
ESH/CLAY KT10 44

Rowans School
RYNPK SW20 32

The Royal Ballet School
RCHPK/HAM TW10 14

Royal Botanic Gardens Kew School
RCH/KEW TW9 7

Royal Hospital
RCH/KEW TW9 14

Royal Hospital for Neuro-disability
PUT/ROE SW15 17

Royal Hospital & Home
PUT/ROE SW15 16

Royal Mid-Surrey Golf Club
RCH/KEW TW9 14

Royal Military School of Music
WHTN TW2 12

Royal Wimbledon Golf Club
WIM/MER SW19 24

The Russell JMI School
RCHPK/HAM TW10 22

The Russell School
RCHPK/HAM TW10 22

Rutlish School
RYNPK SW20 33

**Sacred Heart Catholic
Primary School**
PUT/ROE SW15 16

Sacred Heart RC Primary School
NWMAL KT3 38
TEDD TW11 29

St Agathas RC Primary School
KUTN/CMB KT2 30

St Albans RC Aided Primary School
E/WMO/HCT KT8 34

St Anne's Special School
MRDN SM4 39

St Anthonys Hospital
WPK KT4 39

St Catherines School
TWK TW1 21

St Cecilia's CE Primary School
WAND/EARL SW18 17

St Clare Business Park
HPTN TW12 28

St Edmunds RC Primary School
WHTN TW2 20

St Elizabeths RC Primary School
RCHPK/HAM TW10 14

St Georges Industrial Estate
KUTN/CMB KT2 30

St Ignatius RC Primary School
SUN TW16 26

St James Independent School
TWK TW1 21

St James RC Primary School
WHTN TW2 20

St John Fisher RC Primary School
RYNPK SW20 38

St Johns CE Primary School
KUT/HW KT1 2

St John the Baptist CE Junior School
KUT/HW KT1 2

St Josephs Primary School
WAND/EARL SW18 17

St Josephs RC Primary School
E/WMO/HCT KT8 34

St Lawrence Business Centre
FELT TW13 19

St Lawrence Catholic School
FELT TW13 19

St Lawrence Junior School
E/WMO/HCT KT8 34

St Lukes CE Primary School
KUTN/CMB KT2 31

St Margarets Business Centre
TWK TW1 13

St Marks Catholic School
HSLW TW3 11

**St Mary Magdalens
Catholic Primary School**
MORT/ESHN SW14 15

**St Mary & St Peters CE
Primary School**
TEDD TW11 20

St Marys CE Junior School
THDIT KT7 35

Marys CE Primary School
CHSGTN KT9 ....41 F5
Mary's CE Primary School
PUT/ROE SW15 ....17 E1
Marys CE Primary School
TWK TW1 ....13 F5
Mary's College
University of Surrey
TWK TW1 ....21 E3
Mary's Junior School
TWK TW1 ....13 G5
Mary's RC Primary School
CHSWK W4 ....8 D1
Marys RC Primary School
ISLW TW7 ....13 F1
Matthews CE Primary School
WIM/MER SW19 ....33 H2
Matthews CE Primary School
RYNPK SW20 ....32 B3
SURB KT6 ....36 B4
Michaels & St Martins RC
Primary School
NSLWW TW4 ....11 G1
Michaels CE Primary School
WAND/EARL SW18 ....17 G5
St Michael Steiner School
WAND/EARL SW18 ....17 H3
Pauls Catholic College
SUN TW16 ....26 B3
Pauls CE Junior School
UTN/CMB KT2 ....3 H1
Pauls CE Primary School
BTFD TW8 ....7 E2
CHSGTN KT9 ....41 F3
Paul's Primary School
WMSMTH W6 ....9 H1
Pauls RC Primary School
THDIT KT7 ....34 D4
Pauls School
BARN SW13 ....9 G1
Peters CE Primary School
WMSMTH W6 ....9 F1
Philips School
CHSGTN KT9 ....41 E5
Richards with St Andrews CE
Primary School
CHPK/HAM TW10 ....21 G3
Stephens CE Junior School
TWK TW1 ....13 F4
Cannon Corner Retail Park
PWMAL KT3 ....38 B1
Ken International School
MORT/ESHN SW14 ....15 H2
Ken Lane Health Centre
MORT/ESHN SW14 ....15 F1
Ken Lawn Tennis & Squash Club
MORT/ESHN SW14 ....15 F3
Ken Mount Primary School
CHPK/HAM TW10 ....15 E3
Ken Sports Centre
MORT/ESHN SW14 ....15 G1
Springdale Primary School
WAND/EARL SW18 ....25 G1
Spting Star House
(childrens Hospice)
PTN TW12 ....27 G1
Dewsbury House School
URB KT6 ....41 E1
Priorglade Business Park
CHSGTN KT9 ....44 D5
Quillberry Green Primary School
ISLW TW7 ....6 B5
Throborough School
URB KT6 ....41 F2
Southfields Clinic
WAND/EARL SW18 ....17 H4
thfields Community College
WAND/EARL SW18 ....25 H1
thmead Primary School
WIM/MER SW19 ....25 F1
th Thames College
PUT/ROE SW15 ....16 A4
PUT/ROE SW15 ....17 E3

Southville Infant School
EBED/NFELT TW14 ....18 A1
South West Middlesex
Crematorium
FELT TW13 ....19 F1
Sparrow Farm Community
Junior School
EW KT17 ....43 G4
Sparrow Farm Infant School
EBED/NFELT TW14 ....10 D5
Sparrow Farm Junior School
EBED/NFELT TW14 ....10 D5
Spring Grove Primary School
ISLW TW7 ....5 G5
Springwell Infant School
HEST TW5 ....4 B3
Springwell Junior School
HEST TW5 ....4 B3
Staines RFC
FELT TW13 ....18 B5
Stanley J & I School
TEDD TW11 ....20 D4
Stoneleigh First School
EW KT17 ....43 G3
Strand on the Green J & I School
CHSWK W4 ....7 H2
Strathmore School
RCHPK/HAM TW10 ....22 A1
Strawberry Hill Golf Club
WHTN TW2 ....20 D3
The Study Preparatory School
WIM/MER SW19 ....25 E5
The Study School
NWMAL KT3 ....37 H2
Summit Business Park
SUN TW16 ....26 B2
Sunbury Court Conference Centre
SUN TW16 ....27 E4
Sunbury Health Centre
SUN TW16 ....26 B4
Sunbury Leisure Centre
SUN TW16 ....26 A3
Sunbury Manor School
SUN TW16 ....26 A3
Sun Life Trading Estate
EBED/NFELT TW14 ....10 B1
Surbiton Business Centre
SURB KT6 ....36 A3
Surbiton Cemetery
KUT/HW KT1 ....36 D1
Surbiton Golf Club
CHSGTN KT9 ....40 C3
Surbiton High School
KUT/HW KT1 ....36 B1
Surbiton Hospital
SURB KT6 ....36 B3
Surbiton Natural Health Centre
SURB KT6 ....36 B3
Surrey County Hall
KUT/HW KT1 ....2 B7
Swedish School
BARN SW13 ....9 F2
Syon House
BTFD TW8 ....6 D4
Syon Park
BTFD TW8 ....6 D5
Syon Park School
ISLW TW7 ....6 D4
Tamian Industrial Estate
HSLWW TW4 ....10 D2
Teddington Business Park
TEDD TW11 ....21 E5
Teddington Cemetery
TEDD TW11 ....20 D4
Teddington Clinic
TEDD TW11 ....28 D1
Teddington Lock
TEDD TW11 ....21 G4
Teddington Memorial Hospital
TEDD TW11 ....28 D1
Teddington Pool & Fitness Centre
TEDD TW11 ....21 F5

Teddington School
TEDD TW11 ....30 A1
The Teddington Theatre Club
E/WMO/HCT KT8 ....34 C2
Temperate House
RCH/KEW TW9 ....7 G5
Territorial & Army Volunteer
Reserve Centre
KUT/HW KT1 ....36 A1
Thames Ditton Infant School
THDIT KT7 ....35 E3
Thames Ditton Junior School
THDIT KT7 ....35 E4
Theatre of the Dispossessed
WIM/MER SW19 ....25 E1
Tiffin Girls School
KUTN/CMB KT2 ....30 B1
Tiffin School & Sports Centre
KUTN/CMB KT2 ....2 E4
Tolworth CP School
SURB KT6 ....36 C5
Tolworth Girls School
SURB KT6 ....41 G2
Tolworth Recreation Centre
SURB KT6 ....41 G2
Tower House School
MORT/ESHN SW14 ....15 F2
Trafalgar Primary & Infant School
WHTN TW2 ....20 C2
Travelodge
BTFD TW8 ....7 F2
HEST TW5 ....4 A2
KUTN/CMB KT2 ....2 D4
SURB KT6 ....37 E5
The Treaty Centre
HSLW TW3 ....12 A1
Tudor Lodge Health Centre
WIM/MER SW19 ....25 E1
Twickenham Cemetery
WHTN TW2 ....20 A1
Twickenham Park Health Centre
TWK TW1 ....13 H4
Twickenham Preparatory School
HPTN TW12 ....28 A3
Twickenham Stadium
ISLW TW7 ....12 D4
Twickenham Trading Estate
TWK TW1 ....13 E4
Unicorn School
RCH/KEW TW9 ....7 G4
University of London
Athletics Ground
NWMAL KT3 ....38 B2
University of Westminster
CHSWK W4 ....8 B4
Ursuline High School
RYNPK SW20 ....33 E2
Ursuline Preparatory School
RYNPK SW20 ....33 E2
Victoria Junior School
FELT TW13 ....18 C1
Victory Business Centre
ISLW TW7 ....13 E2
The Vine Clinic
KUTN/CMB KT2 ....30 B1
Vine Medical Centre
E/WMO/HCT KT8 ....28 B5
The Vineyard Primary School
RCHPK/HAM TW10 ....14 B4
The Waldegrave Clinic
TEDD TW11 ....21 E5
Waldegrave Girls School
WHTN TW2 ....20 C3
Wallbrook Business Centre
HSLWW TW4 ....10 C1
Wandsworth County Court
PUT/ROE SW15 ....17 F3
Watermans Arts, Cinema
& Theatre Centre
BTFD TW8 ....7 F2
Waterside Business Centre
ISLW TW7 ....13 G2

Wellington Primary School
HSLW TW3 ....4 C5
West Ewell Infant School
HOR/WEW KT19 ....42 C4
Westfields Primary School
BARN SW13 ....9 E5
West Hill Primary School
WAND/EARL SW18 ....17 H3
West Middlesex University Hospital
ISLW TW7 ....6 B5
Westmoor Community Clinic
PUT/ROE SW15 ....16 B5
Weston Green School
THDIT KT7 ....34 D5
West Park Hospital
EPSOM KT18 ....45 F5
West Thames College
ISLW TW7 ....5 H4
West Wimbledon Primary School
RYNPK SW20 ....32 C5
Whitelands College
PUT/ROE SW15 ....16 A5
Whitton Health Clinic
WHTN TW2 ....20 A1
Whitton School
WHTN TW2 ....20 A2
Whitton Sports & Fitness Centre
WHTN TW2 ....20 A2
William Hogarth School
CHSWK W4 ....8 D2
Willington School
WIM/MER SW19 ....33 G1
Wimbledon Chase Primary School
RYNPK SW20 ....33 F3
Wimbledon Common Golf Club
WIM/MER SW19 ....24 C5
Wimbledon Common
Pre-Preparatory School
WIM/MER SW19 ....32 D1
Wimbledon High School
WIM/MER SW19 ....33 F1
Wimbledon House School
WIM/MER SW19 ....33 G3
Wimbledon Lawn Tennis Museum
WIM/MER SW19 ....25 F3
Wimbledon Magistrates Court
WIM/MER SW19 ....33 H1
Wimbledon Park Athletics Track
WIM/MER SW19 ....25 G2
Wimbledon Park Golf Club
WIM/MER SW19 ....25 G3
Wimbledon Park Primary School
WIM/MER SW19 ....25 H2
Wimbledon RFC
RYNPK SW20 ....32 A2
Wimbledon School of Art
WIM/MER SW19 ....33 F3
WIM/MER SW19 ....33 H2
Wimbledon Squash
& Badminton Club
WIM/MER SW19 ....33 F2
Wimbledon Theatre
WIM/MER SW19 ....33 H2
Wimbledon Windmill
WIM/MER SW19 ....24 D3
Wolfson Medical Centre
RYNPK SW20 ....32 B2
Worple Primary School
ISLW TW7 ....13 F2
Worton Hall Industrial Estate
ISLW TW7 ....12 D2
Wyke Green Golf Club
ISLW TW7 ....6 A2

Acknowledgements

Schools address data provided by Education Direct.

Petrol station information supplied by Johnsons.

Garden centre information provided by:

Garden Centre Association ⬡ Britains best garden centres

🌿 Wyevale Garden Centres

The statement on the front cover of this atlas is sourced, selected and quoted
from a reader comment and feedback form received in 2004

How do I find the perfect place?

AA **Street by Street**   QUESTIONNAIRE

Dear Atlas User
Your comments, opinions and recommendations are very important to us.
So please help us to improve our street atlases by taking a few minutes
to complete this simple questionnaire.

You do not need a stamp (unless posted outside the UK). If you do not want to remove
this page from your street atlas, then photocopy it or write your answers on a plain sheet
of paper.

Send to: Marketing Assistant, AA Publishing, 14th Floor Fanum House,
Freepost SCE 4598, Basingstoke RG21 4GY

ABOUT THE ATLAS...

Please state which city / town / county you bought:

_____

Where did you buy the atlas? (City, Town, County)

_____

For what purpose? (please tick all applicable)

To use in your local area ☐   **To use on business or at work** ☐

Visiting a strange place ☐   **In the car** ☐   **On foot** ☐

Other (please state)

_____

Have you ever used any street atlases other than AA Street by Street?

Yes ☐   **No** ☐

If so, which ones?

_____

Is there any aspect of our street atlases that could be improved?
(Please continue on a separate sheet if necessary)

_____

_____

ML212z

continued overleaf

Please list the features you found most useful:

Please list the features you found least useful:

_____

LOCAL KNOWLEDGE...

Local knowledge is invaluable. Whilst every attempt has been made to make the information contained in this atlas as accurate as possible, should you notice any inaccuracies, please detail them below (if necessary, use a blank piece of paper) or e-mail us at _streetbystreet@theAA.com_

_____

_____

_____

ABOUT YOU...

Name (Mr/Mrs/Ms) _____

Address _____

                                            Postcode _____

Daytime tel no _____

E-mail address _____

Which age group are you in?

Under 25 ☐   **25-34** ☐   **35-44** ☐   **45-54** ☐   **55-64** ☐   **65+** ☐

Are you an AA member?   YES ☐   NO ☐

Do you have Internet access?   YES ☐   NO ☐

Thank you for taking the time to complete this questionnaire. Please send it to us as soon as possible, and remember, you do not need a stamp (unless posted outside the UK).

We may use information we hold about you to, telephone or email you about other products and services offered by the AA, we do NOT disclose this information to third parties.

Please tick here if you do not wish to hear about products and services from the AA. ☐